Praise for Peter Miller and Auth

"There's no better literary representative, anywhere, than Peter Miller. I have found him to be very enterprising, extremely knowledgeable, and tireless in his representation of me. His book is an invaluable source in guiding any author's career."

—Vincent Bugliosi, author of *Helter Skelter,*
And the Sea Will Tell, and *Outrage*

"It is my sincere belief that Peter Miller is the finest literary manager in New York. Peter has a fantastic instinct for what will 'sell.' He was the only agent in New York who had faith in my manuscript—it had been rejected by over a hundred agents and publishers before it came to Peter's desk. Peter snapped it up, and in no time at all five of the largest publishing houses in the world were making me offers! Peter is known as the Literary Lion, but in reality he is a pit bull of an agent, a consummate dealmaker who never stops until he gets the best possible contract for his client. I would never want anyone else to represent me, in any kind of negotiation."

—Anthony DeStefano, author of *A Travel Guide to Heaven*

"Peter Miller discovered me and launched my career as a writer, skyrocketing my first book, *Mitigating Circumstances,* onto the *New York Times* Bestseller List, and at the same time, landed me a major film deal. He's enthusiastic, knowledgeable, personable, and knows what it takes to make it happen."

—Nancy Taylor Rosenberg, author of six *New York Times*
bestsellers: *Mitigating Circumstances, Interest Of Justice,*
First Offense, California Angel, Trial By Fire, and *Abuse of Power*

"This book is a must-read for anyone who has ever been rejected by an agent or a publisher. Do yourself a very big favor and read it."

—Ann Benson, author of *The Plague Tales*
and *The Burning Road*

"Peter Miller sold my very first novel and got me a subsequent two-novel deal. He got my book optioned in Hollywood. He delivers top-flight results and is tireless in advancing the careers of his clients. Not only does he return every phone call and e-mail but he does it immediately and graciously. He is a true 'mensch.' He is a dynamo with a great heart. I love working with him."

—Lynne Kaufman, author of *Slow Hands,*
Wild Women's Weekend, and *Taking Flight*

"For first-time authors, it's a maddening Catch-22: you can't sell anything without an agent, but until you've sold a book no good agent will take a chance on you. Peter Miller immediately recognized our book's potential. One week later we signed with him; within three weeks, several top publishers had made offers for our manuscript and Peter quickly negotiated the deal that launched our careers. He's tenacious, he has an encyclopedic knowledge of the business, and most importantly he gets the job done. We saw the Literary Lion in action, and he proved he's the king of the jungle."

—Rob Wiser and Christopher Curtis, authors of *M.A.C.K. Tactics*

"Peter Miller read my book *Miss Fourth of July, Goodbye,* and within three weeks sold it to Disney. Within a year Disney made my book into a film nominated for four Emmy Awards. This is a kind of miracle in the book publishing and movie business and the kind of accomplishment Peter Miller is famous for. He's absolutely the best."

—**Christopher G. Janus, author of *Miss Fourth of July, Goodbye,***
Search for Peking Man,* and *Angel on My Shoulder

"This book should be every aspiring writer's bible! Peter thrives on the chaos of the literary and film industry and has boundless energy and passion that produces wins for those he represents! As agents go he's untouchable, undoubtedly the king of dealmakers."

—**Tammy L. King, author of *Family Secrets* and *Transparent Leader***

"I can think of many words to describe Peter Miller and his approach to business. Fearless, motivated, energetic, intelligent, and charismatic all come readily to mind, and all are accurate. However, one word moves to the fore. Integrity. Peter is a rare breed, a man who tells you exactly what he's going to do, then goes out and does it. Coeur de Lyon . . . Heart of the Lion!"

—**Liam Jackson, author of *Offspring***

"They don't call Peter Miller the best in the business for nothing. After all, as super literary agent he has sold over a thousand books and counting. The Literary Lion's new book *Author! Screenwriter!* is a dazzling collection of priceless insights and asides about the wide world of film and publishing. You won't be able to put it down!"

—**Harvey Frommer, author of more than forty books,**
including the bestselling *Red Sox vs. Yankees: The Great Rivalry*

"Peter Miller is every author and screenwriter's dream. An agent with an artist's passion, a visionary's zeal, and an entrepreneur's 'never say die' bravado. Like a literary locomotive, he is ten tons of unstoppable forward-moving thrust that will not stop until there's a deal."

—**Michael Chase Walker, author of *Power Screenwriting***

"Peter Miller is a mighty warrior for words and wordsmiths. He fights like a lion. He is honest. Creative people sometimes don't like honest, but a writer without honesty is like a knight without armor. Peter tells you what your chances are and presses forward in your behalf. He takes chances on new writers, struggles to sustain all others, and never leaves the battlefield until every possibility has been tested. I trust him. I can say nothing more than that about anyone."

—**Richard Taylor, author of *The Ghost of Cambria***
(to be published by TOR)

Author!
Screenwriter!

How to Succeed as a
Writer in New York
and Hollywood

Peter Miller

Adams Media
Avon, Massachusetts

Published by Adams Media, an F+W Publications Company
57 Littlefield Street
Avon, MA 02322
www.adamsmedia.com

ISBN: 1-59337-553-0

Printed in the United States of America.

J I H G F E D C B A

Library of Congress Cataloging-in-Publication Data
Miller, Peter
Author! Screenwriter!:
How to succeed as a writer in New York and Hollywood / Peter Miller.
p. cm.
Includes index.
ISBN 1-59337-553-0
1. Authorship—Marketing. 2. Motion picture authorship—Marketing.
3. Television authorship—Marketing. I. Title.
PN161.M54 2006
070.5'2—dc22
2005026048

This publication is designed to provide accurate and authoritative information with regard to the subject matter covered. It is sold with the understanding that the publisher is not engaged in rendering legal, accounting, or other professional advice. If legal advice or other expert assistance is required, the services of a competent professional person should be sought.

—From a *Declaration of Principles* jointly adopted by a Committee of the American Bar Association and a Committee of Publishers and Associations

Many of the designations used by manufacturers and sellers to distinguish their products are claimed as trademarks. Where those designations appear in this book and Adams Media was aware of a trademark claim, the designations have been printed with initial capital letters.

Interior design and composition by
Electronic Publishing Services, Inc., Tennessee

*This book is available at quantity discounts for bulk purchases.
For information, please call 1-800-872-5627.*

Contents

Preface *by Mark Wolper*   vii
Dedication   ix
Acknowledgments   x
Foreword *by Jay Bonansinga*   xi
Prologue *by James Dalessandro*   xiv

Introduction: *The Five Steps to Success as a Writer*   xvi

⌐ Part One ⌐
GET PUBLISHED!

1	Know the Realities of the Book Business	3
2	Create a Sellable Proposal	9
3	Manuscript and Proposal Protocol	17
4	Find a Good Agent/Manager to Represent You	23
5	Working with Your Representative	31
6	The Truth About Nonfiction Books	43
7	The Worlds of Fiction	59
8	Wonderful Circumstances	69

⌐ Part Two ⌐
GET PRODUCED!

9	The Cast of Characters	77
10	Know the Realities of Hollywood	83
11	Packaging Your Work	101
12	Marketing Your Screenplay	111
13	Making It in Television	117

14 Contracts: Watch Your Back!   123
15 Making the Deal in Hollywood   133

⭢ **Part Three** ⭠
PROPOSALS THAT GET THE DEAL DONE

#1: A Biography Proposal   141
#2: A True-Crime Book Proposal   165
#3: A Self-Help/Relationship Book Proposal   181
#4: A Cookbook Proposal   211
#5: A How-to Book Proposal   219
#6: A Health Book Proposal   223
#7: A Fiction Proposal   235
#8: A Television Series Proposal and Script   239
#9: A TV Movie and Dramatic Series
         Proposal and Treatment   255
#10: A Novel Coverage   267

APPENDIXES

Book Publishing Glossary   279
Film Industry Glossary   287
Resources   301

Index   305

Preface

Peter Miller is one of those New York book people who can't stay out of Hollywood. I have known him for going on twenty years and he never stops. My company has made two films with Peter so far. They were based on books and/or with clients he was managing: *Deadly Blessing* (ABC), based on a true-crime book by Steve Salerno, and the remake of *Helter Skelter* (CBS), based on the book by Vincent Bugliosi and Curt Gentry, which was the most successful true-crime book ever published. We also have another film, *Citizen Jane,* in development that is based on a true-crime book Peter manages; he will serve as an executive producer on the film adaptation.

Peter's book *Author! Screenwriter!* is an absolute must for any author, particularly one who believes his or her book has film or television production potential. Peter is the real deal, and he never gives up if he believes in a project or author. He has batteries that never wear down, and if I were an author he is precisely the manager I'd choose to have in my corner. He has a reputation for being a true Literary Lion, and, trust me, he and his company, PMA Literary Film Management, Inc., are the people I would want to have roaring for me. I have been an active producer for moore than twenty years now and have produced well over 200 hours of prime-time long-form and television series programs. I am an expert on the metamorphosis of books into film and television productions, and I know how literary dealmakers like Peter Miller work their magic.

Peter was in my office several years ago pitching me a project and I passed on it. He looked at me kind of funny, and I said,

"Peter, what are you complaining about? You have two projects in development with us and we just produced one. How many companies in L.A. do you have two films set up with now?" That quieted him down a bit. Then he said you're right—and went right on trying to sell me something else. That's Peter: He never stops! My company, the Wolper Organization, is presently working on a few projects with him that are based on books or clients he manages or properties he has optioned. Peter will always try to have a few things set up with us. This is a relationship business, and Peter keeps good relationships and consistently comes up with exciting and viable properties.

Don't just read *Author! Screenwriter!* Devour, memorize, and study it! It's your bible for success in the book and film worlds. It's rare that you can find a book that is jammed with information from the inside of the film and publishing worlds *and* that comes from the point of view of someone like Peter Miller. Peter has been on the battlefield fighting for author's rights for more than three decades and now fights for his own rights as a producer with his production company, Millennium Lion, Inc., an organization that my company, the Wolper Organization, is proud to be associated with.

Good luck getting published *and* produced.

Mark Wolper
The Wolper Organization
Warner Brothers Studios

Dedication

This book is dedicated to my wife Giselle and my daughters Liseanne and Margo, who taught me something more important than how to get published and produced: how to love. And to my late mother, Clare Willamette Lyons Miller who said to me one day, "Son, there is a buyer for everything." She was a great lady, and her energy and wisdom live with me daily. And also to my brother Robert, who told me, "Never limit your horizons." Thanks, Bob—I never have. And, last, to my late and great friend Christopher Cook Gilmore who taught me many things, including, "There is more room on the top than there is on the bottom!" Thank you. Chris, you are my captain and helped me see the light at the end of the tunnel.

Acknowledgments

I'd like to extend a special thanks to all the friends, colleagues, and clients who helped me develop and write this book, beginning with my original editor David Weaver; my editor and friend Lou Aronica (a man of many talents); my former associates: Helen Pfeffer, Jennifer Robinson, Yuri Skujins, Nathan Rice, Julie Hahn, Scott Hoffman, and Greg Takoudes; and my present staff: Betty Ferm, Kelly Skillen, and Leslie Henkel, as well as all of the interns who have worked at PMA: Jonah, John, Ben, Carlos, Tamar, Amy, Amanda, Jessie, Kay, Mark, Samuel, Amanda II, Lauren, Caroline, Joel, et al.

I also want to thank the publishers of the previous edition of this book, Joan and Ralph Singleton and Jeff Black for having the foresight to see the need for this work; and thanks to everyone at Adams Media: Gary Krebs, Jill Alexander, Scott Watrous, and my editor, Larry Shea, for his wisdom and for understanding me.

Additionally, I would like to thank my many friends and many wonderful clients who gave me the right to use their proposals in this book, including Jay Bonansinga, Vincent Bugliosi, Lee Butcher, Joan Detz, the late Christopher Cook Gilmore, Roy Guste, Albert Marchetti, Steve Salerno, Jerry Schmetterer, Rob Wiser, and Christopher Curtis, and all of the authors who have given me the honor of being their literary manager over the years. I was born to develop and sell intellectual properties and I thank God for blessing me with my career.

Also a special thanks to Jay Bonansinga again, the Italian god of contemporary authors, for his wonderful foreword and his belief in me. Keep an eye on the Bonansinga name—this man oozes with talent. Thanks also to that other Big Italian in my life, James Dalessandro, for his unique wit and charm that has helped fuel this literary management engine over the years.

Foreword:
The Keys to the Kingdom

Congratulations! You are holding in your hands the keys to the Publishing Kingdom. But beware. Like the proverbial Excalibur, your success in the book business cannot merely be yanked out of stony obscurity on sheer hard work. It takes a lot more. A lot more than talent. More than luck. More than good looks.

It takes . . . in a word . . . *management.*

Let's stay with the Arthurian metaphor for a moment (because that's what we writers do, we work those metaphors). Arthur had his Merlin, right? Well, that's the kind of management I'm talking about. I'm talking about a mentor in the mythological sense. The trusted *consigliere*. Someone who points you in the proper direction, kicks your butt a little, and sends you on your journey.

Merlin was nothing—he was a piker, an amateur.

I got Peter Miller.

And please don't think of Peter as a mere agent—although he can work his mojo in that area like nobody else. He could agent the spots off a leopard. But he's more than that. He's a literary manager in every sense of the phrase. He manages your literary life.

Let me give you an example. Fourteen years ago I was an out-of-work filmmaker with delusions of grandeur and thousands of dollars of debt. I had sold a couple of short stories to a few underground magazines, and had gotten a bunch of empty promises from Hollywood producers (is there any other kind of promise from Hollywood?). And then I made the best decision of my career.

xii   FOREWORD: THE KEYS TO THE KINGDOM

I took my first stab at a novel, and sent it to Peter Miller. And he rejected it.

(Did I mention he's a sadist, too?)

The truth is, he *should* have rejected it. The novel wasn't ready. But here's the key to Peter's magic: He sent along notes. He took the time to read the submission, and he had some good things to say about it as well as constructive criticism. And that was the beginning of my true education in building a career.

Because that's what Peter does: He builds careers. He *develops* writers. And that's why we clicked. I happily rewrote my manuscript to his specifications, and zipped it back to him, and he was impressed by the *cojones* of this young kid who refused to take no for an answer. It was the beginning of a beautiful friendship.

A year later, Peter called me and said, "The Eagle has landed, Junior."

For some reason, this phrase, which originated with the astronauts finally reaching the lunar surface after an arduous spaceflight, has found its way into business parlance. It has come to mean: The deal is signed, sealed, and delivered—we did it!

And now that I think of it, selling a book is not unlike making it to the moon.

But what Peter Miller was able to secure back in 1992 for my first novel, *The Black Mariah,* was definitely out of this world. Warner Books won the bidding war, and New Line Cinema offered a five-figure option against a mid-six purchase price for the movie rights. The frosting on the cake was the way Peter wedged me into the film deal: I was hired to co-write the screenplay alongside my childhood hero, George Romero, the creator of *Night of the Living Dead.*

My career in the book and movie businesses had officially started with a bang.

But remember: Peter is about the long haul. He's constantly working with me on the next project, the next big book. Developing, brain-storming, editing, polishing . . . selling, selling, selling.

He literally manages my time. "Here's what I want you to work on next," he'll growl at me over the phone in his good-natured New Yawk bark, and then he'll steer me toward the next big deal.

Another aside here: Peter Miller is the consummate New Yorker—a streetwise, whip-smart, fast-talker. But mostly that's his phone persona. In person, he's a big teddy bear. Boyishly handsome, with a big mop of hair, he looks twenty years younger than his fifty-some years. And maybe that's why he's so good at creating deals, creating commercial niches for his clients.

Which is exactly what he has done for *me* with a vengeance. Since *The Black Mariah* was published back in 1992, Peter has sold nine more books for me, with many more pending. He has placed much of my work overseas, resulting in foreign editions in a dozen different languages. He's gotten me a movie deal on every single book—that's right, *every book*. And as this goes to press, we're staring down the barrels of two major motion pictures, one television film, and two television series based on my work going into production in the very near future.

Which brings us back to the handy little tome you now hold in your hands.

Over the years, Peter has taught me a lot, but perhaps the most important thing he's taught me is how to be a professional. And that's what this book can do for writers of all persuasions. In the arts, being a professional doesn't mean selling out. Nor does it mean wearing berets and thumbing your nose at "the man." It means having a career. It means working not just hard but also *smart*.

Which is what's inside this book—the smart stuff.

Read it carefully.

The career it creates could be your own.

Jay Bonansinga
Author, Screenwriter
Chicago

Prologue:
The Four Words That
Matter to a Writer

There is probably not a single other profession in the world for which its fledgling participants are less prepared or less knowledgeable about the art, craft, and business than the rewarding and treacherous world of writing. I believe that 99 percent of the people who set out to write a screenplay have never read one: most don't know even know the rudimentary elements of format. Most nonfiction book writers think the minute details of their lives—"This is about angst in my Italian/Jewish/Chinese/Latvian family"—have some universal importance. There are far too many would-be works of fiction in which plot and character are not revealed, but explained, although occasionally one of this latter ilk does make it onto someone's bestseller list.

I know of no activity that requires more time, more effort, more talent, more luck, more good advice, a thicker skin, a more tolerant spouse, more understanding children, or more tolerant friends than writing. When are they going to invent steroids for writers, so we can hit the dangling participle out of the park? Until then, remember this simple phrase. Writing is not a sprint, it is a marathon. It helps to have the energy of a speed freak, the imagination of Arthur Rimbaud, and better connections than the Pope.

It also helps to have Peter Miller on your side, for a multitude of reasons. He's smart as hell, he has great taste in both literate and commercial pursuits (and the rarest of stories, those that manage to be both), he's loyal and punctual, he never procrastinates, and he loves new writers and new ideas.

Since you don't have him in your corner as of yet, I suggest that you don't read his book. I suggest you study it, perhaps render it to memory. *Author! Screenwriter!* should be mandatory reading for everyone crazy enough to think they can do this work and get away with it. There is more practical knowledge and poignant insights in this volume than you are likely to find in any other of its kind.

There are four words that matter to a writer. THE END. BIDDING WAR. I have accomplished the former on four books and twenty-five screenplays. My novel and screenplay, *1906*, were the subject of the latter, all thanks to Peter Miller.

Like my friend Jay Bonansinga, whose Foreword you may or may not have skipped over because you are anxious to flip to the "How Much Money Can I Make Section," I have a life and a career thanks to Peter Miller. I follow Peter's advice.

I suggest you do the same.

James Dalessandro
Author, Screenwriter
San Francisco

Introduction:
The Five Steps to
Success as a Writer

"Writers aren't exactly people . . . they're a
whole lot of people trying to be one person."
—F. Scott Fitzgerald

After reading all of the complimentary things written in the Preface, Foreword, and Prologue above, you may be asking yourself: Just who is this Peter Miller? And how is he going to help *my* career as a writer trying to make my way in the worlds of books and films?

Well, allow me to introduce myself, and this book. I've been a literary representative since 1973, and prior to my entrance into the publishing business, when I was fresh out of college, I was briefly in the contract packaging business. During my years in the publishing business, I've represented numerous authors and placed more than 1,000 books throughout the world. My first-hand experience with the ups and downs of the publishing world has left me with one constant: my admiration for those with the genius, stamina, and determination to select writing as a profession. Not only do I pray for them, but I have dedicated my life to them. I have been called a "Literary Lion," a moniker I am proud of because I have spent my entire adult life and career defending author's rights and nurturing many writers.

I have been fortunate enough to manage many successful careers, and many of my clients have made more than seven figures from their work. As of this writing my company has represented more than a dozen *New York Times* bestsellers and we have managed countless global bestsellers.

Author! Screenwriter! is a book for all writers, big and small. It's been written with the hope that the wisdom I have gained about the publishing and film industries can make the difference in the success of your writing career. I will attempt—and, I hope, succeed—to bring you as an author into my mindset as a manager of literary and film properties, show you how the publishing and film industries really work for writers, and enable you to chart your own course for success in New York (or wherever your book will be published) and Hollywood. Go into any bookstore and you'll find shelves full of books on how to get your own book published, and numerous other books promising that they will teach you how to make it as a screenwriter. *Author! Screenwriter!* is the only book that shows you how to succeed in both worlds—New York and Hollywood, books and film.

We are regularly told of the willpower and self-sacrifice needed to succeed in other professions, but I say, "Try writing a book!" Nothing challenges the mind, sparks the imagination, or requires more discipline than writing. If you're a writer, this may seem obvious. But too often the basic element of writing—hard work—is forgotten during the hot pursuit of illusory formulas for easy success.

Next to actually writing the book, the greatest problem any writer faces is getting it published. All writers who are serious about their profession face this situation, no matter what type of writing they do and regardless of the quality of their work. As a writer's representative, it is my responsibility to always keep the often harsh reality of the publishing industry in sight and to make sure the writer gets published. I have a quick bottom-line style when evaluating would-be writers and their works, and from years of experience I know what separates those writers who will be published from those who won't.

I'd like to share Five Steps to Success designed to help you get published. Later on in the book, we'll talk about the specifics of book proposals, working with agents and managers, contracts, and more. For now, just know that the following steps are basic parts of any successful career as a book author and screenwriter.

STEP #1: HAVE FAITH IN YOURSELF

This is not as simple as it sounds. Being a writer doesn't end when you've finished typing your manuscript! You may feel confident now, but what happens after a few rejections or some negative criticism? How committed will you be to your writing after your mother and closest friends give up on you? Can you stand to see your writing friends forge ahead, while you have nothing to show for your efforts other than a stack of rejection slips and a case of writer's cramp? It's important to have confidence enough to complete your manuscript, but it's even more vital to have faith in it when you're ready to let someone read it, or when—on that fateful day—you're ready to submit it to a literary representative.

Many of the books I've represented were submitted to a dozen or more publishers and were rejected by all of them. To use a simple analogy, the results of those first few innings did not make the whole ball game. As a writer, your operative word must be *persistence*. The first novel by one of my clients had been previously turned down by another representative. Two weeks later, I successfully represented him in a six-figure, two-novel sale to a major U.S. publisher and later placed the rights in Germany, the U.K., Japan, Holland, Korea, Italy, and Bulgaria and optioned the film rights. The author then wrote a third novel that was also published around the world. Having faith in what you're doing as a writer is what will keep you going until you find your own success.

STEP #2: KNOW THE MARKET

Publishers want books that sell—period—and there are many elements that contribute to the commercial viability of a book. In my more than thirty years of being in this business, I have seen the ups and downs of the book-buying marketplace. As of this writing, the publishing business is booming. However, it is booming for only the right kind of book and author, at the right time, with the right editor and publisher. Therefore, know and accept the current conditions of the literary marketplace. Read magazines written for writers, such as *Writer's Digest,* and those related to the book business, such as *Publishers Weekly,* to get an idea of what publishers are looking for. This doesn't mean you must conform to publishers' expectations, but if you want to succeed, either by their terms or by breaking the rules, you first must know those rules. I'll discuss what you need to know about the ins and outs of publishing in Chapter 1, "Know the Realities of the Book Business."

STEP #3: PRESENT PERFECT PROPOSALS AND MANUSCRIPTS

Although this recommendation seems obvious, I am amazed at the number of sloppy, unprofessionally presented manuscripts and proposals my agency still receives. Aspiring authors, please note: Messy manuscripts do not become books! And if you cannot even produce a polished, clear, typo-free ten-page proposal, why should anyone trust you to create a 300-page book?

Whenever you prepare a manuscript for submission, it should look as professional as possible. An editor will never get past the first few pages if a manuscript isn't in perfect shape—and I do mean PERFECT.

This concept may seem out of style after hearing about assiduous editors plucking literary geniuses from the proverbial "slush pile." However, with the advent of the computer and the huge number of unpublished manuscripts that go along with this new technology, editors are now forced to be more selective. A manuscript's presentation is obviously the easiest element of a manuscript to judge. We'll discuss the specifics of how to format and present your proposals and manuscripts in Chapter 2, "Create a Sellable Proposal," and Chapter 3, "Manuscript and Proposal Protocol."

STEP #4: WORK WITH THE RIGHT REPRESENTATIVE

Make sure your literary manager is working FOR you and FOR the success of your book(s) and career. That doesn't mean your representative should be your buddy: Well-meaning friends can hand out bad advice. You should have a good rapport with whoever represents you; you want to feel that you, your representative, and their staff are playing on the same team and that you're all out to win. It may be worth a trip to New York (as it is the publishing center of the United States) to meet your manager. After all, your choice of representatives may be the single most important decision you make in transforming what was an avocation into a vocation. Don't be afraid to question your representative about all aspects of the business, because he or she should have the answers. And, you are entitled to them (just be polite!). In Chapter 4, "Find a Good Agent/Manager to Represent You," and Chapter 5, "Working with Your Representative," I'll tell you how to find a great representative, and how to maintain a mutually successful, long-term relationship with him or her.

STEP #5: REALIZE THAT YOUR SCRIPT COULD BE A BOOK—AND VICE VERSA

I'd like to take you on a trip to Hollywood. This imaginary journey begins when a new, untested writer comes to me thinking he has just written the next *Da Vinci Code*. After taking the initiative to write the screenplay of his story he comes to me, convinced that he's a shoo-in for an Academy Award. At this point, I must bring everything crashing down to Earth with my last bit of advice: It doesn't happen like it does in the movies. If the publishing world is a jungle, then the film world is a jungle on another planet. Whatever the script's merits, the "political" nature of the film industry combined with the incredible cost of producing a film makes any sale a highly complicated affair. And this happens to even the greatest of screenwriters with regularity. So a screenplay by an unknown writer is next to impossible to sell.

In my experience, the key to success in the film industry is packaging—that is, associating "proven" elements with an original, untested product. Ideally, packaging would mean the combination of a bestselling book, a well-known screenwriter, a recognized and successful director, and bankable stars. Without all of the elements (or at least one major one), the packager might attempt to option or sell the property by obtaining a star's interest in the screenplay and then by capitalizing on that star's power. This act would move a project into "development."

Although an unknown writer has little chance of attracting the interest of established people in the film industry, I try to develop ways of giving this aspiring screenwriter a chance at fulfilling his dreams. My strongest piece of advice is to turn a screenplay into a novel. If I find a good script, I'll ask the author to flesh out a few chapters and develop a proposal for the novel (if they can write prose). Then, if I really believe in the writer and the project, I'll submit everything (the chapters, proposal, and the original screenplay) to an editor. This demonstrates the validity of the project as a book and illustrates the obvious potential it has to become a film.

You may have thought that books are adapted into screenplays, and things just don't work the other way (except for novelizations of finished films). Not so—as I've described above, the ways that the book and film industries intertwine are more complicated than that. In the chapters in Part Two ("Get Produced!") of this book, you'll learn how to navigate the world of Hollywood as the writer of a book or screenplay—or both. And in Part Three, you'll have the chance to study a number of examples of well-crafted proposals for nonfiction and fictional books, as well as for movie and TV productions. Your journey to success as an author and screenwriter has just begun. Let's get going!

PART ONE

Get Published!

CHAPTER	
ONE	Know the Realities of the Book Business
TWO	Create a Sellable Proposal
THREE	Manuscript and Proposal Protocol
FOUR	Find a Good Agent/Manager to Represent You
FIVE	Working with Your Representative
SIX	The Truth About Nonfiction Books
SEVEN	The Worlds of Fiction
EIGHT	Wonderful Circumstances

CHAPTER ONE

Know the Realities
of the Book Business

*"The average trade book has a shelf life of
between milk and yogurt."*

—Calvin Trillin

So you want to become an author, but the great big world of book publishing seems just a little bit intimidating to you, not to mention discouraging?

It's not surprising. The current literary marketplace is so glutted with submissions that a new or struggling writer—even one with a good idea or a promising manuscript—has less of a chance of being published than ever before.

FEWER PLAYERS, TOUGHER TIMES

One reason that getting published has become more difficult is that the total number of major publishers is shrinking; hence, there are fewer big buyers. For example, as a result of corporate takeovers and mergers, Random House and its many imprints (Random House, Knopf, Crown, Broadway, Doubleday, Bantam, Pantheon, Presidio Press, Ballantine, Del Rey, Clarkson N. Potter, etc.) is now owned by the huge German conglomerate Bertelsmann. The Penguin Group Worldwide acquired the Putnam Berkley Publishing Group and is now called Pearson; now it too has many imprints (Viking, Penguin, Putnam, Dutton, Berkley, Riverhead, NAL, Onyx, Gotham, Chamberlain Bros., Puffin, Perigee, etc.). Time Inc. merged with Warner Communications, which then merged with AOL and is now called the Time Warner Book Group, making it part of what was the largest entertainment company in the world . . . until Disney bought ABC. Who knows what's next? At the time of this writing, Viacom owns Simon & Schuster (which consists of many imprints: Simon & Schuster, Pocket Books, Atria Books, Scribner, Washington Square Press, Touchstone/Fireside, Little Simon, The Free Press, and more), Paramount, CBS, MTV, Showtime, VH1, and countless other major entertainment and real estate interests. Viacom may sell its publishing interests or expand them; no matter what they do, the number of major publishing players is more likely to continue to shrink than to grow.

The publishing industry is continually going through enormous changes. During the past several years, there has been an overall tightening of purse strings, partly as a consequence of this takeover of publishing houses and the general downsizing that has resulted. Many senior editors, for example, no longer have assistants—and, in the past, those assistants may have been the people who would help more experienced editors to get through piles of submissions to find your gem of a manuscript.

Certain common practices in the book industry have also made publishing more difficult. For example, publishers of trade books basically sell them on consignment. This antiquated policy ends up with large quantities of books—50 percent on average for mass-market paperbacks—being returned from bookstores unsold. Despite all the bestsellers and publishing successes you read about, there are also many flops that go unnoticed by the public.

What does all this mean for you as a potential book author? From my own experience, fiction has become harder to sell than it ever was; my company will only manage a novel if it is truly stellar. Nonfiction is easier to sell than fiction. Because the stakes are higher, though, all publishers are looking for authors who are more of a sure thing (or at least as sure as anything can be in the uncertain world of book publishing). This means that a publisher will likely insist that a potential nonfiction author have a platform. A *platform* is having a media presence, such as a radio or television talk show, a newspaper, magazine or ezine column, or an affiliation with a major popular Web site. Authors with platforms are more likely to receive promotion, publicity, and notice when their book comes out—and less likely to see their works disappear without a trace.

HOW PUBLISHERS DECIDE WHICH BOOKS TO PUBLISH

Many publishers today use the committee system to make decisions. This means the publisher has an editorial board meeting that usually takes place weekly, and that editor has to request an opinion from several other editors who will then discuss it at the meeting and vote. Recently, I was involved in a situation in which a major publishing executive phoned me to say that he and a colleague loved a book my company managed. And then, one day later, he phoned again to say that his committee didn't. I don't like committees, but those are the rules by which the publishing game is played. Therefore, having an enthusiastic editor on the side of your book becomes an absolute necessity. Since this editorial process takes place in many publishing houses, it is necessary for an editor to have the support of several other editors for a positive decision to be made.

One thing to note about the publishing business: Publishing has always been called a "gentleman's business," and in some ways it still operates this way. However, it is now a gentleman's business that is substantially run by women or, simply put, a woman's business. Remember this: It is very likely that the majority of the editors in that committee meeting who will need to approve your book are women. In many ways, women rule the publishing industry!

Once an editor is hooked, and the publisher's committee concurs, the publishing process begins. You've sold your work! The publisher has literally "sold itself" on your book and hopefully on your future career.

FINDING YOUR PLACE IN THE MARKETPLACE

The question arises: If getting a book published successfully (or at all) is so difficult, why are so many people—people like yourself—still trying so hard to do it?

Well, for one thing, the publicity—and money—received by well-known bestselling writers, such as Dan Brown, John Grisham, Tom Clancy, Mary Higgins Clark, and Patricia Cornwell, is phenomenal. Just to give a few examples of the amazing success stories of enormously popular authors: Stephen King's four-book deal with Viking Penguin (for a reported advance of $40 million); Patricia Cornwell's three-book deal for about $24 million; Tom Clancy's three-book $40 million deal; the $8 million advance to Charles Frazier, the author of *Cold Mountain,* from a one-page synopsis of his next novel; and the $40 million deal for Tim LeHay, the author of the *Left Behind* series. Michael Crichton, John Grisham, and Mary Higgins Clark have also all hit enormously large paydays. For the biggest book contracts, the trend is up. If you're a talented writer, your chances of striking it rich may at least be better from writing a book than from buying a lottery ticket.

Unfortunately, though, the promise of quick success and easy money is really an illusion for almost all other authors besides the big names mentioned above. You must be most concerned about your own writing, not the success of other writers. Every author has his own problems and every book is unique, especially when dealing with the marketplace.

Every author wants the biggest possible financial commitment from the best possible publisher. Every author and his representative also want that publisher to promote the book as heavily as they can. Experienced writers know that books can die if every aspect of their publication, especially promotion, is not coordinated carefully and pursued aggressively. Currently, there are approximately 200,000 new books published in the U.S. every year, so competition is fierce. When you think about this number, you have to consider all aspects of the publishing industry, including trade fiction and nonfiction in hardcover, trade paperback and mass market editions, as well as all the professional, educational, and children's books being published.

It's not just about writing a great book; this book must also be advertised and promoted in a major way. I used to say "sell the hell out of it," but since I started managing Anthony DeStefano and his wonderful book, *A Travel Guide to Heaven*, I now say "sell the heaven into it."

SOMETIMES DREAMS DO COME TRUE

Many years ago, I took on a new client, an Australian writer named Roland Perry, who submitted an intriguing first novel to me, *Program for a Puppet*. The novel dealt with industrial espionage and the manipulation of the American political scene. What clinched my enthusiasm for it was Perry's belief in his work and his willingness to hang in there for the long haul. I decided to hold my first literary auction. The difference between a simultaneous submission and an auction is that, in an auction, you designate a specific date (and some time, like on or before 4 P.M. Thursday, October 20th) to conclude the sale of a work(s). Simultaneously, I submitted the book to fourteen publishers, asking them to read the manuscript in two weeks and to come back to us with an offer of not less than $50,000. I had a nibble from one of the publishers, but it wasn't above my established "floor bid." I was shocked! It was like throwing a party and having no one show up! I met with Perry and one of my associates to plot our next strategy. Roland did not lose heart; in fact, he set about editing and fine-tuning the manuscript. His resolve encouraged me: I redoubled my efforts to place his novel.

A month or so later, I was in London. Of the various projects I considered presenting to the group of British publishers I knew, none seemed more deserving than *Program for a Puppet*. I submitted the revised manuscript to an English publisher and, happily, it was accepted. It was a case of the right publisher at the right time. Soon after, I arranged for the author to co-write a screenplay based on his novel. Having garnered one publishing agreement, I used that foundation to auction off the American rights to the book for the second time and then I received a $50,000 advance in the U.S. The novel was published in the U.S. and Canada, Italy, Germany, Spain, Mexico, and Japan—in hardcover and in paperback. The author's faith in himself and his writing, which directly affected my belief in him, paid off. We won!

YOUR NEXT STEP

When, after taking a look at the marketplace and at your own work, you believe you're ready to be published, you should do all you can to find a determined and dedicated agent, manager, or representative. We're out there and we need you . . . and not just because of the money. There's no bigger thrill for me than telling an author I've just found a publishing home for their book and that it will be published at long last. Ask yourself, do you write to live, or live to write? Well, I live to manage (and manage to live), and that's why I'm referred to as a literary lion. I love to ROAR and I can ROAR really loudly when the writing is there.

Good projects don't sell themselves! That's why I am writing this book, in order to help you sell your work and know how it is sold. Of course, there are many excellent writers who have written wonderful books that have yet to sell, but remember: Publishing is a tricky business. One more piece of advice: I know it's a little common, but writers . . . WRITE ON!

CHAPTER TWO

Create a
Sellable Proposal

*"The only reason for being a professional
writer is that you can't help it."*
—Leo Rosten

If you are a writer, and you want to go very far in the world of
book publishing, you are going to need representation. And if
you're trying to succeed as a writer in Hollywood, having a good
agent or manager working for you is even more of a necessity.

As your first step when first seeking representation, you'll
need to prepare a "query" letter and a book proposal, manuscript,
screenplay, or teleplay, etc. My formula for a successful query letter
is this: an opening statement, followed by two or three paragraphs
about the book, then (if possible) a paragraph about your next
book(s), and finally a paragraph about yourself. If your book is
nonfiction, you may want to include some concise facts about the
book's market and the demographics of its intended audience.

Before you submit anything to a prospective representative,
share it with as many people as you can. Value their feedback
but weigh it carefully; don't give up your artistic integrity. Make
sure your work is perfectly edited and typed. If you're writing a
nonfiction book proposal, be sure it is properly developed.

If your work is a novel, particularly a first novel, your proposal should basically be a completed manuscript. It used to be

possible to sell a first novel with a proposal, but this opportunity is shrinking because the market for first-time novels—which fall in a category known as "midlist fiction"—has been slowly vanishing. The market has changed and is continuing to change, due to the consolidations and upheavals discussed in Chapter 1. Publishers often have larger inventories, meaning they are less anxious to sign new deals with unknown authors, unless it's a book that seems to have the potential sales of *The Lovely Bones*. Remember: The decision to publish or not to publish always gets right to the bottom line, and publishers don't want any "fat" on their lists.

WHAT AGENTS AND EDITORS LOOK FOR

My literary agency receives queries and submissions of all kinds from writers all around the world. These 200 to 500 queries per week (yes, per week) come in the form of faxes, e-mails, treatments, proposals, letters, synopses, manuscripts, and screenplays. Like most representatives, we usually measure a writer's ability and originality by the quality of their "query" letter. Therefore, we look for those well-written, perfectly edited, typed, and presented letters and/or proposals, or—better yet—manuscripts.

I always advise an author to write a one-page synopsis of his property so publishers and editors can get a thumbnail sketch of what the book is about. In addition, when I have a meeting with a potential publisher, it's easier for me to take a one-page synopsis than it is to carry a bulky manuscript. (If I ever write my autobiography, I think I'll call it *Born to Schlep!*) If the editor likes the idea, I then follow up by sending the complete manuscript; this way, I save myself stress AND lower-back problems. Fortunately, these days some editors accept e-mail attachments. A few years ago, I began asking our authors to add to the package a paragraph or two about themselves. I have successfully sold this book-and-author package many, many times.

DEVELOPING PROPOSALS

Occasionally, in the pursuit of editors, I've taken a new and rather unusual approach with some projects, particularly novels. Usually, editors require complete novels—a MUST for a first-time author—before making a judgment. Let's say I represent a novel that is reasonably complete. The author and I develop a proposal that consists of the first three to six chapters, as well as a good synopsis of the entire book. I submit this proposal to editors. The editor is now faced with a far less formidable reading burden and I can anticipate a quicker and more flexible response. If the answer is favorable, we proceed to an evaluation of the entire manuscript, or even to the negotiation of a contract based on the proposal. If the answer is not favorable, we are still in a position to incorporate the editor's suggestions (if we are lucky enough to have them) into the manuscript. This allows the author to make a second attempt to sell the book to that editor.

Nonfiction proposals often sell this way because the book is usually dependent on its subject matter rather than on the author's storytelling abilities or writing style. The author researches the subject, writes a brief synopsis (including Introduction, Preface and/or Foreword, and a Table of Contents) and attaches a few chapters for evaluation (more details on this are found in Chapter 6). If the author has published before, a book proposal on an interesting subject can be placed for an advance with relative ease.

BAITING THE HOOK

Throughout Part One of this book, I'll be talking about how to approach potential representatives and publishers in order to turn your great idea for a book into reality. Chapter 3 discusses proposal and manuscript protocol, for example, and Chapter 6 covers the specifics of creating proposals for nonfiction works.

(With nonfiction, the proposal is usually what sells the book to a publisher, while in fiction it is usually the manuscript itself that does that.) In Part Three of the book, you'll see examples of proposals for nonfiction in a variety of genres—biography, true crime, cooking, and more—as well as an article that was used as part of a proposal to help sell a novel.

But here's the million-dollar question: How do you know if your idea for a book really *is* that great? This is a question that is impossible to answer in a simple way, as the potential ideas for great books are nearly endless (and the potential ideas for bad books probably *are* endless). The best book ideas are often the ones that are the least expected and the hardest to quantify.

Kelly Skillen, one of my associates at PMA Literary and Film Management, offers the following advice (from here to the end of the chapter) to aspiring authors who need to know if their idea for a novel or nonfiction book has what it takes to make editors and representatives sit up and take notice, and who also may be wondering if they really can write what they love and still succeed in today's publishing world. To the second question, Kelly's answer (and mine) is a definite "Yes!" Here's what she has to say:

There are many reasons to write—all of them valid—but when it comes to getting published, there are certain rules that must be adhered to. Isn't it enough just to be good? Of course not. Think of the publishing industry as an exclusive soiree to which you have not been invited; you're going to have to crash, and you'll never get past the doorman without the right shoes and some serious swagger. But don't despair; getting published is not tantamount to *selling out*. Furthermore, obeying industry conventions can actually enhance the quality of your work, rather than diminish it. I swear. Here are four rules you must follow to break into today's ridiculously competitive, oversaturated market that *don't* require selling your soul to the gods of commerce at the expense of your art.

Rule #1: Yes, you need a hook.

Those of you who write commercial fiction are most likely aware of this, but you literary types need one too, as do those of you who write narrative nonfiction or chronicle current events or pop culture. The hook is the thing that garners immediate interest from a stranger in the space of a sentence—a sort of blue streak of recognition. It takes a lot to get the attention of representatives and editors these days, so make your hook a good one. Our agency recently signed a commercial Dead Sea Scroll mystery involving the lost gospel of Jesus Christ, a literary tale of a woman who becomes emotionally involved with the man responsible for the death of her son, and a dating guide that applied the art of hostage negotiation to finding the ideal mate. Each, in its own way, offers a compelling hook.

But a hook just gets you past that glowering doorman; it's not enough to keep you at the party. You must have supple prose, flawless pacing, and wit to burn if you want to stay. It's true that without a big idea, you don't stand a chance, but a hot concept with lukewarm execution is going leave prospective publishers unsatisfied—maybe a little angry at you.

Rule #2: Yes, it has to appeal to idiots.

I'm aware that just by typing this, I'm contributing to the "dumbing down" of American society. But before you fire up your well-earned indignation, I never said that your book couldn't appeal to thoughtful, hyper-intelligent people as well. I'm simply noting that literary successes from *King Lear* to *The Da Vinci Code*, whatever their measure of brilliance, have an undeniable mass appeal—universal ideas that speak to everyone, even idiots.

The truth is, if you expect strangers to part with their hard-earned cash for the privilege of reading your book, it is your obligation first and foremost to entertain. If your book can't succeed on this level, it fails on every other. But once you've fulfilled this fundamental requirement, you can continue to inform, inspire, and ponder the very nature of Everything—or not. It's up to you.

Rule #3: Yes, publishers will try to pigeonhole your book.

They will want to know which genre it belongs to, and precisely which shelf it will sit on. Pigeonholing has become increasingly tricky, because genres are continually merging. For example, the dichotomy between literary and commercial fiction has blurred, and experimental forms such as "fictional biographies" and "faction" abound. But the reality remains that if you're going to sell your book to a major publisher, someone's going to have to figure out what to call it.

As an agent, I tend to make this stuff up. I fall madly in love with books—as well as people—that cannot be easily categorized. But this hasn't made my life any easier. I once alternately described an incredible novel I represented as "sly social commentary disguised as realistic science-fiction," "commercial horror," "literary horror," and "a bad-boy thriller filtered through a literary sensibility." Somehow, they were all true, and what made the book difficult to describe was ultimately what set it apart.

Rule #4: Yes, you must know the market.

As an aspiring professional author, it is your job to pay attention to the market. It's stunning how many writers embark on a book, whittling away endless, over-caffeinated hours, basking in the spooky glow of a computer monitor, without considering who their readership will consist of. I mean, who's gonna read this thing? There are a great many reasons to write, but if you are crafting a memoir for therapeutic purposes, or to provide your future grandchildren with a cautionary tale of your misspent youth, you are the sort of author that Publish-on-Demand was created for. In such a case, you are writing for a small and specific audience—in some cases, an audience of one. And that *has* value—just not to a major publisher.

But beware: An over-awareness of the market can lead to calculated, soulless writing—the sort that seeks to ride current trends all the way to the *New York Times* extended list. Here's a hint: By the time you identify a discernable trend, such as paranormal chick-lit, say, or books narrated by characters beyond the grave, the *market is already glutted*. Editors and representatives are already inundated with proposals, and by the time those proposals grow into book and are hatched into bookstores, the fickle public will likely have moved on to something else. (Some trends never die, of course. Vampires pretty much always sell.) More importantly, trying to catch those elusive trends places you in danger of losing your heart. Write what you love—it's no guarantee that your prospective editors or representatives will love it too, but if you aren't passionate about your story, you can't expect anyone else to be either.

It really is possible to break into the publishing industry without compromising your ideals—as long as those ideals include a healthy dose of respect and consideration for your readers. No one wants to toil in obscurity forever, not just because it isn't profitable or rewarding in the material sense, but because it defeats the point of being a writer—to reach people, to allow strangers to connect with your words, to contribute a small fragment to the greater story of humanity. So mind the rules of commercial publishing, to the extent that they make sense, and get the message out.

CHAPTER THREE

Manuscript and Proposal Protocol

"Manuscript: something submitted in haste and returned at leisure."

—Oliver Herford

When you are submitting a manuscript (or a proposal), your goal should be to achieve the opposite of Mr. Herford's definition above. Don't just send in a slapdash piece of work to an agent or publisher. Instead, take the time to craft a manuscript and proposal that will effectively sell your book, and that will sell yourself as a potential author now and for the future. Then, you might not have to wait forever for a response, as an agent or publisher may even be eager to contact you to discuss your book. (Although, as we shall see, you should never pester agents or editors for immediate feedback; give them time to do their own jobs carefully as well.)

PROPER PROTOCOL FOR MANUSCRIPTS AND PROPOSALS

Every writer interested in having his book published or his screenplay produced should follow correct protocol when presenting his query letter to a potential representative or buyer. Not only does this fall under the rubric of good etiquette, but it also goes a long way toward convincing potential buyers that you are a professional who is aware of and observes professional norms. In this sense, writing is no different from any other business: Small details matter in a large way. Your proposal or manuscript is only a tool to help you make the sale, but the better looking the tool, the better chance you have of success.

One surprisingly common violation of protocol that crosses my desk is the submission of a handwritten manuscript. (Yes, it may be hard to believe, but this really still happens.) It's safe to say that when one of these is received, the writing is usually illegible. But even if you have the finest handwriting in the world, it is still an unacceptable submission, especially given the widespread availability and affordability of home computers and the reasonable cost of typing services. As a result, the readers for my company are instructed never to read a handwritten manuscript; they should, instead, move on to a submission by a writer who cares enough about his work to take the time to present it in a clean, legible format.

Similarly, all correspondence accompanying a submission should be typewritten; your prospective representative or publisher will not have to decipher what you've written and miscommunication between the two of you will be kept to a minimum. I also still strongly believe in letters—not faxes—especially for the first communication with a prospective representative. I was shocked—and not happy—when an unsolicited author e-mailed his complete manuscript to me! However, I must admit that my company does now accept e-mail queries if we ask for them. Then, if we request an attachment with more material you can send it. It is impossible with the volume of submission traffic we have to download every submission. When you are contacting agents or publishers with your own queries and proposals, try to find out as early as you can how they prefer to be contacted.

NEATNESS COUNTS

Another violation of protocol is the submission of a sloppy manuscript. This could be defined as:

- A manuscript in poor condition, i.e., dog-eared or dirty pages, sloppily typed, smells of cigarette odor, etc.
- A manuscript printed on a low quality or weak printer, making a photocopy of it especially difficult to read
- A manuscript that is improperly bound

The proper manuscript is, in fact, one that is unbound (the pages are left loose for easy handling by the reader), typed on 8.5 by 11-inch bond or semi-bond paper (one side only), and mailed in a strong cardboard box. Binders or folders are NOT recommended: They make the manuscript too awkward to handle when reading.

Equally crucial is correct pagination. The main purpose of paginating an unpublished manuscript is to facilitate finding a particular page in a hurry.

I once received a manuscript from a published writer—which means he should have known better—that was not only typed sloppily, but printed on a weak printer and unpaginated. We were under a deadline to get this manuscript to a publisher when we discovered that it had been incorrectly photocopied. As a result, we had to re-collate the manuscript and we very nearly missed the deadline. The unpaginated manuscript was a mistake that might have caused serious professional embarrassment to the writer and to us.

Proper pagination for a manuscript begins on the first page of the book—not on the Title page, the Table of Contents page, the Acknowledgment page, or the Dedication page—and it proceeds to the end of the manuscript without pause. Pagination is not broken down by chapters; all illustration pages are included. In addition, simple pagination (numerals printed in the upper right-hand corner or centered on the bottom) is best.

The dogmatic insistence upon pagination may seem irrelevant to the quality of the writing, but a small matter such as this can affect a reader's judgment of the overall work, which could tip the balance when decisions are made.

CREATING PERFECT PROPOSALS AND MANUSCRIPTS

All proposals and manuscripts should:

- Have (at least) one-inch margins
- Be double-spaced
- Be left-justified
- Be typed in a Pica font (such as Times New Roman or Courier, 12-point size on a computer, 10 pitch on a typewriter)
- Be free of all typographical errors
- Be printed on a high quality printer
- Come enclosed in a sturdy manuscript box (Photocopied versions must have dark and legible print)

I am a salesman, but any sales effort I make when representing a writer is only a reflection of the quality of the work I manage. It's not about how good the representative is; it's about how good the author's writing is. I will not represent or submit a work unless it is in impeccable condition. Take the time to present your project in the best possible manner and avoid the saddest fate in publishing—an UNNECESSARY rejection. Although computers are a great asset to authors, bear in mind that your manuscript should be presented simply, not riddled with different typefaces like some recent books. These books are specifically designed by the publisher to appeal to a certain (younger) market demographic. Your job in presenting a manuscript is not to demonstrate your ability as a trendy book designer—it's to highlight the quality of your writing and your idea for a book.

The bottom line: When you present your work to an agent or a publisher, there should be nothing in it that stands in the way of its quality shining through bright and clear. If your manuscript is hard to read or understand, then a busy agent or publisher will decide—in a heartbeat—not to read it at all. Which means that no one else will ever have the chance to read it, either.

CHAPTER FOUR

Find a Good Agent/Manager to Represent You

"Dear Contributor: Thank you for not sending us anything lately. It suits our present needs."
—A note received by the aspiring author Snoopy, in a *Peanuts* cartoon

A re rejection slips from publishers, some even more cruel than the one above, piling up on your desk? You need to find a good agent.

Finding a literary agent, who can also be known as a literary manager or representative, will be one of the most important decisions you can make in your career. Obviously if your mother went to school with Mort Janklow (one of the most successful agents in the world) and they were best of friends and she tells you he owes her a BIG favor, I would allow Mom to make the introduction for you. However, the introduction to any representative is only going to be as good as whatever you have written or are proposing to write. Although I will share many war stories with you in this book, this book is really about how you can learn to navigate your own course through the tricky waters of the publishing and the motion picture and television industries. You will have to discover the way to finding an agent that is best for you and for the type of books that you write (or hope to write in the future).

DO YOUR HOMEWORK

There are many ways to find a literary representative, beginning with the yellow pages. However, the yellow pages in Akron, Ohio, have few literary agents, if any; New York is the publishing capital of the United States, and probably the world, so you should look in the direction of the Big Apple. Try to find a representative in New York, as that is where the action is. Depending on where you live, you may be able to find an agent or representative closer to home who can do the job, but an agent based in New York is more likely to have the strong connections in the book publishing industry that you will need.

One commonly used resource for finding an agent is Jeff Herman's annually updated *Guide to Book Publishers, Editors, & Literary Agents*. Another book to check out is the annual *Guide to Literary Agents* published by Writer's Digest Books, which has listings for hundreds of agents. (The annual *Writer's Market* guidebook, also from Writer's Digest, includes a shorter listing of agents.)

You also might just try Googling "literary agents" or "literary managers" and see what you come up with. There are hundreds of agents out there, but you will only need to choose one to manage your career.

SORTING OUT THE LISTINGS

What are you looking for when you see an agent's listing? Well, the *Guide to Literary Agents* includes sections for each agency that tell you the following:

- **Member Agents:** This gives you the names of agents to contact, sometimes with their specific areas of specialization (fiction, nonfiction, children's, etc.).
- **Represents:** This section describes the general types of works as well as the specific areas (cooking, military history, women's fiction, etc.) that an agency represents.

- **How to Contact:** Some agencies accept e-mail queries; others insist that you mail in your proposal or manuscript with the traditional SASE. Some accept submissions sent simultaneously with other agencies; some want to receive exclusive submissions. An agency may prefer to initially see a proposal, or a sample chapter, or an entire manuscript.
- **Recent Sales:** A short list of book titles (including their publishers) that the agency has placed in recent years.
- **Terms:** The levels of commissions that an agent receives, and the various costs (postage, etc.) that a client may be charged.

All of the above information can be useful for evaluating whether or not to contact an agent, and how to submit a query or manuscript. The most important thing, though, is to make sure that your book fits in with what the agent represents. *Please* don't send your novel to an agent who is described as representing "Nonfiction only"! If you can't picture your book fitting in comfortably with what the agent has represented in the past, the agent won't be able to, either.

If you need to know still more about a particular agency, you can send them a query letter requesting such information. Many agencies (certainly the larger ones) have Web sites, like my own company's site at *www.pmalitfilm.com*. You should check out the site of any agency you are considering contacting in order to find out the most up-to-date information on who works for the agency, what types of works they represent, what books they have sold, and how they prefer to be contacted and sent submissions. At my agency, we think of our site as continually "under construction"; because we constantly sell books and make deals, our Web site is *always* in the process of being updated.

I can't emphasize this enough: Do your homework and be extremely selective in which agents you decide to contact. Agents don't like it when they are approached by a "wannabe" author who has gone to dozens of other agents and is comparing notes and feedback from all of them. Literary representatives are extremely busy people and don't like to play games, and I can assure you that, as with other agents, my company and I will be very direct with you about this if you contact us. Research the history of the agent you're approaching to make sure you have found the kind of person and company that you want to have represent you and your career for years to come.

PERSISTENCE PAYS OFF

Finding a representative is not easy. One example of an author's lengthy search for an agent is that of my client, Anthony DeStefano, who claims he wrote to 100 agents regarding his first book, *A Travel Guide to Heaven* (Doubleday), and that only half replied at all. Of the fifty that did reply, only three of them (including my company) expressed interest in representing him. Anthony says that of those three I was the manager he wanted, and I agreed to represent him. Fortunately, for both of us, this was a marriage made in heaven, and I successfully placed two books for him. The second book, *Ten Prayers God Always Says Yes To,* will be published next year. It is unfortunate that the process of finding representation took Anthony DeStefano many months and quite a lot of effort, but ultimately he made the right choice, and you will too. However, not every marriage is made in heaven, so, I repeat, do your research.

GO WHERE THE REPRESENTATIVES ARE

When you are trying to find the right literary representative, query letters and e-mails are essential parts of your search. But meeting someone face to face can often move along the process more quickly and effectively. The question is, how can you get to meet an agent or manager? (Without hanging around in front of his or her office, that is—something that is definitely not recommended.)

One great way to meet agents and managers, as well as editors, is to attend writers' conferences. Scott Hoffman, one of my associates at PMA Literary and Film Management, contributes the following account of how one writer took advantage of the many opportunities available at a writing conference for advancing one's career:

 Whether you're a novice scribbler, on the verge of finishing The Great American Novel, or trying to find an agent or literary manager to sell your completed, polished book, writers' conferences can help you take your craft to the next level and forge the right partnerships that will allow you to get published.

Here at PMA, we get nearly 500 query letters a week from writers who want us to represent their work. Because of the sheer volume of submissions we receive, it's virtually impossible for us to devote more than a minute or two to each aspiring author. All of us, however, speak frequently at conferences and seminars, as do other literary representatives and many editors from major publishing houses.

Often, as part of these conferences, industry professionals will agree to one-on-one meetings with attendees. These meetings, which are usually about five to fifteen minutes long, are an excellent opportunity to showcase your ideas and your writing to a group of people who can help make your writing dreams come true.

Even if you're not fortunate enough to get one of those one-on-one meetings, there are still numerous opportunities at writers' conferences to buttonhole agents and editors to talk about your work. Consider the story of Mario Acevedo. I met Mario at the Rocky Mountain Fiction Writers' Conference in Denver, Colorado. Mario wasn't able to get a formal meeting with me, so he made sure to track me down after I had given a talk.

Mario gave me the elevator pitch for his book—literally in an elevator. Every writer should have a prepared "elevator pitch." That's a description of your writing that is so short and so exciting that when you happen to be on an elevator with an editor or an agent you can convince him or her to read your work by the time you reach the lobby.

Mario's pitch, was, well, unconventional, to say the least. By the time he was done describing his novel, the only thing I could think of to say was, "That's the strangest idea for a book I've heard of in my entire life." But because I'm always looking for quirky projects, novels and nonfiction books that break the rules, I added, "So you have to send it to me immediately."

By the time I got back to New York, the manuscript was on my desk. I started reading it, and just couldn't stop. The book, *The Nymphos of Rocky Flats*, was about a Latino vampire private detective given the job of investigating an outbreak of sexual misconduct at the Rocky Flats Nuclear Processing Facility. I called the author immediately after finishing the book and signed him as a client.

We went through a light edit of the book and I sent it out to publishers. A little over a week later, we had a three-book deal with HarperCollins. *The Nymphos of Rocky Flats* is scheduled to be published soon and will be available at a bookstore near you—in fact, at just about the same time as the book you're reading right now.

Of course, this doesn't happen to everyone—but if your project is even a little bit outside the mainstream, it can certainly pay to meet an agent or an editor in person. Most of my colleagues have similar stories. Even if we're a little skeptical about the project itself, if we sense how enthusiastic you are about it, there's a good chance we'll agree to take a look.

So what are you waiting for? Get on the Internet, find a writers' conference near you, and make plans to attend. I'll see you there.

AGENTS VS. MANAGERS

I call myself a literary manager (though I prefer to be called a literary lion) because at my company we manage author's careers. And, of the hundreds of New York-based literary agents, we differ as a company in that I am actively involved in the development of the motion picture and television rights to most all of the projects we manage that have a film potential. Agents don't normally produce films, but managers can and sometimes do. This is the main difference between agents and managers. I have regularly traveled to Los Angeles for more than twenty-five years to cultivate many relationships in Hollywood—as with book publishing, the film industry is very definitely a relationship business. This practice of keeping connections on both coasts is why my company specializes in managing authors who write books with film and television production potential.

Different representatives have different specialties. Some only represent nonfiction, or children's books, or science fiction and fantasy, or illustrated and packaged books. Other agencies are eclectic, like we are. In my opinion, a good book is a good book is a good book! Whichever type of agency you choose, be sure that it is one that is experienced in the area of the book you are writing. And if you believe your book has the potential to be turned into a film, try to choose an agency that has some experience with such adaptations.

HOW TO CHOOSE BETWEEN REPRESENTATIVES

Researching your agent's track record before you approach them is extremely important. Obviously, if you Google an agent on the Internet and find several articles that say they are being sued in a class action suit by a dozen authors who have not been paid, you need to look elsewhere. As in every profession, there are good and bad agents and representatives.

When doing your Internet research, you need to carefully evaluate what you find. If you do your research on me, for example, you may find that I was once sued in a completely frivolous lawsuit that was thrown out of the courts and dismissed, and the several appeals that followed were all denied. (Lawsuits are an ugly business to be in, but in the words of several friends and colleagues, to be in business as long as I have and only been sued once is a blessing.) Additionally, you might find that I once sued a multibillion dollar corporation and well-heeled production company when one of my clients, a producing partner, and myself had our project stolen. We sued, and fortunately settled the case without it going to trial, but it took four years and was a lot of hard work. The point is that you should make sure that you choose a reputable representative, one who will protect you and stand up for your rights, and one who doesn't have a history of abusing authors and their rights.

The worst things that a representative can do to you are neglect your career, submit your work to the wrong publisher(s), and not present an accounting to you on a regular, timely basis. A good representative has an obligation to be fair, reasonable, and completely honest in all dealings with the authors they represent. After all, a representative works for the author and the author owns what the representative represents. You might compare it with properly managing real estate. Your career is your apartment house and you want the managing agent to take care of the property. The only difference is that your work is intellectual property as opposed to physical property. Intellectual properties and an author's career need special handling and this is why choosing proper representation will be so critical to your success.

CHAPTER FIVE

Working with Your Representative

*"What an author likes to write most is his
signature on the back of a check."*
—Brendan Francis

Have you heard the one about the agent and the author who
fly to New York from Los Angeles to meet with a publisher?
The three go to lunch and when it is over, the publisher promptly
pays the bill. The agent then says, "I guess we can now discuss
the advance for my client." The publisher slams his hand down
on the table and says, "What do you mean? I just paid it!"

My experiences as a literary agent and currently as a literary
manager have involved me in the representation of many kinds
of writing, including nonfiction and fiction, for domestic and
foreign book and magazine publishers and now Web sites. I call
myself a manager, and my company a management company.
We do everything literary agents do, but we are also involved
in shaping the motion picture and television rights to many of
the books we represent, along with the long-term goals for our
clients' careers. When you work with your own agent or representative, you need to make sure that your representative can
handle the various aspects of your career, and, most importantly,
that he or she is working to help your writing be successful for
years to come, not just until the next commission is received.

BEING A TEAM PLAYER

Working closely with your representative means that both of you should be willing to listen to each other. If you're the star quarterback of the football team, then your manager is the coach. Listen to your coach! Your representative shouldn't try to force you to do anything to your book that violates your writing integrity. (It is very important for you to remember that any move a representative makes on behalf of your book is subject to your final written approval.) However, your representative also can't change the realities of the publishing world. It's a representative's business to know what is marketable and what isn't.

If you already have experience dealing with the publishing world, my suggestion that you rely on your agent's judgment may be hard to accept completely. However, this recommendation is crucial to any writer who is trying to develop a professional attitude. A representative does do more for his client than collect a commission. I can honestly say that I fight for every author I have ever represented and I train everyone on my staff to do the same. Once a contract with a publisher is signed, you have to live with it. So your representative had better make sure it is as good for you as it can possibly be.

Editors are dedicated and extremely individualistic people, and most have very specific tastes. Literary representatives who understand this will be able to help their clients. For example, I have spent a great deal of time developing solid relationships with and nurturing the interests of dozens and dozens of editors over the years at every major publishing house I have dealt with throughout the world. In order for me to grow as a manager, I have to be very selective about who and what I represent. It's easier for me to place a big six-figure book than to sell a smaller book. Publishers are more interested in growing their author slate with name-brand, potential multibook authors than with single midlist projects. I can say without a doubt that a representative can make the difference between his author getting published and being rejected. Often, an editor relies on a representative's endorsement of an author's credibility: The representative offers his reputation as a form of "collateral." A representative's integrity is valuable, but only when coupled with a suitably professional and perfectly polished manuscript.

RELATIONSHIP PROTOCOL

In Chapter 3, we talked about the protocol you should use in creating and sending proposals and manuscripts. There is also a protocol for writers to follow when interacting with representatives and publishers.

First of all, any relationship with a representative or publisher should be treated as a business relationship. For example, when I agree to consider a proposal or manuscript for representation, it is not tantamount to my agreement to represent it. Authors who understand this will allow a reasonable amount of time for me to evaluate their work and to come to my own conclusions about its viability. Pressure from a writer trying to "sell" me usually has an adverse effect; it is more than likely to turn me off from his project altogether. I consider myself the "hunter," not the "hunted." Novice writers must understand that most reputable agencies handle an enormous number of submissions and, quite frankly, because their submissions are from unpublished authors, they are placed at the bottom of the reading pile. Your hard work and determination—and patience—can change that. So, when you do secure representation for your writing, it still does not exempt you from the editorial protocol laid out in this chapter.

Agents and managers, like editors and publishers, are extremely busy people. It is not that we're unfriendly or that we don't want to know about your new project; it's just that we need to restrict communication to matters of real importance. Too many worthless phone calls and too much correspondence requiring responses harm your representative's ability to work productively for you and for other authors he represents. Some writers expect their representatives to be hand-holders or psychiatrists or publicity gurus or lawyers or bankers or friends. Some writers ruin their relationship with me before it starts with too many e-mails and a nagging attitude.

Principally, representatives negotiate the best possible sale for an author's work—this is what we're paid to do. Sometimes, as with my company, a representative or manager may do much more than just sell a client's work. We have gotten many of our clients national publicity, offered important editorial advice, and even given authors ideas for books. On the other hand, we do not do publicity, but I try to help all our clients whenever I can. It is true that your representative does work for you, the author. However, you should establish clearly with your agent how and when you can turn to "your employee" for help.

AGENTS, WRITERS, AND EDITORS

Your agent or manager should answer any questions you have about contractual details concerning your book(s). Unfortunately, a writer sometimes becomes so engrossed in his work as his publishing deadline approaches that he cannot resist talking directly to his editor. The result? The writer tries to dictate to his publishing house how to publish his book (into which the house has likely already made a substantial investment); the editor's excitement for the project is dampened by constant author harassment; and the writer receives far fewer answers than he was hoping for.

Many basic queries from a first-time author can be answered without difficulty by an experienced representative. The questions they cannot answer will likely require the additional weight of their reputation when brought up with an editor or publisher. (This is when the representative begins the conversation by saying, "In all my years as an agent. . .")

Frequently, the writer and his rep can play the good cop/bad cop scenario with the publisher: The author is responsible for the terrific writing and the devotion to his project, while the complaints about the contract, advance, royalties, tardiness in editorial response, expenses, etc., come from the representative. This scenario is editorial protocol at its finest—everyone knows his job and treats each other with respect: The writer is successfully published, the representative secures a potentially lucrative new client, and the publisher gets a great book.

GETTING THE SUPPORT YOU NEED

What can an agent do for a writer? Here's one example. One of my clients, at work on his second book, was dissatisfied with the way his first book (about the psychology of the stock market) was promoted by its publisher. After his hard work, the first book had been published in hardcover and sold about 35,000 copies, an excellent number in my estimation. However, his frustration made him angry with me and with the publishing process in general. In fact, he threatened to quit writing. I explained to him how foolish this threat was: The market would definitely support the next book he was planning to write. I convinced him to write a three-page outline for the second book and he did so reluctantly. He later consented to let me submit his brief proposal to a different publisher. The brief outline, along with his previous book's success, was presented to one of the most important men in the publishing industry. He bought the proposal, paying a handsome advance for it. Of course, the author was delighted and immediately began to work on a proposal for a third book.

The author is now one of the most successful investment bankers in the country; his once privately held company recently merged with a large firm that manages more than $8 billion in investment funds. He attributes much of his success to the publicity he received from his books. His third book was a *New York Times* bestseller!

AGENTS IN NEW YORK AND HOLLYWOOD

In general, New York representatives mainly deal with book publishing and related industries. On the other hand, Los Angeles agencies and management companies mostly deal with writers of movies and television and therefore don't spend as much time representing book authors. L.A. agents often have relationships with New York-based agencies to facilitate contact with writers who are working in publishing; conversely, New York agencies often have relationships with Los Angeles representatives who are well-versed in handling movie rights for their authors.

As mentioned, I am one of the few New York managers who represent all types of writing—in New York, Los Angeles, and worldwide. Besides my management company in New York, PMA Literary and Film Management, Inc., which deals mostly with book authors, I have established myself in the motion picture, cable, television, DVD, and video industries and produced movies with our brother company, Millennium Lion, Inc. In addition, my bicoastal work has afforded me the opportunity to meet all types of writers. This, in turn, has paid off in the growth of my company and in the expansion of our client base.

Here's an example: I once met a famous actress at a party in Beverly Hills; I suggested she write a book on beauty. In a few weeks, we were talking to Simon & Schuster about it; they published it and it became a national bestseller and was on the *New York Times* bestseller list for fourteen weeks. Apart from a cookbook she had already written and self-published, she was unpublished. I was able to help my client because she needed a New York literary representative, not a Hollywood talent agent, business representative, or attorney—all of which she already had.

MAKING CONNECTIONS

The process of networking cannot be underestimated—it is of crucial importance to the management business. I meet many potential clients this way and pride myself on having an "open door" policy with the attitude of trying to help all authors even if we don't represent them. Unfortunately, this policy is not easy to maintain because of the volume of work offered to us, and this is why all authors should not solicit representation until they are absolutely ready and professionally confident that their work is ready to be sold.

The art of networking is contagious. The more you do, the more likely you are to succeed. I'm where I am today because my enthusiasm for my business is so high that if I am walking down the street and I see someone walking to the post office with a manuscript box or shipping envelope, I could approach them, find out that they are carrying a novel, read it, and sell it. This is true networking or just plain aggressive sales or maybe I have just developed a "sixth sense" about authors.

One of my favorite sayings that I've heard in Hollywood is: "Life is like a fishing trip—if you want to catch a big fish, you've got to go where the big fish are." When you set out to look for a literary agent, it's important that you choose one who is actively involved with and visible in the marketplace. Literary representatives do not simply sell an author's work and negotiate the advance. In some cases, the representative must know how to package (or even repackage) and market the project and your career. The primary goal is, however, to sell your work to a publisher. You may have heard that the well-respected British author Doris Lessing sent two of her manuscripts to publishers under a pseudonym. Every editor, including one at Ms. Lessing's own publishing house, rejected them. As this case shows, it's not always the writing that makes the difference.

SOMEONE IN YOUR CORNER

Your literary representative must know the market and the people working in it. If your literary representative's relationships in New York and the world publishing marketplace are solid and well grounded, then you have a decided edge. A literary representative also must have confidence in his or her writers and in their work.

Selling a novel by my client Christopher Cook Gilmore included one of the most unusual experiences I've had as an author's representative and in defending an author's rights. I sold the synopsis and a few sample chapters of Gilmore's second novel, *Watchtower*, to a publisher who had previously hired him to write a novelization. The two had a good relationship. Gilmore finished the novel, and renamed it *The Bad Room*. However, after the editor read it, she called to say, "Christopher Gilmore didn't write the book I hired him to write. He's going to have to do a lot of editing." Gilmore felt his novel was fine the way it was and he wasn't going to change a word for an editor who didn't appreciate the book. When I relayed this information to the editor, she said, "We don't want to publish this book. We want our money back." I offered to give the editor and publisher a check in the amount of the author's advance, post-dated sixty days away, and I would try to resell it. Actually, I had no obligation to return the advance, as the author's representative and Gilmore had already spent his original advance money, but I was confident in the novel and that I could resell it. In two weeks, I received an offer from Avon Books for double the advance that I had previously negotiated for Gilmore and with nearly double the royalties—and he didn't have to change a word in the manuscript. The book was very successful and optioned several times as a film.

DO YOU NEED A CONTRACT WITH A REPRESENTATIVE?

A contract is only a piece of paper but a relationship may last forever. When someone asks me for a business card, and I don't have one (as I usually have handed them all out), I tell them that I don't have a card, but that I do have a reputation.

Yes, you should have an agreement with your representative, but the relationship between you and your agent is more important than the agreement. Different representatives have different agreements.

Normally, in my agency we do not offer our management agreement to our clients until they agree they want us to manage them and we agree to represent them. However, many long-term clients of mine have been working on handshake agreements for years. PMA Literary and Film Management, Inc.'s basic terms and conditions are that we charge a 15 percent U.S. and Canadian commission and a 25 percent foreign commission (from which we may also pay any foreign agents with whom we work, if we decide to do so). Additionally, if we are involved in any producer role on the motion picture or television rights production adaptation to any author's work(s) we manage, we normally reduce our management commission to zero if and when a film actually goes into production and I am paid to be a producer on the production.

The terms you have with your own representative will vary, depending on their policies, and the type(s) of writing you do. Just make sure that any agreement you have covers the various ways your work may be sold or packaged, now and in the future.

HOW TO TREAT YOUR REPRESENTATIVE (AND HOW YOUR REPRESENTATIVE SHOULD TREAT YOU)

Your relationship with your representative is one of the most important relationships you can have. Don't abuse it! In my agency, our clients from hell used to just call, write, or fax us too much. Now, thanks to the ease of using the Internet, they e-mail us too much. This sometimes tells us a lot about how insecure and/or disturbed an author can be.

An author should only e-mail his representative when it is important and not waste their time with too much correspondence. I ask all my clients not to communicate with me unless it is absolutely necessary, though they can always query my assistant with any questions they may have. An author's greatest sin with his representative can be bugging them too much. Our best clients, and the ones who earn the most money and have the most fun, are the ones who let us do our jobs.

However, your agent is obligated to discuss with you a strategy or overall game plan for how to market your work including who might be the best editor(s) and publisher(s) for your book(s) and how and when it (or they) should be published. Additionally, your representative and his company should give you at least a biannual accounting (most publishers pay royalties biannually) and account to you regularly as monies are paid in on any subsidiary rights sales. Such sales might include audio, foreign, electronic, special sales, and motion picture or television options or licenses.

Being properly represented is like being happily married. But, as you already know if you are married or in a serious relationship, all successful relationships need to be worked on. There is no perfect anyone for anyone in any relationship, and I have seen many authors (and their relationships with their representatives) self-destruct with their success. So, if you get a good representative, try your best to stick with them. If they breach any of their fiduciary obligations to you, or treat you unfairly, then you may consider changing representation. But a strong indicator for long-term success as a writer is a solid long-term relationship with a representative who is fighting on your side.

CHAPTER SIX

The Truth About Nonfiction Books

*"The profession of book writing makes horse
racing seem like a good, stable business."*
—John Steinbeck

A nonfiction work is defined as writing derived from fact;
or, for the most part, it is a piece that is fact-based. From a
literary representative's point of view, selling a nonfiction book
is easier than selling a novel. Works of nonfiction include the
following genres:

- Biography (authorized, "as-told-to" or unauthorized)
- Crime (true or anthology)
- How-to (on any subject)
- History (including performing arts, religious, and enter-
tainment histories)
- War
- Science
- Performing arts and entertainment
- Travel
- Cookbooks
- Basically, any fact-based account on any subject

Virtually all of the nonfiction books my company and I have represented (which make up a bit more than half the books we have placed in total) have sold from a proposal.

An editor once told me that a nonfiction book proposal should anticipate and then answer all questions that any editor might be inclined to ask about the book. Aside from the book's topic and other related details, these questions might include the following:

- How long will the book be (in pages and in word length)?
- Will the book be illustrated (with what kind of illustrations)?
- How long will it take to write?
- And (most importantly), why is the book unique? And if it is not unique, why will this book be better than any other book on its subject that has ever been published?

Some years back, my company considered representing a book on female infertility. The book was eloquently written and the author was knowledgeable on the subject. However, after looking at *Books in Print* (the reference book that lists every title currently in print from all U.S. publishers), we discovered there already were dozens of books published on the topic. We decided not to represent a book that might not stand out in what was already an overcrowded marketplace.

Today it is even easier to find out what nonfiction books have been published on various topics. Let's say that you are considering writing your own book on some aspect of female infertility. You go the books section of Amazon.com and type in the word *infertility*. Almost immediately, a list of 658 books with the word "infertility" in the title pops up on your screen.

Now, most of these 658 books related to infertility will probably not be that similar to your own proposed book. Some, for example, will be medical texts intended for a professional audience, while your own book might be aimed at women in their late thirties or older who are trying to overcome fertility problems through natural means that don't require the use of drugs. What you will need to do is to determine what books your own proposed book will be competing against in the bookstores. Ask questions like the following:

- Which books treat a similar topic and are meant for a similar audience?
- Which ones were published recently and which ones are clearly outdated?
- What sets your book apart from all similar books and makes it the one that a significant number of readers will want to turn to?

To find out all of this information, you may need to do a fair amount of research. Besides Amazon, you can run searches on Barnesandnoble.com and on more general search engines. You should also do some more old-fashioned research: Head to the nearest large bookstore and to your local library and take a look at the shelves with books in the field you're considering writing about.

A few pieces of advice about Web searches: You will need to make sure your searches are not too broad or too narrow to find the types of books you're looking for. For example, if you include both the words *female* and *infertility* in your basic Amazon search, you'll get a list of more than 13,000 books—every one that includes *either* of those two words in its title. And if you type in "female infertility" in quotes, you'll get only the fifteen books that have both words together in the title. A good way to fine-tune any Web search is to choose an "Advanced Search" option whenever one is available. On Amazon, this option allows you to search by subject (not just titles), publication dates, and other criteria.

By the way, I have had my own personal experience with the process of seeing where a nonfiction book fits in the marketplace. While I was originally considering the possible market for the book you are reading right now, I learned that many, many books on writing were readily available. However, I also discovered that:

- No book was written specifically from the agent's or manager's point of view.
- Few addressed the topic of what an author can do to make his work more saleable.
- No books for writers thoroughly covered both the book and film possibilities of the profession.

Lastly and most importantly, I decided that the passion I have for my profession and my thirty years of experience in it would enable me to create a book that hits home with readers looking for guidance on its particular topic. I therefore patterned this book for the available market, and I made sure to include useful elements such as samples of book proposals for potential authors to study (as found in Part Three). In the end, all of the research I did spoke to me and said, "You are a Literary Lion! Go out and roar for all of the authors out there who need this book."

WHAT READERS NEED

Several years ago, I sold a book called *Open Boundaries* written by Howard Sherman and Ron Schultz, to Addison Wesley for a $75,000 advance. The author incorporated tips from Richard Carlson's philosophy on selling into his own proposal to help him sell his idea. (Mr. Carlson was the president of the Carlson National Group, a national communication and sales consulting company.) As adapted for the particular world of bookselling, Carlson's philosophy puts the process of publishing a book into the following steps:

1. The decision to publish a book is based on the Verified Need, which is the discovery of too few books (or too many inadequate books) on the same topic. This Need is based on factual information, not hearsay or guesstimation. To verify this need, you will need to do the sort of market exploration discussed above.

2. The Felt Need, which is based on opinion, asks, "Why is the Verified Need intolerable or unacceptable?" In other words, why does it appear that the market for this topic is not being met? This opinion should not belong solely to the author, but it also should represent the opinion of experts.

3. According to Carlson, the Felt Need is followed by the Verifiable Benefit, which asks, "What will the reader gain from this book that can't be found elsewhere?" Like the Verified Need, the response to this question is based on fact and evidence, not on the hopes and wishes of the author.

4. Finally, the author should provide the Felt Benefit, or, how long the book will succeed in fulfilling a need. The Felt Benefit is based on the author's opinion.

As Carlson states, "When all four of these issues are addressed in this particular order, there is a reason to buy and an opportunity to sell."

Schultz made sure that these four points were incorporated and addressed within the first three to four parts of his book proposal, yet he did not specifically highlight them, so the reader is almost unaware of this successful sales technique. In your own book proposal, you can address these issues as well; it will help to create a convincing argument for the market appeal and likely success of your nonfiction book.

NONFICTION PROPOSAL GUIDELINES

Given below is a brief description of what my company has used as a guideline for developing a nonfiction book proposal. Of course, nonfiction book proposals will vary depending on the genre of the book being proposed and its particular attributes, but most often, they incorporate the same basic points. This is a tried-and-true format, so it should be invaluable for creating your own proposal.

Before a publisher can make an offer to a writer, or a literary representative can agree to represent a book, he or she must know some basic, pertinent facts about the book. These facts should be included in every proposal:

- The approximate number of pages
- The total number of words (Note: 75,000 to 125,000 words is an average length for a nonfiction book. Usually manuscript pages are 250 to 300 words per page, depending on typeface, margins, and spacing)
- The type of format
- The number and type of illustrations and how the illustrations will be presented (i.e., color, black and white, graphs, charts, etc.). Additionally, an author must have the legal right to use any kind of illustration. Signed releases are now necessary on each and every image before a publisher will publish any kind of illustration.

The publisher needs all this information in order to calculate the advance payment against the writer's anticipated earnings during the book's first year of publication.

The following is the standard format our writers use when presenting a nonfiction book:

1. A Book/Author Sheet that would read like the copy on the book jacket; it should include several paragraphs about the book and one paragraph about the author.
2. An Introduction, Preface, Prologue, and/or Foreword to the book. (Note: Ideally, a famous or respected authority could write one of these for you. Just make sure you can deliver what you promise; don't suggest that Dr. Phil will be writing a glowing foreword for you, when you've never met him and have no possible way of doing so.)
3. A few paragraphs addressing the publisher's main question: "Why should we publish this book?" You should

discuss the book's available market and how your book would differ from others on the same topic.

4. A Table of Contents, briefly listing the chapters and including a few sentences about each chapter. This is also known as an annotated table of contents.

5. A few sample chapters, normally the first three, unless there is a cogent reason to provide later chapters. The samples should illustrate your writing ability and show that you are a professional and that you can deliver publishable, acceptable prose.

6. If your book includes illustrations or photographs, samples of these also should be included. Note: Do not suggest using any illustration unless you are completely sure you can obtain the rights to do so.

I also suggest to authors that they obtain endorsements and quotes for their work and build Web sites; these can be used to showcase their work and demonstrate that they are serious about their careers as writers. An author can never do enough to promote their book(s) and career!

All of this material should be assembled in a neat, professional matter. All pages should be typed, double-spaced, on bond paper; wide margins should be used. If the book is typed on a computer, only a letter quality or laser printer is acceptable. All photocopies should be of the highest quality. Organizing an attachment, preferably in Microsoft Word, is also acceptable to some representatives and editors, but make sure you verify this with them first before sending any attachments. For computer network security reasons, some representatives will not download any files from people they don't know.

In Part Three of this book, you'll find several samples of nonfiction book proposals; these have been used successfully to market works by authors my company represents. Before creating your own nonfiction proposal, be sure to look at this section for ideas on the proper style, format, and content of a proposal that will sell your own book as well as possible.

THE RIGHT MARKET AT THE RIGHT TIME

Any author setting out to write a proposal or book should have a clear understanding of precisely who the market is for the book, as well as which publishers are the right sales targets for it. A good manager or agent who works with you can help you focus on a particular publisher's needs. However, if your manager tells you the business strategy book you are writing is perfect for Harlequin Romance, fire them immediately, and take a walk or have a drink to calm yourself down. Harlequin does not publish nonfiction! Any good manager will know this!

Frequently, publishers are looking to grow certain categories of books within their list. If an author and his manager are fortunate enough to submit the right kind of book at the precise time a publisher is expanding their list in that area, then that is what we all strive for. It's called good timing!

In addition to books that benefit from good timing, there are always books that achieve publication through their uniqueness and perfect fit in the marketplace. For example, I took on the management of a cutting-edge business philosophy book, *The Power of Breakthrough: How the World's Great Companies and Top Leaders Achieve Impossible Growth* by Dr. Bart Sayle and Dr. Surinder Kumar with Tammy Kling. In the words of my clients, this book was the missing book in all the business leadership strategy books in the marketplace, which is why it warranted an auction and commanded a significant six-figure advance. When authors say that their book is unique in a category, and they are able to back it up, publishers pay attention. It goes without saying that the reading audience is always open to a new "cutting-edge" philosophy. The strategy described in *The Power of Breakthrough* is that good management grows good employee relationships first, and consequently good products are grown, which equals good business. This same strategy is applicable to good books. If you manage your writing correctly, in concert with your representative, good relationships with publishers and editors will develop, which will lead to good books being produced, and ultimately a successful career for the author. I am proud of our work with *The Power of Breakthrough* and its authors, as I obviously am proud whenever we place books at high levels. This is a win-win-win situation: It is good for the authors and their future careers and for PMA Literary and Film Management, Inc.'s reputation in the industry, as well as good for other projects and clients PMA may represent.

Let me emphasize once more here the importance of the relationship between an author and his or her representative. The value of a literary manager's belief in his client's work and the manager's assistance during the selling process cannot be underestimated. The cost of a good representative is negligible compared to the gains earned for the writer by setting up a strong and profitable business relationship with a publisher. In every deal I negotiate, I always try to earn the author more so they will never regret paying me or my company a commission. I take the necessary time to "tune up" a deal—higher royalties, better splits, flow-through (an accelerated pay-out to the author after their advance earns out)—you name it and I'll try to get it for our clients. So, let's take a positive approach to writing: Any author who is determined to succeed and has an awareness of the marketplace—and who has read this book!—can improve his or her writing so it will be worthy of representation and saleable.

TYPES OF NONFICTION BOOKS

Over the many years I have been in this business, I have represented almost every kind of book. The key to success in selling a work is the quality of the proposal and the potential significance of the work in the marketplace, juxtaposed against who the author is and what their platform may be. I am only as good a representative as the quality of the author's work that I am managing. Some types of writing may not necessarily require representation; the most likely examples of these are found in academic writing or textbooks. However, I would generally advise an author to never enter into an agreement with any publisher without some kind of representation.

The following sections discuss some of the more popular varieties of nonfiction books.

Sports Books

Some types of nonfiction books remain staples in the industry and are easier to sell than others. For example, sports or sports-related books seem to never stop selling. Recently my company placed two: one by noted sportswriter Harvey Frommer on the 1927 Yankees, placed with Wiley, and another on USC's Trojan Ten by Barry LeBrock, with Chamberlain Brothers (a division of Penguin). One advantage sports books have is that most of them relate to a specific team, player, or sport. This means that such books often have a ready-made audience of fans (which is short for "fanatics," of course) who will buy just about any book about their beloved Green Bay Packers, or Boston Red Sox, or their idols such as Tiger Woods or Michael Jordan. In some ways, this kind of specific identification can limit the potential overall audience. On the other hand, a rich, dramatic, and well-told sports story, like the one in Laura Hillenbrand's *Seabiscuit: An American Legend*, can reach a large group of readers and sell millions of copies to people who have never been to a racetrack in their lives. Of course, it also can help to sell a lot of books if a sports story is turned into a high-profile movie like *Seabiscuit*, or, more recently, *Cinderella Man*, which no doubt helped to sell many copies of Jeremy Schaap's book of the same name about the boxer James J. Braddock.

Business Books

Business and finance books also seem to be a staple, but an author needs to find the right niche. For example, hundreds or even thousands of books on leadership have been published in recent years, so that is not an area I would suggest writing about, assuming that you don't want to face a lot of tough competition in the bookstores. However, there are always new trends, and sometimes these trends may expand just as books on them are starting to be published. Globalization, outsourcing, and nano- and digital technologies are all areas of business that are being written about extensively at the moment. All business books also need to be considered against the always volatile and changing financial climate that, as we all know, is drastically dependent upon such impossible-to-predict factors as war, terrorism, the rising costs of oil, and more.

Biographies

Biographies have also always been a staple of the publishing industry, but it is a matter of finding the right biography and writing it at the right time. It seems that a year or so before every election, there are a plethora of books about new presidential candidates, as well as the president, their families, and other well-known political leaders. When a publisher is deciding if you are the right person to write such a book, your experience in the field and your access to inside information will be important factors.

Historical biographies about noted figures are always a possibility. For example, a new client of ours is fascinated with Sigmund Freud and is at the moment feverishly researching a Freud biography. He has come up with some amazing information that he claims has never been written about before, and, hence, he has a unique take on Freud's relationship with his family, particularly his wife's sister. After all the many books written on Freud, an author needs to give publishers, book reviewers, and readers a reason to believe that his book will contain something that is new and worthy of attention.

Of course, if your name happens to be David McCullough, the author of hugely successful biographies of Harry Truman and John Adams, you can be sure that any biography you write will be sought after by publishers and noticed by readers everywhere. Just about everyone else writing a book on a major figure will need to find a particular angle. One well-received 2005 book, for example, was Stacy Schiff's *A Great Improvisation: Franklin, France, and the Birth of America*. Franklin is a familiar subject in many books, of course, but Schiff's book focused on his eight years spent as America's envoy to France. It thus capitalized both on the current fascination Americans have with our Founding Fathers (as exemplified by the bestselling books from McCullough and others) and on the enduring interest we have in France and all things French.

In Part Three of this book, the first sample book proposal, on page 142, is for a biography of Steve Jobs, the legendary co-founder of Apple Computer. It demonstrates how you need to prove to publishers that your subject is worthy of a book, and that you are just the person to write it.

Fleeting and Enduring Trends

Pop culture is another high-growth category in nonfiction publishing, but it is a matter of finding the right person, group, trend, or piece of culture to write about. A pop culture book could be about an actor, performer, musician or group, as well as current trends in fashion and design that are popular.

One problem with writing about pop culture is that it is very difficult to be timely enough. A newspaper article about a current musical sensation could be written today and published tomorrow. A magazine article could be published next month. A book, on the other hand, may not appear for a year or longer (unless it is a slapped-together "instant book"); by that time, the interest many people have in the book's subject may have waned or disappeared. The long-term sales potential for pop culture books is not very great, either, as those who wrote books on the Backstreet Boys already know, and those writing books on *The Apprentice* will someday find out.

Other trends may be more enduring. Religious books of all kinds have become enormously successful. After the shocks of 9/11, the book-buying public appeared to begin seeking a higher consciousness and a quest to find out the true meaning of life. Consequently, religious sales have grown tremendously. To give the most prominent example: *The Prayers of Jabez: Breaking Through to the Blessed Life* by Bruce Wilkinson has sold more than eight million copies to date.

True-Crime Books

Over the years, as a result of my management of Vincent Bugliosi, the author of *Helter Skelter*, I have become a target for many reporters or journalists who have a true crime or crimes that they want to write about. I have sold dozens of crime books, but the market has changed. It used to be that a good true-crime book would be published in hardcover and sell 15,000 to 25,000 copies and then sell a 100,000 (or more) in mass market. Now, because there are so many true crimes covered in the media, they are usually only published as mass market originals, and an average printing is around 50,000 copies. This doesn't translate to much income for an author, so my advice is if you want to write true crime, pick a big one. I am presently working on the biggest crime story that I have ever encountered, an account of a New York cop who infiltrated the Cosa Nostra and lived (and still is living) to talk about it; the book describes how he went undercover again and again; and how his story chronicles the New York Mafia over the last forty years. My client had a front row seat for every major crime family in New York and how they operated for decades. This is the sort of story that may become a

BIG hardcover book and then a television series. My specialty as a literary manager is just this sort of book that has major motion picture and television potential.

Proposal 2 in Part Three (on page 167) is a proposal for a true-crime book by Steven Salerno about a dramatic murder case. My introduction to the proposal highlights some of the difficulties and concerns that come from writing about actual cases that become involved in the criminal justice system.

SPECIALTY BOOKS

Many years ago, there was a book published called *Real Men Don't Eat Quiche*. It was extremely successful and was the seminal book of a genre called the Non-book, or Specialty Book—that which is not considered a serious book.

Have you ever seen a book called *The Nothing Book*? The perfect example of a Non-book, it consisted of a black binder with blank pages in between. It sold millions of copies.

There are various categories of Non-books, or Specialty Books, including humor (Dave Barry), cartoon (such as *Garfield* or *Peanuts* books) and gimmick (*Real Men Don't Eat Quiche*, for example), and a book of lists (rationalizations for women who do too much work while running with the wolves). Unbelievably, these publishing programs have become extremely successful. Think about it: Every time a new fad is created or a new invention hits the market, there is the possibility for a new kind of Non-book.

When telephone answering machines first became popular, publishers everywhere were producing books about how to play practical jokes on friends utilizing them. My company represented one such book called *At the Sound of the Beep*.

It may seem that joke books were on the upswing, and they were a staple of Specialty Books for perhaps a century. Every manifestation of a joke book has been published from *Truly*

Tasteless Jokes to *Gross Jokes* to *The Worst Jokes You Have Ever Heard* to a series called *Joking Off*. Some of these joke book series have been published in numerous volumes and continue to be staples of publishing. However, with the Internet craze of everyone sending everyone jokes via e-mail, this genre has waned.

Now, you may wonder whether or not you should write a Non-book or a Specialty Book. My advice to you is to consider this very carefully. It's easy to imagine the success you might have publishing a book that sells 100,000-plus copies. But, finding the right gimmick and the right publisher is not easy.

Many years ago, the *Questions* books had been successful and, as a result, I received a number of proposals for similar books; none has been placed. However, recently I received a proposal for a book called *Stuck on You* by Katie Gates and Tim Knight that I thought was really cute. It was a tiny book, less than twenty-four pages that included patches that the reader would put on their arms during various stages of recovery from a failed relationship. Everyone in my office hated it. I loved it and placed it with Chamberlain Brothers. This little book might spawn a major *Stuck On* series, so keep your eyes on the bookstore shelves around the globe. The book is gorgeous, and this is a perfect example of authors being lucky enough to find the right editor/publisher with a vision greater than their own. It's called synergy! As a literary representative, I offer my congrats to Katie and Tim, and I have major respect for Anna Cowles and Carlo DeVito at Chamberlain Brothers for displaying the vision to see the book's potential.

Research the marketplace carefully before considering the development of any Specialty project. Just because you have a gimmick doesn't mean you're going to sell it. Many agencies may have the same philosophy we do: We represent authors—professional writers with long-term careers ahead of them—not one-shot wonders.

LOOK TO THE FILM AND TELEVISION POTENTIAL

If you are an author who wants to write nonfiction books, I would suggest that you try to find stories that have definite motion picture or television potential. Why not? If you are going to do the work, wouldn't it be better to try and focus your energies on something that does indeed have that potential down the road? The trick is to find something that clearly has such film potential. There are many recent examples of blockbuster books that became blockbuster films: *A Beautiful Mind, Midnight in the Garden of Good and Evil, A Perfect Storm*—I think you get the idea. Choose your book projects very carefully. Given the choice, what author would want to go through all the hard work and suffering to write a book and then not have the potential reward of having a motion picture or television production made based on their work?

CHAPTER SEVEN

The Worlds of Fiction

"There are three rules for writing a novel.
Unfortunately, no one knows what they are."
—W. Somerset Maugham

Just as there are many categories of nonfiction (as explained in the previous chapter), there are many categories and genres of fiction. The main difference between marketing fiction and nonfiction is that your representative can sell a nonfiction book based on a proposal but for a novel—particularly in the instance of your first novel—you need a completed and perfect manuscript. Yes, I said perfect!

The most common categories of fiction today are as follows:

- Literary
- Historical
- Romance
- Romantic Suspense
- Chick Lit
- Mystery
- Suspense/Suspense Thriller
- Young Adult, Young Reader, Middle Grade, Preschool Fiction
- Sci Fi/Fantasy
- Horror
- Western
- And just plain old Mainstream Fiction or the Great American Novel

The main difference between literary fiction vs. mainstream or genre fiction is that literary novels tend to be more character driven and atmospheric, whereas commercial and genre fiction tend to be more plot and circumstance driven. In my experience as a representative, we have managed many different variations of fiction including instances of novels being hybrids—for example, a mystery suspense thriller or a thriller with horrific overtones.

The main thing that I ask all authors to strive for is a great book—not a good book or an okay novel, but a fantastic, superior work, no matter what genre it is. Quite frankly, in today's market, a company such as mine cannot take on the management of any fiction unless it is stellar—and I do mean stellar in every respect! The old saying that "a good book is a good book is a good book" has now been changed to "a good book must be a great book to get published today." I know what you are thinking: What about all the crap that gets published? I can assure you that if you are a beginning author who wants to attract the interest of a reputable and effective representative, and then be published by a top-notch publisher, you will need to provide high-quality work.

TRENDS IN FICTION

As with nonfiction books, trends in fiction come and go. Perhaps the most popular recent trend in mainstream publishing is the emergence of what has commonly been referred to as Chick Lit. You might describe Chick Lit as another version of the romance novel, but with a younger, hipper audience in mind. One novel my company placed, *Slow Hands* by Lynne Kaufman (Mira/Harlequin), was sophisticated Chick Lit about two sisters, thirty- and forty-something, who inherit over a million dollars when their mother suddenly dies. However, there is a catch: They cannot use the money for twenty-five years unless they create a business plan that passes muster with their mother's estate attorney. They decide to open a bed and breakfast, which is a disguise for a full service spa where women can go and have their every need attended to by Zen student monks. This was a terrific premise for a book, and someday may be a motion picture as well.

Often a retelling of historical facts can be a way for an author to write a novel. Look at E.L. Doctorow's *Ragtime* or Michael Shaara's Pulitzer Prize–winning novel *The Killer Angels* (the basis for the 1993 film *Gettysburg*). Many thousands of novels have been based on true events or actual events in history that have been embellished by novelists who took artistic license to create a story around them. One of our clients, David Maine, came to our attention when he sent us a manuscript for *The Preservationist* (based on the biblical legend of Noah's Ark), from Pakistan, of all places, where he lives. After we had plucked that manuscript from the slush pile of submissions, my associate, Scott Hoffman, gave David an idea for a second novel, *Fallen* (based on the biblical story of Cain and Abel). David has also completed a third biblical epic, *The Book of Samson*. The first two books were published in 2004 and 2005 in hardcover by St. Martin's Press, with trade paperback editions to follow. These books have been sold in a dozen countries throughout the world as of this writing, have been licensed to several book clubs, had audio versions made, and have been heavily and favorably reviewed. Essentially, this author has for the moment cornered the market on biblical fiction being retold in a modern way. And—you won't be surprised to hear—we are in discussions about how to turn these epic stories into major films.

CHOOSING A REPRESENTATIVE AND A PUBLISHER

When you are exploring who should represent your fictional work and who might be the best fit for the kind of writing you do, there are several things you have to take into consideration. For example, my company is not heavily involved in the worlds of science fiction and fantasy; other agencies may specialize in that kind of fiction. However, if you think your work has surefire film potential, you may want to choose a representative with strengths in the motion picture and television worlds, and not give quite as much consideration to the genres they specialize in.

You also need to consider whether or not your potential manager has a presence in the foreign market. Some agents and managers do and many don't. For my clients, we try to retain foreign rights whenever we can and it can be a real battle. On the aforementioned David Maine novels, for example, St. Martin's Press controls them on the first two novels, but we did not do a world license on Maine's third novel, *The Book of Samson*, so we will be placing that novel directly with foreign publishers.

Assuming you have more than one candidate for managing your novel (if so—congratulations!), you need to carefully weigh where you think your career will be best managed for the long run. And, once you have representation, you then may have the same choices to make in a publisher, and hopefully you will. I have seen many publishers drop the ball on many authors and literally let books die. Promoting fiction is a lot harder than promoting nonfiction, unless there is some way that the author's work can be tied into a contemporary news item or series of events.

Additionally, when choosing a publisher it is important to know how many similar books or authors are on that publisher's list. Obviously, you don't want to wind up with a publisher who has too many authors writing about the same things. The decision of who to represent you and who will publish your work are probably the two most important decisions you can make after you have decided what you want to write.

CAN YOU TAKE THE CRITICISM?

Everyone who creates—whether it is a novel, nonfiction book, movie, piece of art—must deal with criticism. This sounds easy enough to accept, but for most creators, accepting criticism is as difficult as the act of creating itself. And criticism is not just something you will encounter down the road when your novel is reviewed by the local newspaper (you should only be so fortunate that it in fact is reviewed or even mentioned). You'll also have to face criticism of your work throughout the publishing process: from when you submit your work to your potential future representative, to when your rep tries to sell your book to publishers, to when your editor pushes you to improve your work.

A former colleague at my company, Jennifer Robinson, wrote the following piece (from here to the end of the chapter) on how writers need to learn how to accept and benefit from criticism:

Two Thumbs Down: Dealing with Criticism

At a recent writers' conference, a client was asked when she felt her novels were completely finished. "When I'm signing copies in a bookstore," she replied. "I like to change things constantly." A writer who is not just willing but eager to rewrite (and rewrite and rewrite) is worth his or her weight in gold.

During the years I've worked with Peter Miller and PMA Literary and Film Management, Inc.—on virtually all the fiction we've represented—I've never seen a book leave our office without having been reworked extensively.

While fiction may seem intimate and personal—a total, individual expression of who you are—it doesn't mean the piece won't need the fresh eye of an astute reader in order to flower fully. Indeed, it's probably because fiction is so personal that it needs constructive criticism—the writer is too close to it and is unable (or unwilling) to see its flaws. Your novel is your baby; quite literally, you gave birth to it. And so, to you, it may seem like a beautiful, flawless jewel. But, in most cases, it's not. The sooner you realize this, the sooner you will admit that someone else might see its flaws. Then, the faster you'll correct them and the closer you'll be to having your work published. Taking pride in your work is vital; seeing every word as sacrosanct is deadly.

Everyone is going to make comments about your novel; your literary representative will be the first in a line of many. As representatives, we find it necessary to do some editing—sometimes minor, sometimes extensive—on every novel we represent. Selling new fiction is difficult in any case, but if the work is imperfect ("close but not quite"), it's nearly impossible. When we submit a novel to editors, we must feel confident that the book is in the best shape possible, then the editor will come into the picture. Editors have their own opinion on a piece, their own ideas of how a novel can improve. However, after you are published, the criticism doesn't stop. If you're lucky, you'll get lots of reviews; if you're not so lucky, those reviews will be sparse or bad. If you have no patience for your literary representative's criticism (remember he or she is the one who loves your book and wants it to succeed), then the cold, cruel world of publishing (and snarky reviewers who love to flex their muscles by wittily trashing others' efforts) will be intolerable.

The clients we work with best, those who navigate the shoals of publishing most expertly, are the ones who listen to criticism and, in fact, relish it. They're the writers who are excited by new ideas, new directions, new possibilities for their work; they're the ones who know that any good idea or interesting alteration will only make their piece better and that having the best book possible is, after all, the whole point. Writers who revile criticism, who won't listen to it or who shy away from writing after they receive it, run into stumbling blocks throughout their careers. They certainly will have difficulty getting a representative, getting published, and finding an audience.

Criticism can be a writer's best friend.

As a writer, you must:

- Learn to accept criticism
- Be able to learn from criticism
- Get to love criticism

Otherwise, your work (and your career) will never be as successful as it can be.

In an attempt to present unpublished writers with the idea of accepting criticism and to loosen them up a bit, I created the following questionnaire for a writers' workshop on criticism I attended. This obviously is a lighthearted attempt at teaching novice writers how to deal with criticism, but the underlying message is serious. So, take the test and see what your Criticism IQ is.

WHAT IS YOUR CRITICISM IQ?

1. *When I finish a draft of my work I. . .*
   FedEx it to Judith Regan.
   Put it in my sock drawer.
   Give it to a trusted friend to read.
   Have a martini.

2. *I have considered joining a writers' group because I'm. . .*
   Lonely.
   Interested in the expressive flow if ideas and criticism in a nonthreatening atmosphere where I might learn something and improve my craft.
   Addicted to the free donuts.
   Anxious to read the work of writers who are worse than I am.

3. *Maxwell Perkins was. . .*
   That guy on Mutual of Omaha's *Wild Kingdom*.
   The inventor of instant coffee.
   The chauffeur on *Hart to Hart*.
   Legendary editor of Hemingway, Fitzgerald, and Wolfe.

4. *When someone tells me he doesn't like my work I. . .*
   Kick him where it hurts.
   Go off to a corner and cry.
   Thoughtfully consider what they are saying and why.
   Fill out my application for air-conditioning repairman school.

5. *I consider the optimum number of drafts on my work to be. . .*

   One.

   Two.

   Thirty-two.

   However many it takes.

6. *People who criticize my work are. . .*

   Unhappy, unfulfilled wannabe writers who hate me.

   Messengers of Satan.

   Trying to help my career.

   Sorry as soon as I get hold of them.

7. *If someone who critiques my book gives me a new idea that I use, I will. . .*

   Be revealed as a shameless fraud on *Oprah*.

   Become impotent.

   Never write anything good ever again.

   Still get my name on the book cover.

8. *I believe that every word I write is. . .*

   Golden.

   English.

   Really quite bad, but don't tell anyone.

   A work-in-progress.

9. *An editor's central function is to. . .*

   Give me vast sums of money.

   Become my best friend.

   Offer extensive and detailed criticism of my work so it will be as good as it can be.

   Yell, "Stop the presses!"

10. *An agent who offers editorial advice is. . .*

    Cruisin' for a bruising.

    Suffering from delusions of grandeur.

    Wasting time when he should be on the phone making me a deal.

    Trying to make my book more marketable.

11. *I won't change my work unless. . .*
    I'm paid an enormous advance.
    Someone offers me some clever advice.
    Michelle Pfeiffer/Andy Garcia gives me a foot massage.
    Hell freezes over.
12. *I will only take advice from. . .*
    Sonny Mehta.
    My mechanic about my car, but only if I'm sure he's not
       trying to fleece me.
    Anyone with something valid to say.
    Dionne Warwick and her psychic hotline friends.
13. *The best criticism is. . .*
    No criticism.
    In the *New York Times*.
    Honest, respectful, and constructive.
    Offered by me.
14. *The most important thing about writing is. . .*
    Having a good computer with all the latest software.
    Being a lawyer from Mississippi.
    Having a first cousin who works at Simon & Schuster.
    Rewriting.

Now, let someone you trust read your novel and give you his or her comments. They should be thorough, and they could be merciless. Listen to their criticism and take it with strength. Then go and criticize someone else's work: at least it will make you feel better.

CHAPTER EIGHT

Wonderful Circumstances

"Most writers can write books faster than publishers can write checks."
—Richard Curtis

L et me tell you a story of what can happen when everything works just about as well as it can for an aspiring author much like yourself.

On the first Saturday of January 1992, I went to the post office, collected my mail, went to work, and began sorting though the barrage of correspondence and submissions that day. In 1992, my company was receiving between twenty-five and 100 new submissions each week. Currently, we log between 200 and 500 per week.

One of the submissions I opened that day was headed for the "slush pile," it was an unsolicited submission from an unknown author named Nancy Taylor Rosenberg consisting of a substantial portion of her first novel, *Mitigating Circumstances*. It was logged and given to a new reader in the company, Catherine Garnier, who began reading it and was immediately impressed. Having previously worked for a major film producer, Catherine was struck by the compelling story and also by the work's obvious film potential. On the basis of her evaluation, I read the first chapters and was dazzled. I forwarded the manuscript to our senior reader and Director of Development at the time, Jennifer Robinson. I wanted Jennifer to read the entire manuscript and give me her comments; as one of my senior associates, I trusted her judgment implicitly. Next, I arranged to meet Nancy Rosenberg in San Diego, California, the following week. I like to meet potential clients in person. I had already planned to be in San Diego to speak at the Southern California Writer's Conference and Nancy's home was in nearby Laguna Niguel.

When we met, Nancy handed me the latest draft of her manuscript and asked if PMA would give her advice on rewriting and polishing it. I agreed to have this done for her. From the first moments of our meeting, I was struck by her former association with the Dallas Police Department and by the fact that she is a native Texan.

My affinity for Texans dates back to 1987, when I gave my first speech at the University of Texas at Dallas. I have had a lot of positive activity with Texas authors over the years: My company has successfully represented more than seventy books by Texans alone! And, most importantly, my wife Giselle hails from Fort Worth.

On the plane back to New York, I read a substantial portion of her revised manuscript and I was riveted. Nancy's storytelling style draws the reader in as the plot unfolds: She adds layer upon layer of suspense and intrigue. It is a wonderful experience to read a novel that only gets better and more suspenseful as it progresses. It was a real page-turner, simply a compelling and riveting read.

Two weeks later, although our report on her manuscript was not quite finished, I called her. She asked me directly, "Do you want to represent me?" I responded, "Yes!" Nancy then mentioned that several other agents had offered to represent her and were inundating her with calls. I told her how effective my company would be for her, particularly when books have motion picture potential. I promised to send her our notes the next day, to be followed up by a contract. Nancy was impressed by our six-page report; she wanted to sign with us and asked me how to handle the other agents. I told her to be as honest and direct with them as she was with me.

When a representative is ready to sign an author, it's like a man proposing marriage to a woman: The agent offers the writer a "ring" because he wants to "marry" the author; the author, then, should do the right thing and show the other "boyfriends" the engagement ring and tell them to quit knocking on the door. Nancy is an indefatigable writer, capable of working twelve hours a day, nonstop. She is, quite simply, the stuff literary representatives and publishers dream of. Based on our notes, she quickly completed a revised version of her book. Jennifer spent an entire day reading the manuscript one more time. We faxed Nancy our notes and she promised to tend to the last polish immediately.

Nancy was about 75 percent completed with the manuscript when I began calling publishers. I knew that many were seeking new female authors, especially those who wrote women's suspense fiction. Women buy approximately 75 percent of new fiction. Publishers try to capitalize on this market.

Nancy's novel was perfect! I decided to submit the manuscript simultaneously to fourteen hardcover and hard-soft publishers whom I thought would be interested. (Fourteen is my lucky number.) Because I had been in the business for so long, I had established relationships with many senior editors, so I tried to select the editors I thought would fall in love with the project. On a Tuesday in February, fourteen manuscripts were hand-delivered in special boxes that I had found. That Thursday, I was in Fort Worth to celebrate my father-in-law's birthday and to host a luncheon for sixty Texas authors. On Friday, I phoned the office and learned that I had received a phone call from a major New York publisher regarding *Mitigating Circumstances*. There was no indication from the message of the editor's degree if interest so I called her. She told me that when her lunch was canceled the day before, she stayed in the office and read Nancy's manuscript—she couldn't put it down! There were a few minor problems but she told me she wanted to buy it. She wanted to make a deal to include Nancy's second—and at the time unfinished—novel, *Prince of the Oaks*. In representational terms, this was a minor miracle! Not only had an editor actually read the manuscript (not a reader or assistant), but that editor was willing to make an offer for not one, but two books! As you may imagine, I was tremendously excited by this quick turn of events, but I had thirteen other phone calls to make, to see if the other publishers were equally interested.

On Monday, back in New York, I received a call from Michaela Hamilton, at the time the Editorial Director of New American Library's mass-market lines (now Dutton-Signet, a division of Pearson). She wanted to acquire another book I represented called *The Secrets of Seduction*, by Brenda Venus. I was happy about that but I also wanted to know her interest in the sizzling women's suspense thriller for which I believed I would receive an offer from a different publisher the next day. I then called the remaining publishers. (Although the manuscript had been in the marketplace for only several days, and I didn't want to appear pushy, I had to kindle their interest in it.) Early Tuesday morning, Michaela Hamilton phoned three times; she wanted to buy the Brenda Venus book—and both of Nancy Taylor Rosenberg's novels! I then proceeded to solicit a floor bid.

I received a bid of $600,000 for a two-book, hard-soft world rights deal, then set an auction date, offering NAL, the floor holder, a 5 percent topping privilege. (This is the right to win the book by topping any other offers by 5 percent.) The phones didn't stop ringing—and not just from New York but from Hollywood producers, too. Random House offered a whopping $750,000 for two books, hardcover rights only. NAL exercised its 5 percent topping right and we ended up placing Nancy's two novels for $787,500. Simultaneously, TriStar Pictures, a division of Sony Corporation, offered to option the feature film rights for $125,000, against a high six-figure sum, outbidding all other interested film companies.

One reason TriStar Pictures paid so much money for the film rights option is because director Jonathan Demme (*Silence of the*

Lambs, Philadelphia) wanted to direct and produce it through his Clinica Estetico Productions, which had a deal at TriStar (now Sony). The film rights were optioned; the film is still in development, but unfortunately, a dead development. Demme's company and TriStar (Sony) still hold the rights to *Mitigating Circumstances*, because they purchased the movie rights.

Director Agnieszka Holland (*Europa, Europa; The Secret Garden*) had co-written the screenplay with Jean-Yves Pitoun and Shawn Slovo and Agnieszka was slated to direct the movie, but the film never got made.

This episode turned out to be the beginning of Nancy Taylor Rosenberg's publishing career. One publisher offered NAL $500,000 for a floor bid to the paperback rights to the two books. But NAL executives didn't want to sell the paperback rights and asked me to consider a four-book, hard-soft deal with them. Nancy agreed to the deal. I wound up negotiating a four-book, hard-soft $3 million contract for Nancy, loaded with what I call "bells and whistles."

When a publisher really wants an author, or a particular book, it is willing to make large concessions in the contract, which is a rare occurrence. The contract we negotiated for Nancy is filled with the following phrase: "Not to be considered a precedent."

Nancy Rosenberg has been published in twenty-eight countries. The first four books of this contract—*Mitigating Circumstances, Interest of Justice, First Offense*, and *Trial by Fire*—were all *New York Times* paperback bestsellers. I also placed *California Angel*, Nancy's next book; this, too, became a *Times* bestseller. I then negotiated a second four-book contract for Nancy at a substantially higher advance than her first at $5 million. The events evolved into what I will always call "Wonderful Circumstances."

I sincerely hope that someone who reads this book will create a book as "red-hot" as *Mitigating Circumstances* was then and that I'll be able to represent them. Then, the next time I update this book, I can write another chapter called, "More Wonderful Circumstances."

─ PART TWO ─

Get Produced!

CHAPTER

NINE   The Cast of Characters

TEN   Know the Realities of Hollywood

ELEVEN   Packaging Your Work

TWELVE   Marketing Your Screenplay

THIRTEEN   Making It in Television

FOURTEEN   Contracts: Watch Your Back!

FIFTEEN   Making the Deal in Hollywood

The Cast of Characters

*"An associate producer is the only guy in
Hollywood who will associate with a producer."*
—Fred Allen

You may be a writer with an idea for a book—or you may
have completed a book—that would make a great film or
TV series. Or perhaps you've written a movie screenplay or TV
script and don't know how to go about getting it produced.
Unless you already work in Hollywood, your knowledge of
the TV and film industries might not be much more than what
you've picked up from years of watching *Entertainment Tonight*.
You just don't know where to get started.

Don't worry: In this chapter, we'll give you a guide to all the
important players on the Hollywood scene. As a writer, knowing
how Hollywood works is the first step to becoming an important
player yourself.

THE WRITERS

So you want to be a writer who makes it in Hollywood? Well,
let's look at who is making it. If you are a novelist, it is instruc-
tive to look at the wildly successful careers of Tom Clancy, John
Grisham, Michael Crichton, Stephen King, Dan Brown, and

Nicholas Sparks. All of these novelists have had numerous films made based on their novels, with the exception of Dan Brown, whose *The Da Vinci Code* has broken all-time records for fiction with more than ten million copies sold and is being turned into his first film. These authors have written a number of bestselling novels, many of which have plot-driven, high concepts that were easily adaptable to films. So if you are a novelist, definitely try to write a book with motion picture and television potential. If you have that God-given talent, then why not?

Many of the authors that my company has managed want to adapt their own work into screenplays, and I always advise them to not be in such a hurry. Not everyone is Michael Crichton, and Hollywood's studio executives and their development teams usually call the tune when it comes to hiring screenwriters to adapt books into films. Quite frankly, it's a process that I have difficulty understanding. An author may slave over a 100,000-word book for a year, and then the studio will have some screenwriter—who clearly doesn't know the story as well as the novelist—adapt the book into essentially a 20,000-word synopsis as a screenplay, and get paid ten times as much for the adaptation. Go figure. My responses to this situation are "Don't fight City Hall" and "Don't bite the hand that may feed you" and, sadly, "If you can't lick them, join them." Ultimately, it is more important that a film get made based on an author's work than who wrote the screenplay. You have to look at the Big Picture, and getting a movie made based on your novel is worth millions of dollars of publicity for your career.

Good screenwriters are high-priced commodities in Hollywood, and oftentimes they are the reason that a film gets made. Here's one story I recently heard in Hollywood: The original screenwriter who was going to adapt James Ellroy's book *L.A. Confidential* had to pass because he couldn't crack the story. In fact, the book was originally supposed to be adapted into a television movie. It was ultimately adapted into a screenplay by Brian Helgeland and Curtis Hanson, who succeeded in cracking the adaptation of what was an extremely complicated book. And they won Academy Awards for doing so.

The point to be made here is that a screenwriter's "take" on the material can be the difference in getting a film made, and perhaps this is why Hollywood relies on well-known screenwriters and script doctors to make a film adaptation work. So, you may be thinking, how can *I* become a Big Name Hollywood screenwriter and be hired to adapt a classic novel into a star-studded major studio film? Well, first, write something fantastic! Then, get yourself a good agent or manager who believes in your work. Then, write something else and then do it again and again and never look back.

In the world of television writing, the big dogs are those writer/producers who are called "show runners." Those who create successful series, like Steven Bochco or David Milch, have gigantic and lucrative careers. Despite the plethora of reality-based shows, many of which don't really require story ideas and scripts, there are still opportunities in the written television series business. Look at the success of shows like *CSI, Alias, 24,* and the ever-lasting *Law and Order* franchise, as well as the cable shows like *The Sopranos* and *Deadwood.*

By the way, if you ever want to know anything about any writer, show, or movie, check out the Web site called the Internet Movie Database *(www.imdb.com)* to find out anything about anyone in Hollywood. You'll find me in there, too. (And, just in case you do try to look me up: I'm *not* the Peter Miller who did the makeup on the 1985 film *Fright Night*; I'm the one who produced the 2004 adaptation of *Helter Skelter*, among other films.)

THE AGENTS

As a New York–based manager who can't stay out of Hollywood (in the words of producer Mark Wolper), I have worked with many of the BIG agencies (CAA, ICM, William Morris, Endeavor,

UTA, APA, and others) on behalf of many of our clients and projects. The verdict is that there is good news and bad news about working with Hollywood agencies. The basic reality is this: "If you are hot, you are hot—but if you are not, you are not."

What does this mean for you as a writer who is starting out in the business? Well, the really big L.A. agencies tend to pay attention to their major clients, and if a star client wants a "hot" book or script they will do anything to placate their talent. However, stars change their minds like the rest of us change our underwear, at least once a day. I am quite gun-shy about the possibility of working on a book with an author for years to develop it, and then letting its success in Hollywood be controlled by another agency. However, there are times when I might agree to this—and your own representative might have to—if the other agency promises to place some of their "A" list talent like a director, star, or screenwriter as part of a "package."

THE STUDIOS AND PRODUCTION COMPANIES

What is the difference between a studio and a production company? Studios distribute product and finance production companies; in a best-case scenario for a production company, they just distribute. Networks and their production policies have changed over the last several years in that they are doing a lot of what is called "in-house" production. In past years, they received programming from many so-called "suppliers" or independent production companies. The bad news is that if a network or studio finances and distributes content then it is less likely that there will be significant "back-end" profit participation for the artists, unless of course you are Jerry Bruckheimer or Steven Spielberg.

THE PRODUCERS

Some people might say that producers rule Hollywood; others hold that it's the agents and managers with the upper hand. But if you really look at where the money is, it's the stars and directors, then the producers, and then the writers. Stars get paid more money than anyone, but if a certain producer has a certain relationship with Tom, Brad, Harrison, Julia, or J-Lo, that might mean that a movie will get made. The word "producer" means what it says—the person reasonable for producing the work—and if you look at the credits of any movie you will see that there are many producer credits, from Executive Producer to Co-Executive Producer to Producer to Associate and Assistant Producers. Then you have line producers and consulting producers and other credits. All producers and production companies have supporting staff like development executives and readers.

CHAPTER TEN

Know the Realities of Hollywood

"You call this a script? Give me a couple of $5,000-a-week writers and I'll write the script myself."
                    —Movie producer Joe Pasternak

One of the greatest pleasures an author can experience is having his work published. And, when the manuscript metamorphoses into a visual image—thereby reaching a far greater audience—the author's pleasure and monetary reward increase substantially. I'm proud to say that the works of many of my clients have made the transition from written word to film. Unfortunately, as hard as it is to place a manuscript with a publisher, the process of selling a screenplay, a television script, or the film rights to a book is even more difficult. The reason is simple: Books may cost thousands of dollars to publish, but movies cost dozens of millions of dollars to produce. As I said in this book's introduction: If the publishing business is a jungle, then the movie business is a jungle on another planet.

In the field of television, approximately 5 percent of the scripts that are controlled by major television networks ever reach production. The percentage for feature films is even lower. Film and television executives look at books—all books, regardless of how prestigious or obscure they may be—as raw material for their movie-making machines. In fact, they are bombarded with so much material (books, scripts, plays, etc.) that they often become oblivious to the mystique presented by a really good book. Unlike publishers (who will often—though not always—buy a manuscript they really love and baby it through publication), producers are not always so committed to a project they profess their love for. Producers, studios, and networks may buy a project because it's "hot" (that is, topical) or because it's perfect for an actor they want to work with. But what if the subject or the actor cools? The project is shelved. Some projects are bought with every intention of being made; others are purchased so no one else will have the story. As pessimistic as this sounds, an upside exists: There is an ever-growing demand for new product to feed to movie theaters, television, and cable, and to the pay-per-view and DVD and videocassette markets. This is all good for writers.

There are a number of ways a writer can increase the chances of successfully moving his work off the page and onto the screen. The most important thing to do is obtain representation, which is crucial at this juncture. A good representative should have valuable contacts in the film and television industries; in addition, he or she should be knowledgeable about which networks or studios are buying new properties and, especially, what *kind* they're buying. Here's one example: several years ago, Turner Network Television (TNT) began producing original programming; suddenly, there was a new entity in the marketplace—and an alternative to the major networks (NBC, CBS, ABC, Fox)—where a writer could sell his material. Now we also have Lifetime, USA, WB, TBS, UPN, FX, Oxygen, Spike, The Discovery Channel, The Disney Channel, The History Channel, Court TV, ESPN, and even more networks. For the writer whose representative is aware of the various nuances of Hollywood (which executives are where; which network is looking for what kind of property, etc.) a sale can be made easily and swiftly. Additionally, a good representative will know intimately about the development process and how to present properties to the appropriate actors, directors, or production companies. A positive response from a "name talent" will prove the property's viability to studio executives and thus make the sale that much easier. Representatives involved with Hollywood often spend as much of their time "packaging" projects (matching directors, actors, and other talent, to a script) as they do selling scripts.

FINDING AN AGENT IN HOLLYWOOD

As we discussed in Chapter 4, there is no easy way for an aspiring writer to find representation. If you are looking for an agent to represent your work for film and television production, you can start by doing one of the following:

1. Contact the Writers Guild of America (WGA) and request from them a list of agencies that will read unsolicited materials from new writers. (There are New York and Los Angeles branches of the Writers Guild.) However, bear in mind that most major agencies only take on major talent, so it is really tough to even get read.

2. Consult a number of the well-known writer reference books (*Writer's Market*; *Literary Marketplace*; *Jeff Herman's Writer's Guide to Book Editors, Publishers, and Literary Agents*; *Hollywood Creative Directory*; *Studios, Agents and Casting Directors Guides and Film Writers Guide*; etc.), which list agents and managers and the types of writing they represent.

Do not approach a representative with your work until you are absolutely certain you are ready to be represented. Agents are not editors or teachers—they are dealmakers. Your understanding and respect of their function are necessary elements in any potential writer/agent relationship.

Before signing with an agent, you must ascertain whether or not he or she has the contacts necessary to represent your work successfully. For example, most traditional New York literary representatives do not directly handle film or television writers. For the film and television rights of their own literary writers, they usually have ties to West Coast reps who handle the sales for them, splitting the commission on those rights. Conversely, there are reps who work only in film and television with "sister" agencies in New York to handle the publishing side for their clients. And, some representatives, of which I am one, have connections on both the East and West Coasts and are comfortable closing the sale of both literary and film properties. On the *Mitigating Circumstances* sale discussed in Chapter 8, I handled the New York book world and Hollywood simultaneously as Nancy Taylor Rosenberg's manager and worked in conjunction with a lawyer Nancy hired.

When searching for a representative, consider the following:

- Find out the number (and type) of film and/or television, or literary, deals the representative has already made.
- Ascertain whether the agent has continuing buyer and client relationships (speak to some of his clients, if you can).
- Find out how much experience and skill the representative has in the areas of negotiation, rights and contracts, as well as the level of their activity.
- Try to determine if the agent is interested only in a specific project you have written or if he will work with you as a writer on developing your career. For example, in 1992 my company, PMA, converted itself from being a literary agency into PMA Literary and Film Management, Inc. because we manage authors' entire careers.
- Get a copy of the representative's client list, if they'll give it out, or go to their Web site and check out any lists of clients or sales made.

In addition, you want someone who will stick with you through your dry periods, and not just during those times when your work is selling (all professional writers know there are dry periods during a career).

Selecting the appropriate representative depends upon your goals as a writer. If you are primarily interested in writing a book, with the possibility of developing a screenplay from it some time in the future, a New York literary representative is probably your best option. If your primary interest is writing for film or TV, a West Coast representative is preferable. I would even suggest considering moving to Los Angeles if you really want to be in the Big Game.

It is my opinion that, during the next few years, a greater consolidation of these two fields of representation will occur, just as we have seen mergers between publishing and film companies which have resulted in huge media conglomerates. As the proliferation of media giants continues to occur, writers will need to be especially vigilant in protecting their work. Therefore, it is crucial that your representative believes in you and your work.

USING AN ATTORNEY

You can retain an attorney to represent your material. An attorney who specializes in entertainment or contract law could possibly negotiate a solid contract, which would put you at a decided advantage. However, while your contract might be well drawn, there is no guarantee that all the provisions regarding subsidiary rights licenses and other aspects of that contract are good. Also, your attorney may not have a thorough knowledge of the ins and outs (including the players) of the marketplace. This can be reflected in the length of time some attorneys take to negotiate a simple deal. A literary representative is in the marketplace on a daily basis and therefore may be able to expedite a sale.

It's a good representative's job to know the trends and the players of the industry. Few attorneys have the time or the inclination to watch the business as closely as an active literary manager does.

Bear in mind that, unlike representatives, many attorneys do not work on a commission basis, so there could be the specter of a substantial legal bill when the contract is completed. If you are using an attorney to negotiate your contract, you should do the following:

- Try to predetermine the legal costs and insist that the attorney give you a minimum and maximum fee.
- Negotiate these costs with the attorney prior to hiring him. Perhaps you could establish a "ceiling" on the entire bill, or a flat fee.
- Realize that attorneys in the film and television industries who don't work on commission generally may negotiate to work for a percentage (typically, 5 percent of the writer's fee) or on a retainer, or both.

SELLING YOUR PROJECT

As I've mentioned before, a novice screenwriter may have a better chance of getting his script produced if he adapts his unproduced project into a book. If the book is published, it can be optioned and then adapted into a screenplay—with a studio's input and at the studio's expense. The motion picture, television, and cable industries purchase the rights to hundreds of books every year (especially bestsellers) in their search for new material.

Made-for-television projects generally cost far less to produce than what it costs a network to broadcast a major theatrical film, so television, in particular, likes to look to publishing as a source for story ideas.

A book that already has been published and has found an audience obviously has an advantage over an unproduced screenplay that has been making the studio rounds for a while.

Besides screenplays, film studios look to all traditional sources for their film projects, including books (the *Harry Potter* series,

Jurassic Park, The Hunt for Red October), stage plays (*A Few Good Men, Driving Miss Daisy*), or musicals (*Chicago, Evita, A Chorus Line*).

Book authors should realize that roughly 200,000 books are published in this country every year, but, in the United States, only approximately 1,000 movies (including movies-of-the-week and cable movies) are made. The odds are not in the writer's favor, but trying to sell a project is certainly worth a try because the rewards can be phenomenal.

Lawyer-turned-novelist Scott Turow received $1 million for the film rights to *Presumed Innocent*, his first novel; Warren Adler, author of *The War of the Roses*, scored a record-breaking $1.2 million for the rights to his next novel. John Grisham and Michael Crichton have broken the $5 million mark more than once with such novels as *A Time to Kill* and *Jurassic Park:The Lost World* respectively. And one doesn't have to look far to see the phenomenal global success of Tolkien's *The Lord of the Rings* trilogy and J.K. Rowling's *Harry Potter* franchise.

THE METAMORPHOSIS
FROM BOOK TO SCREEN

"I never metamorphosis I didn't like."
—Christopher Cook Gilmore

The art of dramaturgy—writing a play, a screenplay, a television movie, or a miniseries—is very specific and vastly different from the art of writing prose. Simply stated, not all authors are suited to adapting their own books, nor do they wish to.

"It was like passing a scene of a highway accident and being relieved to learn that nobody had been seriously injured," responded author Martin Cruz Smith, when asked how he liked the movie version of his novel *Gorky Park*.

First off, when the rights to a book are sold, the studio, network, or producer usually has the right to change it without approval from the author. If this happens, it's often because the purchaser is unwilling to let the author write the screenplay; sometimes it is felt that the screenplay should veer drastically away from the source material. If you have strong feelings about these issues (i.e., adapting the work yourself; guarding against major changes, etc.), you should consider these elements prior to selling your work. It is important for you to know what you want when selling the rights to your work. Your feelings will determine the exact form of the deal, including who will be able to purchase the rights (if there is more than one bidder). For example, if you're interested in a second career as a screenwriter, you might take less money for the book rights in exchange for a deal to write the script. Other permutations are possible, but if this can be negotiated, do it—and then do everything within your power to write a script that is pure dynamite. Just don't take the money and run.

If you are an author who wants to make it in Hollywood, one book you should definitely read (well, besides this one, of course) is William Goldman's 1983 *Adventures in the Screen Trade*. Goldman provides an excellent example of a book author who has adapted his novels into screenplays (i.e., *The Princess Bride*, *Marathon Man*, *Magic*) and who has found enormous success in Hollywood. His scripts have won him two Oscars: one for his original screenplay for 1969's *Butch Cassidy and the Sundance Kid*, and one for his adaptation of 1976's *All the President's Men*.

Goldman's fees range upward of a million dollars per script, although it took him years to reach such heights. Of course, if you are William Goldman, John Grisham, or Michael Crichton—in other words, your name is synonymous with "success"—you can write your own ticket.

Sometimes, the author is not the only person who controls the rights to a story. This is particularly true in works of nonfiction. My client Steve Salerno's *Deadly Blessing*, a true-crime book about a bizarre murder in Texas, was eagerly pursued by a number of television production companies before it was sold to David L. Wolper Productions, a producer for Warner Bros. Television.

An Errors and Omissions Policy (requested by networks when dealing with a work of nonfiction) was taken out with an insurance company for the proposed adaptation. This expensive policy protects the network from litigation in case someone involved in the case should sue the network for libel or defamation of character. Warner Bros. soon realized that Vicky Daniel, one of the principals involved in the case, had *not* agreed to sell *her* rights to the story. So, for *Deadly Blessing*, Warner Bros. purchased *all* the court transcripts of the case: 16,000 pages at $1.50 per page. The transcripts were used as background material by the screenwriter, John Ireland. With the E&O policy in place, the production company proved it acted in reasonable "good faith" and with "due diligence" to produce a realistic version of a story that was in the public domain. Without Warner Bros. willingness to invest its money at this early stage—before the script was written—the project would not have gotten off the ground.

As it turns out, the resulting script was actually very sympathetic to Vicky Daniel; the project was produced and aired on ABC television in 1992 under the title *A Bed of Lies*.

BREAKING INTO TELEVISION

Sometimes, an unproduced writer can break into television by writing a treatment (an outline of a story) for a movie or a proposed series rather than a full-length teleplay. The reason for this is simple: If the idea is a good one, the producer will buy the story idea from you (thus providing your break into television) and then hire an established television writer to adapt your idea into a teleplay.

Partly because of the necessity of writing for commercial breaks, writing for television is harder than it looks, and this is why producers and networks can be uneasy with new writers. Usually, television networks have strict criteria for hiring writers, so a novice writer will need to prove his or her worth to those in television.

Experienced TV writers understand that TV movies are interrupted by twelve to fourteen minutes of commercial time per hour and usually are adept at designing scripts with "cliff-hangers" before each break. They manage to retain the story's basic integrity and continuity despite the constant breaks.

A treatment, no matter how brief, is evidence that a writer can write. The producer may not be sold on your story, but he may be impressed enough with your writing ability to hire you for a different project. In both films and television, it is essential to sell the writer over the project. This is particularly true because it is common for a property to take years to reach completion. If the producers are sold on the writer from the start, it is possible that they could be encouraged to work with him or her again—and sometimes before the writer's project has finally seen the light of day.

Treatments usually run between eight and fifteen double-spaced pages and include a full synopsis of the story. There are no other hard-and-fast rules as to what else should be included in the package. If your treatment is, say, a true-crime story for a TV Movie of the Week, you may wish to supplement the synopsis with some well-chosen newspaper articles illustrating the widespread interest in your subject. Or, if the project is a straight drama, you might want to break down the idea into separate acts to exhibit the strength of the story's dramatic structure. If your idea is a comedy, include sample dialogue to prove that you can write funny lines.

Some treatments include descriptions of the main characters so the producer can imagine actors appropriate for the roles. (Sometimes, reference is made to a well-known actor: "This character is a Clint Eastwood type . . .")

When writing a treatment, you should make it as powerful and eloquent as possible. But a treatment is only as good as the screenplay that will follow. I once placed a prominent author's work with a network days after I secured the publishing rights for his book—and the book wasn't written at the time. The entire deal was based on a nine-page treatment. In this case, the key was the involvement of a "prominent author." (The same author sold his next book as a miniseries, also without a completed manuscript.)

A treatment is, at best, a vehicle by which a writer makes a deal to write—it is not really writing itself. If your treatment is not selling, re-examine your commitment to your story idea. If you are convinced that it is THE movie you want to write, begin writing the screenplay and hope you'll sell the idea with a completed script. If you have doubts about the idea, put the treatment away, at least for a while, and begin writing something else.

If you have an idea for a television series, the best way to attract the attention of a production company or a network executive is by writing a treatment that includes an overview of the entire series, brief descriptions of the major characters, one-paragraph synopses of thirteen episodes (thirteen represents about half the number of episodes for a full-season commitment from a network, though a "full season" can now be as few as twenty-two episodes) and perhaps a completed script of the series pilot. Be forewarned: of all the deals discussed in this book, selling a television series is the one least likely to be made. The networks receive vast numbers of proposals for series; only a few of them get to production, and most of these are from established writers, producers, and stars. In fact, a 500-page book—*Unsold Television Pilots: 1955-1988* by Lee Goldberg—has been published that describes television series concepts that reached the development stage and were not produced. And just think how many more failed ideas for television series have been developed in the years since 1988!

One successful way of selling an idea is to keep abreast of news events. Buy the rights to someone's story and develop it into a movie or miniseries idea, write a treatment, and then, in conjunction with your representative or packager, present the proposal to a network or to an independent television producer or production company. Networks always like to get in on the ground floor of a potentially bestselling, high-ratings idea, which is why there often is a proliferation of news stories-turned-movies. The Jessica Lynch story and the Scott Peterson murder trial both quickly became the subjects of TV movies. During one week, a major publisher received fourteen proposals for a book based on the Stuart murder in Boston (the story of a young white man who murdered his pregnant wife and stirred up controversy by claiming that a mysterious—and completely fictitious—black man had done it). The books being written on this story in turn resulted in tremendous interest in Hollywood.

Occasionally, material strikes such a chord that a producer is willing to invest his time, energy, emotion, *and* money to develop it for the screen. This happened to me after I read an epistolary novel called, *Miss 4th of July, Goodbye*. I optioned the book with a partner. Set in a West Virginia coal-mining town around the turn of the century, the book is about a young girl who defends the rights of a black man victimized by the KKK. The story is even more poignant because the girl, as an immigrant, is subject to bigotry herself. We submitted the book to Disney Television and received a very positive response. Just as the situation looked promising, Disney shelved the project: It no longer was interested in historical dramas. To me, it felt like a personal rejection. I could only imagine how the author must have felt. However, we were fortunate because everything did work out for the project: It was made into a movie for the Disney Channel, retitled *Goodbye, Miss 4th of July*. It starred Louis Gossett Jr. and Chris Sarandon, and was directed by George Miller (*The Man from Snowy River*) and was nominated for four Emmy Awards.

During my long association with author Vincent Bugliosi, we worked together to see that his nonfiction book *Till Death Us Do Part* successfully made the transition to the screen. Published in the late 1970s, the book won the Edgar Allan Poe Award and was a hot property. But it was rejected by nearly twenty-five producers—for any number of slight or insignificant reasons. Vincent and I had an enormous amount invested in this book, an investment of conviction and emotion—feelings that go far beyond money. We finally sold the book to a production company, and in 1992 it was made into an NBC Movie of the Week starring Treat Williams.

As an aspiring television writer, you may be tempted to write a sample script for an existing show, in the hope that it will sell or at least prove your ability to write episodic TV. This exercise is more futile than you might expect. In fact, I don't recommend this option unless you live in Los Angeles and can devote your time to breaking into the television business. If you insist on this exercise, write an episode of your favorite show, but try getting it to the producers of a *different* show. Producers of a successful show often do not want to even *see* a script for their show written by anyone they are not already working with. The reason? They are afraid that they may be sued for stealing an idea if something similar to an element in the spec script appears in their show sometime later. Basically, breaking into episodic television is extremely difficult unless you know the executive producer (known as the "showrunner") to a specific show.

THE TELEVISION MINISERIES

Ever since *Roots* (the nonfiction book by Alex Haley that traced the author's heritage to African slaves), network television has been in love with the miniseries (a long-form TV movie broadcast over several nights), and producers and networks have frequently turned to bestselling books as a source for this form of TV entertainment. *Rich Man, Poor Man; Lonesome Dove; Stephen King's The Shining*—all of these successful, popular TV miniseries were based on bestselling novels. However, in recent years, miniseries are becoming less popular; networks are now often developing what are called "limited series." What originally would have been a three-night miniseries of two hours each would now be a six-night limited series of one hour each.

Helter Skelter, based on Vincent Bugliosi's book of the same name, was made into a miniseries in 1976, and it is a prime example of a successful television miniseries. It dealt with a sensational, true-crime story; the characters (including beautiful actors and actresses and hippies-turned-murderers) were larger than life; and it offered, through Bugliosi's point of view, some redeeming social value. The original miniseries based on the book was so successful that I was able to convince Warner Bros. to remake the film. It aired on CBS as a three-hour "event" movie in May 2004. We originally sold it as a four-hour miniseries, but CBS ultimately decided to do it as three hours, as viewership loyalty for a second night of a miniseries is not as great as it once was. I served as an Executive Producer on this with Vincent Bugliosi and Mark Wolper.

In another specific area of movies and miniseries based on real-life crimes, journalists and attorneys have an advantage: They are often among the first to learn about interesting, marketable crime stories and, as such, they can begin developing a treatment for the idea long before other writers have heard of the case. When a true-crime story cannot be found, a mutation is created: the "docudrama," a combination of fact and fiction, has become an accepted genre of the TV movie or miniseries.

AVOIDING CATCH-22

Catch-22 is, of course, the phenomenally popular Joseph Heller novel that was later adapted into a film (with a screenplay by Buck Henry). Unfortunately, "Catch-22" also can be used to describe your situation if you are a writer trying to break into television. Typically, people who write for television are members of the Writers Guild of America (WGA), which means they have sold at least one script to a production company that is a WGA signatory (this includes most network shows, some syndication, and some cable shows). Signatories rarely hire writers who are not members of WGA. Yes, it's a "Catch-22" situation: You can't become a member of the WGA without selling a script; but you can't sell a script without being a member of WGA. There is a chance that a producer will be so enamored of your work that he will buy your project or make a deal with you to write an episode of his show, thus allowing you to become a member of WGA at a later date—but it is a slim chance. Success in television is difficult, but if you make it, you'll almost certainly make it big.

Many years ago, I represented a writer named David Burke, who co-wrote the pilot for a television series called *Crime Story*. Since then, he has worked his way up the TV ladder from Story Editor on the show to Executive Producer and also director of the critically acclaimed series *Wiseguy* and *Seaquest DSV* (writing many episodes for both series as well).

Writers Guild scale for a one-hour episode of a prime-time series is around $38,000, plus a guaranteed rerun payment; on top of this, there are potentially lucrative foreign sales possibilities (anywhere between $15,000 and $50,000)—all for a sixty-page script. Writing revenue from syndicated series can also be quite lucrative.

THE DEVELOPMENT DEAL

Once a writer sells a producer on his ability, and the producer shows a desire to hire the writer, the writer's agent sets up a development deal with the producer. A typical development deal (for feature films or television) works like this:

- A producer options the writer's property for a set period of time, usually a year (with an opportunity to renew the option for a second year). A one-year option represents a down payment of approximately 10 percent of the full purchase price of the property.
- For that year, the producer controls the property exclusively and can promote its sale (to a television

network, production company, or studio). If the property is purchased by the network, production company, or studio, then the producer recoups his option payment, along with other development costs he incurred. (Some prominent producers have what is known as an *output deal* with a specific network or studio; this guarantees that a certain number of their projects will be made each year.) The author receives his full payment (the remaining 90 percent of the full purchase price) and the process of developing the script for production (either by the author or by a different screenwriter) begins.

Here's an example of how it works: Mike Cochran, a well-known Associated Press reporter with more than thirty years of experience, and one of my former clients, published a nonfiction book called *And Deliver Us from Evil*, a compilation of true-crime stories set in Texas. One episode concerned an innocent man accused of murder who then became a fugitive from justice. Mike optioned the rights to this chapter to a television producer for one year and the story went into development. At the end of the first option period, the producer had not sold the story. At this point, the producer could have paid Mike the remaining purchase price to own the story outright or he could have renewed the option for another year and continued to shop it around. He renewed the option and the film was made and aired on CBS as *Fugitive Among Us.*

TRENDS IN TELEVISION AND FILM

There has never been such a diverse amount of material available to the viewing public. Big-budget blockbuster-type movies and miniseries always seem to find an audience. Currently, offbeat stories have a better chance of being optioned than at any other time in recent memory. Several years ago, a front-page headline in *Daily Variety* summed it up: "Warts and All: TV Embraces Fact and Flaws and Frailties." In the article, the author noted that the leading TV series at the time were shows like *Roseanne* and *The Simpsons*, which present a less-than-perfect view of contemporary America. The success of *The X-Files* indicated that viewers are willing to embrace an offbeat and dark show. Now there is another evolution of shows that mix dark and comic elements, from *Desperate Housewives* and *Lost* on network television to *The Sopranos* and *Six Feet Under* on cable.

Many distributors feel that the primary audience for movies is comprised of kids. Only kids, they rationalize, have the time, energy, disposable income, and fanaticism necessary to see a movie seven or eight times in a theater. The original trilogy of *Star Wars* films was the perfect example of this. However, the days are past when any film set in outer space with expensive special effects is a guaranteed box-office blockbuster. The trend for popular entertainment films these days is to look for something that will appeal to kids while also keeping their parents happy. A perfect example is the *Batman* series, films that work very hard to strike this kind of balance. The same is true with *Harry Potter, The Lord of the Rings,* and the *Shrek* films. Is there anything that will definitely sell? No. But lately there has been a trend in Hollywood toward comedy films—specifically, films that mix comedy with action and more spectacular "event" films.

Any writer should be aware of the constantly changing trends in the television and film industries and should be prepared to adapt to these changes—at the drop of a hat. In fact, the writer who is truly successful in movies or TV doesn't follow the trends—he writes stories that interest him and, in the process, may SET the trends.

There is always room for a quality screenplay. Although the quality may not necessarily be recognized immediately, and it may not receive its financial due, there is a producer somewhere who is willing to make a film simply because it should be made.

Many major actors now have their own production companies and make an effort to alternate between commercial and less commercial fare.

In Hollywood, the competition is fierce but the rewards can be substantial. So, go west, young writers! There's success and big money in them thar Hollywood Hills!

CHAPTER ELEVEN

Packaging Your Work

> *"Did you hear about the screenwriter who submitted his first screenplay to a major studio? A week later, he received two rejection letters: one rejecting the current script; one rejecting a future script."*
>
> —Joke overheard at
> a Hollywood party

The entertainment industry believes it can best avoid severe financial loss by combining compatible marketing "hooks," whether they are two bankable actors; a star actor and a star musician (for the possibility of a hit movie and soundtrack); a star director and a bestselling author, etc. Should a project not do well in one area, there are other elements to pick up the slack and improve the total financial performance of an entertainment property. That's why motion picture and television deals today emphasize the package. A package, then, is not an afterthought or an accidental by-product of the filmmaking process. Rather, it has become the prerequisite of virtually all studio deals and the constant objective of representatives, packagers, directors, producers, and would-be film investors. Indeed, some films are more famous in the industry for their packaging efforts than for their quality. The 1996 film *The Cable Guy* appeared to be a no-lose package, matching wildly popular comic Jim Carrey with hip, talented director Ben Stiller and popular leading man

Matthew Broderick. It was a colossal bomb. An example of successful packaging is 1998's *Rain Man*; this film was produced because of Michael Ovitz's strong belief in it. Then president of Creative Artists Agency, Ovitz packaged the film several different times and saw it through many screenplay drafts before it finally went into production. It eventually married the talents of superstar actors Dustin Hoffman and Tom Cruise with A-list director Barry Levinson. The film went on to win Oscars for Best Picture, Best Director, Best Actor (Hoffman), and Best Original Screenplay (for its script by Ronald Bass and Barry Morrow).

GREEN LIGHT MEANS GO

Before studios give their approval and "green-light" a project, they want to know what the package is; industry players no longer attempt to merely place the film rights to a property or sell an original screenplay—they always try to package the property.

As one studio executive once said to me, "Peter, you always have terrific projects, but who's going to make the film? Bring me a filmmaker. Then, try to put together as complete a package as soon as possible."

The package may also include co-production financing or foreign pre-sales (including production financing, prints and advertising, or even negotiable bank guarantees based solely on creative talent).

The average cost of a movie these days is upward of $60 million; many major studio films have budgets close to or above $100 million. (The mega-successful James Cameron film *Titanic* had a budget exceeding $200 million.) That's a lot of money to risk on unknown actors or directors. Competition is fierce, especially when the goal is to match the billions in worldwide revenue racked up by such recent hugely successful film franchises like *Shrek*, the *Harry Potter* films, the *Lord of the Rings* series, *Pirates of the Caribbean*, the *Men In Black* films, or the *Star Wars* saga. It's almost impossible to compete with these juggernauts . . . unless, of course, you've got a "can't miss" package.

The film package that begins with a bestselling book (100,000 or more hardcover copies sold) has an advantage. Unfortunately, very few books published in this country ever reach such sales or status. These properties, like John Grisham's *A Time to Kill* or Dan Brown's huge success *The Da Vinci Code*, are heavily pursued and are optioned quickly by major studios, networks, or well-connected independent producers.

A more modestly successful book may still have strong screen or television potential, especially if the book contains an inherently cinematic concept or deals with a topical subject. Perennials—books on subjects that are always popular, i.e., true crime—are always good projects to package. In fact, true crimes have been the rage on television for many years; most of these TV movies have been packaged around books that originally brought the crimes to national attention.

However, even bestselling books cannot overcome all the obstacles inherent in the filmmaking process. The sad fact is that fewer than one out of ten books optioned by film or television producers goes into production (the odds are even worse for an optioned original screenplay). Typically, the reason is because a satisfactory package could not be assembled. Also, studios will sometimes hire and fire multiple writers on a single script, in an effort to "get it right." Sometimes this leads to a script that finally strikes the correct combination of plot, character, tone, etc. However, just as often, this process exhausts executives' enthusiasm for a project, and a script can die in what's called "development hell."

IT ALL STARTS WITH THE STORY

Independent producers or production companies—those entities that function without specific connection to a studio or network—are usually active buyers of book properties. This is especially true if an independent has a "first-look" deal with a studio. Then, the independent is compensated by the studio for the purchase of the rights and for office overhead; sometimes, the company receives base salaries against future production fees.

But it all starts with the story: The book is a major element of any package. It is usually developed as a screenplay by the original writer or by a screenwriter brought onto the project. When the first-draft screenplay (or some written form of the material) is completed, its film potential should be self-evident. The script should be simple, concise, clear and without artistic pretension. Remember: The audience wants to see a film, not a photographic reproduction of the printed page.

Despite rumors to the contrary, it isn't true that producers "can't read." They simply like to prioritize their schedules. So, keep your ideas and scripts simple. Whenever I go into a meeting, I try to rehearse the pitch so that I present the property in one paragraph—two to five succinct sentences, or maybe even one (if it's a high concept idea).

Besides the story, all packages should have:

- A director interested in the property (it helps if he is as much a "star" as any actor).
- A "star."

Creating a package without star names is like baking bread without yeast—your project won't rise, no matter how long you bake it. If there is an extraordinary angle, i.e., a Top-10 hit song or a mass media event like the O.J. Simpson or Scott Peterson trial, a project could move forward without stars. But, generally, stars are critical to the final deal. An actor who is on the verge of stardom or a director who has made one or two critically acclaimed but small films are not significant enough to package.

In the basic law of packaging, a package is as strong as its weakest element. Any movie with A-list talent, i.e., Dustin Hoffman, Clint Eastwood, Tom Hanks, Julia Roberts, Harrison Ford, Brad Pitt, Tom Cruise, Jodie Foster, Michelle Pfeiffer, Steven

Spielberg, Ron Howard, John Grisham, Michael Crichton, etc., has an excellent shot at being made. But, how often are A-list talents available? Therefore, packaging efforts sometimes resemble sleights-of-hand. If you have two really strong elements, perhaps a star actor or actress and a strong property, the package may be able to overcome one weaker link, such as a director who hasn't yet made a major film, particularly if a major actor wants to work with the director. This kind of packaging "magic" makes it an art.

The 1996 film *The First Wives' Club* was a package made in Heaven: It was based on a popular novel by Olivia Goldsmith and starred a trio of Hollywood's most popular actresses—Bette Midler, Goldie Hawn, and Diane Keaton. As another example: Before the ink was dry on the film rights to *Steel Magnolias*, it was almost guaranteed a green light: It was based on a hit play by Robert Harling and starred Academy Award–winning actresses Shirley MacLaine, Olympia Dukakis, and Sally Field. The cast also included country music star Dolly Parton and popular young actresses Daryl Hannah and Julia Roberts; it was to be directed by the acclaimed Herb Ross and produced by film mogul Ray Stark, who saw the potential in the play and was wise enough to purchase the rights.

Then look at the packaging genius of the 2004 hit *Sideways*, a film that wasn't packed with all the well-known stars of the above examples. The combination of the directorial talents of Alexander Payne (*Citizen Ruth, Election,* and *About Schmidt*) with the cast of Paul Giamatti, Thomas Haden Church, Virginia Madsen (a beautiful but underappreciated actress), and Sandra Oh (Payne's wife at the time) produced a magical chemistry that was essential to the success of the film, as was the extraordinary dialogue, from an Oscar-winning screenplay by Payne and Jim Taylor. And here's a part of the package that may inspire you if you are an aspiring author/screenwriter: The film was based on the first novel by Rex Pickett, a screenwriter and director of several forgettable films in the 1980s and '90s. Frustrated with his lack of success in the movie business, Pickett wrote a semi-auto-biographical novel, with its main character being a depressed, unpublished author. The novel was rejected by fifteen publishers before Payne, who was represented by the same agency as Pickett, saw the manuscript and decided to develop it into his next film. Before the movie went into production, St. Martin's Press finally accepted Pickett's novel and gave him a small advance, which quickly earned out. Pickett now says (quite happily) that he earns an additional dollar every time someone buys his novel. As you can see, persistence, and the willingness to try something different in your career, really can pay off in a big way.

LET'S TALK MONEY

Once the talent is in place, it's time to finance the picture. Financing without a good package is like a well without water; no matter how deep the well, it's just another hole in the ground.

When producers of a film give up their equity in it in exchange for additional financing from an outside partner, *co-production financing* has occurred. In this case, a partnership is created, whereby profits are split because some of the rights to the film—e.g., foreign, video, DVD, television, etc.—are pre-sold. Besides raising equity capital for production, a pre-sale may also involve a negotiable bank guarantee. When this happens, a potential buyer agrees to pay a certain amount of money when a final print of the film is available. Such a letter of commitment, combined with the filmmaker's reputation, is then used to obtain credit from a bank.

Below-the-line financing refers to production costs. *Above-the-line costs* are defined as those other than for the physical production of the film—i.e., acquisition of the property, talent (director, producer, and actors), etc.

What makes packaging a business—and not just an art—is the fact that a financial scheme is necessary to make the whole production click. As with everything else in Hollywood, it comes down to money: In the case of a film or television package, production costs, financing arrangements, subsidiary sales, pre-sales, escalations, step deals, videocassette and DVD advances, back-end guarantees, and many other variations on the theme must be considered.

Most programming (particularly long-form) on Home Box Office (HBO) is based on a combination of financing arrangements, which makes any one of their productions a safe, almost guaranteed investment.

While many people working in Hollywood package deals with talent, only a few can be referred to as packagers—those who put the financial arrangements in place. If one of these players is on your team, it could make the difference in getting your work produced. Just as Don Quixote was not stopped by the realities of his world, packagers are likewise not intimidated by the windmills of Hollywood: It doesn't matter that they're selling a commodity that doesn't exist. Generally, packagers pre-sell certain subsidiary rights or territorial rights to the film. Before the film is completed, the packager collects money for these rights so the film can complete production. Subsidiary rights include such elements as television syndication rights, product licensing rights, videocassette/DVD rights, game rights (also known as interactive multimedia rights), and anything anyone else can think of. In fact, even some rights that no one can even imagine may be part of the package. The contract could apply to rights "now known in any form, or to be invented, throughout the universe for the history of recorded time." If all goes well, your packager may manage a network or cable television pre-sale for substantial money.

The marriage of a good talent package and proper financing for an independent production is no easy task. Each element interacts with all the others until the right pieces come together. The process of packaging is a tedious, cut-and-paste effort. This can easily take several years of work.

Therefore, a successful packager often has many of the qualities that a successful representative has—the ability to deal with people under pressure, to negotiate, to mediate, and to compromise. In fact, quite a few agents and representatives have gone on to success as packagers and/or producers. The processes are so similar, it seems almost inevitable that a representative will be drawn to the packaging process if he or she is interested in the film market. Representatives who become involved in the film industry can help push an author's career far beyond his or her expectations.

A FEW WORDS OF ADVICE

The industry is rife with original screenplays, but, unfortunately, most are not as well written as those developed from books. If a book has gone through the New York publishing mill, it should have—at the very least—a fully developed story; Hollywood respects that. In the words of mega-producer Jerry Bruckheimer, "If it's on the page, we will put it on the stage."

As a film manager, I prefer to represent an original screenplay only as part of a package. Screenplays considered by themselves are very difficult to sell or place. I usually repeat the same advice to all aspiring writers: Consider writing a novelized version of your screenplay to create interest in the property for packaging purposes. If the property works as a book, it has a good chance of being placed; then it's in a better position for others to evaluate its true film potential. This approach also can triple your income: You earn money from the book's publication, from the sale of movie rights, and, one hopes, from the sale of your screenplay adaptation of it.

I currently represent several developed properties, new screenplays, various novelists, and a few directors. The package is always what spurs me on. My original company's sister company, Millennium Lion, Inc., has grown exponentially since its founding and currently has more than a dozen films in development. Part of our success is due to our good taste in clients and their work and our responsiveness to them and to the market. But equally important is the fact that there is real talent out there waiting to be discovered.

Hollywood loves a good package. So if you are a writer and you want your project made into a film, find a producer (either in association with your representative or do it yourself) and work with him or her to put together a package with recognizable actors, director, etc. Then, get a distributor. You may need to negotiate pre-sales to raise production funds—hopefully you'll do this without bargaining your rights away and giving up too much too early on a good property. You should then have a viable package. If your luck holds and your team puts together a quality film, you can check out the results shortly at your local cinema.

CHAPTER TWELVE

Marketing Your Screenplay

*". . . the single most important fact, perhaps,
of the entire movie industry:
NOBODY KNOWS ANYTHING"*
—Author and screenwriter
William Goldman

You may find William Goldman's famous quote about how clueless everyone in Hollywood is a little discouraging. But let's consider the rest of what Goldman had to say:

> *"Not one person in the entire motion picture
> field knows for a certainty what's going to
> work. Every time out it's a guess—and, if
> you're lucky, an educated one."*

It's true that no one *knows* which screenplays or upcoming films will turn out to be big hits (and don't believe anyone in Hollywood who tells you that they do!). You can, however, try to make yourself more educated and experienced about the ways of Hollywood. This will give you a better idea of what properties are likely to be sellable and—cross your fingers—successfully produced someday.

In my early years in the New York publishing industry, I believed that the experience I acquired in dealing with both publishers and writers would eventually help me if I ever decided to become involved in the movie industry. I was right!

The publishing and film businesses are similar: They are both schizophrenically split between creativity and commerce. Furthermore, my involvement with hundreds and hundreds of properties over the years has allowed me to analyze which works have the potential to be successful films and which will probably never make it off the page.

As of this writing, I have successfully represented and placed more than 1,000 books with publishers all over the world. Despite the fact that I've been involved in dozens of motion picture and television rights sales, options, and screenplay development deals, only eleven films have been produced based on properties with which I've been involved. One was an original screenplay, *The Treasure of the Moon Goddess*; another, *We, The Jury*, was an original treatment. Several were book adaptations: *Goodbye, Miss 4th of July; Deadly Blessing; Bed of Lies; Till Death Us Do Part; The FBI Killer; Helter Skelter; A Tangled Web;* and *A Gift of Love*. Another film, *Fugitive Among Us*, was based on a chapter of a book. There are two lessons to be taken here. One is that films can be derived from a number of different types of properties. The other is that the vast majority of properties never end up making it to the screen.

As a writer, what can you do to beat the odds? The marketability of some of these books we manage as movie properties is often greatly increased by the author's willingness to write the screenplay adaptation. When this happens, the author and the book become something of a package that can be offered to producers—an attractive proposition because the property always feels closer to production when a screenwriter is attached. You should realize, however, that even if you adapt your own work, it does not guarantee that your screenplay is the draft that gets made. Producers and executives are notorious for having second thoughts—even third and fourth thoughts—about projects. In many cases, the writer is the victim of these extra thought processes. To producers, the fact that you, as the original writer, may have lived with this material for years may not be a compelling enough argument to make the property a successful movie. And, if an element of the package changes (i.e., an actor drops out or the director leaves, citing "creative differences"), the script is usually rewritten to accommodate the new elements in the package. A screenplay will probably end up looking a little different if the actor playing its protagonist has been changed from Kevin Spacey to Sylvester Stallone. It never hurts for the writer to be flexible regarding quick changes and adaptable to rewrites.

Some time ago, I took on the representation of a novel called *The Strokers*. The book's author was a well-known former music agent and manager who had represented a number of hit recording artists; it was his intimate knowledge of the industry that enabled him to write a fictionalized "insider's account" of the music business. While in the process of soliciting the sale of the movie rights to his novel, the author wrote a screenplay adaptation; this move enhanced the attractiveness of the project enormously. Potential backers could see the metamorphosis from novel to screenplay and got a good idea of how the screenplay would evolve with further rewrites. A purchase offer for the movie rights was made; the project was nearing production when the company went out of business. The author was paid for options and screenwriting. Without his commitment to the project, his book would not have reached the pre-production stage so quickly.

So many writers want to break into the business that screenplays are often written at no cost to the producer (these are called *spec scripts*); the writer hopes his script will sell or perhaps he'll win an assignment as a result of the exposure his writing received on the spec market. For members of the Writers Guild of America, the minimum fee for a screenplay of a medium-budgeted film is approximately $58,000 plus, while the payment for a low-budget feature film would be roughly 60 percent of that.

I negotiated the option for Jay Bonansinga's novel *The Killer's Game* (Simon & Schuster, 1997); it was purchased by Andrew Lazar's production company, Mad Chance. Andrew developed the script with screenwriter Rand Ravich. When the script was sold,

Ravich received a $700,000 payday, and Bonansinga gets his payday when the film is made, hopefully soon. It has been in development going on eight years now and the author has earned hundreds of thousands of dollars in option payments. It is now with Paramount so hopefully we will be able to see this in the theaters soon.

TREATMENT VS. SCREENPLAY

Many beginning screenwriters try to sell their ideas via the treatment to save themselves the time and angst of writing a full-length screenplay. Treatments usually sell for less money than a full-length screenplay. In addition, treatments do not always exhibit the writer's talent.

The best way to sell a treatment is to package the story idea with an appropriate writer and develop a first-draft screenplay. Then, try to sell this quality product to a production company or studio. First-time screenwriters with completed screenplays are in a stronger position to make a sale than those with a treatment or idea.

One of my clients, Paul Davids, finished his adventure-fantasy, *Starry Night*, before attempting to sell it. The premise centered on Vincent van Gogh returning 100 years after his death to avenge the wrongs done to him when he was alive. The project was optioned to an Australian film producer; when it lapsed, it was picked up by William Dear, who had directed the films *Harry and the Hendersons* and *Wild America*. The project was in development as a major motion picture for a long time but was never made. Because of the author's indefatigable efforts to continually improve his story, he wound up producing and directing the movie himself, and it was released in 1999, and is now available on DVD and distributed by Universal Pictures.

A screenwriter, like a playwright, should realize that no screenplay is ever truly finished while it is still on paper; changes will be made throughout the production and sometimes even into post-production. The axiom that the screenplay is just the blueprint for the film is undeniably true.

WRITING THE SCREENPLAY

In all this talk of deals, packages, financing, treatments, and such, it may seem that we have not paid much attention to one very important part of your experience as a writer in Hollywood: actually writing the screenplay!

There's a reason for this. My goal in this book is to teach you, as an aspiring or somewhat experienced book author or screenwriter, how to get your work published and produced in the best possible way. We're mostly talking here about what can be sold in today's market, and where and how to sell it. The one essential underlying assumption of all of this is that you can come up with the goods to sell.

I don't have the space here, or the expertise, to talk about all the fine points of screenplay construction, any more than I can tell a book author when he should use an adjective or an adverb (I rely on my own editor to tell me that!). With that said, let's talk a bit here about screenwriting.

In your attempt to write the best screenplay possible, you should check out the many excellent books available on plot construction, dramaturgy, and the art of screenwriting. Keep in mind the bottom line: Your writing must be entertaining. I highly recommend all of Linda Seger's books on writing, including *Making a Good Script Great*; and I strongly suggest you check out Chris Vogler's *The Writer's Journey*.

It is crucial to maintain a firm grasp on the central concept of the script while writing it. "High concept" scripts are those whose basic idea can be clearly summed up in one or two sentences. These scripts are often most attractive to Hollywood. Often, writers who are unable to describe their scripts in one or two sentences lack a clear focus on what they are writing. It can be helpful to distill your story by focusing on what the simple concept is.

Your screenplay must involve the reader to the fullest degree. For that reason, I prefer to read scripts that aren't cluttered with camera direction or lengthy descriptions; in the best-written scripts, the screenwriter takes into account the special rhythms of filmmaking. To keep your screenplay compelling, you must constantly ask yourself if your story will be of interest to anyone other than you or your immediate family. Plot, character development, visual details—all of these elements must be juggled constantly in order for a successful screenplay to result. While producers may open hundreds of screenplays, only those screenplays that grab and hold the reader's attention are read to the final page.

I once met a police officer who served as a consultant on several films, including such successes as *Beverly Hills Cop, Beverly Hills Cop 2*, and *The Presidio*. Because he worked full-time for the Los Angeles County Sheriff's Office, screenwriting was only a hobby. But, he was vastly interested in improving his hobby. He came to me with his first completed screenplay and I gave him advice on how to improve it. He acted on the criticism, writing several subsequent drafts. Because of his tireless efforts, we were able to option the script to Five Rivers Productions.

If you aspire to be a screenwriter, you should look upon your work as a process that will come to fruition over time—perhaps a long time. One screenwriter we worked with put his first screenplay through five rewrites before we would submit it for him. It was sent to twenty-five producers; it was rejected by all of them. The twenty-sixth submission hit the mark: The screenplay was optioned and is in development.

Even if you are extraordinarily fortunate and sell your first screenplay, it might be a long time (maybe even years) before it reaches the screen, particularly if it is a feature as opposed to a TV or cable movie. Remember: Every piece of writing in circulation that carries your name is establishing you as a writer in the minds of those who read it. Therefore, be certain that every piece of your writing is your absolute best effort. If you think seeing your name in print is exciting, wait until you see it on the screen.

CHAPTER THIRTEEN

Making It in Television

"Television has proved that people will look at anything rather than at each other."
—Ann Landers

Television is a big business. Unlike other facets of the entertainment industry, where it seems only the producers or studios see any profit, television offers numerous opportunities for gifted writers to receive lucrative rewards for their efforts. If you write for TV, you can be remunerated for:

- Original treatments
- Series proposals
- Teleplays

In addition, you can receive residuals from royalties, foreign sales, and from the rerun and syndication markets. Times have never been this good for the writer who specializes in television. The Writers Guild of America reports that royalties and residuals paid to its members are constantly increasing.

To participate in this payday, you first must break into the business. This is not a simple ambition. However, the advantage all writers have is that television is renowned for being a writer's medium: It has a voracious appetite for writing, particularly good writing. For example, the normal season-long pickup for sitcoms and dramatic series is twenty-two episodes; some series sell for longer terms (*3rd Rock from the Sun* and *Beverly Hills,*

90210 each had multilayer renewals, as have other shows like *Law and Order, Homicide,* and *NYPD Blue).* It is commonplace for a show to have several writers working on each episode, another benefit for writers.

A writer entering TV should understand certain basic rules. Good writing in episodic television is defined as that which:

1. Faithfully remains within the confines of its genre
2. Provides a plot easily grasped within the first few minutes of the show
3. Features strong, dynamic roles for the program's stars

Good episodic television writing is NOT subtle. Perhaps more than any other kind of writing mentioned in this book, television writing is a mechanized process; it does not pay to become too attached to it or to be too experimental. The bulk of episodic television programming is comprised of stalwart cop or medical dramas or family comedies—writing that is not likely to challenge the writer's deepest resources. However, in response to the burgeoning cable market, the broadcast networks are attempting to push the envelope on standard TV fare. This helps to explain the appearance of shows like *CSI* (and its various offshoots), *Desperate Housewives,* and *Lost,* which traditionally would have been considered too radical for mainstream television.

CABLE AND SYNDICATION

For the writers who do not wish to explore the network television arena, there are other markets, the most high-profile of which are cable and syndication. The cable industry has undergone an unprecedented expansion and continues to grow. Specialty programming prevails in cable, as there are channels devoted to history, biography, children's programming, etc. Your prospects in this area as a writer can be difficult to assess, since the possibility of finding work is dependent upon your ability to fit these specialized needs.

Ironically, the new writer's best opportunity for breaking into cable TV is probably by writing shows resembling those found on network TV. HBO, for example, began solely as a movie channel, but now it initiates a large amount of original programming, mostly in the form of TV movies or miniseries. USA Cable continually produces original "made for cable" movies—all in the $2.5 million budget range (and often lower). The chances of winning a writing assignment on a cable series may be slight, but overall, there are still opportunities to get involved on the movie or miniseries fronts if you have the right property and package.

It's best to have a completed screenplay or teleplay that can be used as a calling card. Then, make sure your representative is knocking on the right doors—i.e., executives who can green-light a picture or a producer who can hire you to write an episode for his show because he has an "output" or "put" deal in place.

Syndicated television originated because broadcasters realized that there are more programming hours in the day than any network can program with original shows. When local television stations (circa 1950) found that producing their own programming was prohibitively expensive, a syndication market of low-cost programming (such as game shows and talk shows) that could be sold to stations around the country began to surface. The syndication market has not significantly changed. Original programming that goes into syndication today is still low in cost, often being limited to one set and a host (think of any game show or even a high-end syndicated show like *America's Most Wanted*). Virtually all of these shows are produced by independent production companies that utilize a staff of writers.

The secret to breaking into network, cable, and syndication, then, becomes similar to breaking into other areas of writing—create the circumstances for your own employment. In other words, create a proposal for a program that is not just viable but that also demonstrates your ability to write. Most independent production companies (television or feature) have a development department. Getting in the door to see a development executive at a cable or syndicated channel often is easier than at the networks. In addition, they are usually more inclined to listen to new ideas; independents are always striving to find the next big project. The rules of what is desired and acceptable keep changing with shows like HBO's *The Sopranos, Six Feet Under,* and *Deadwood.*

In Part Three of this book, on page 240, you'll find my own co-attempt at creating a syndicated series. *True Murder Mysteries* is a project that I developed with Vincent Bugliosi. Conceived as a half-hour or hour-long weekly series, the show is intended to feature America's most famous murder cases during the last century; Bugliosi would be narrator and host. Once we had a proposal that we felt accurately represented our project, we enhanced its marketability by creating a "presentation script." This script would make the show a reality in the minds of the producers we were pitching. The concept has sold as far as options several times but it has yet to be made.

One of the lessons here is a rule for this business that can't be stressed too often: Just because you sell a property, it doesn't mean it will be produced. Prepare to have your heart broken many times before seeing your ambitions realized. As a matter of fact, sometimes Hollywood not only breaks your heart, but it may rip it out of your chest and roll over it with a bulldozer too.

Also in Part Three, on page 256, you'll find a proposal for a dramatic series. Called *The Inside Man,* it is written by Jerry Schmetterer, a well-known newspaper and television journalist. This proposal includes a treatment for the two-hour movie that would serve as a "back-door" pilot (i.e., the movie would stand alone or it would set up the series by being its first episode).

Off-network syndication programming is an area of television syndication that generates tremendous sums of money. Popular TV series, like *Seinfeld* or *Frasier,* went into syndication after they had aired on network television for several years, often selling for well over $1 million per episode. With little in the way of overhead or production costs to weigh it down, the show earns nearly 100 percent profit throughout its syndicated run. For example, *The Cosby Show* earned approximately half a billion dollars upon its initial availability for off-network syndication. With money in this range, even the writers—usually Hollywood's low men on the totem pole as far as profit participation goes—have had reason to smile.

Remember the golden rule for all writers in Hollywood: Pitch yourself as well as your project. The project could be forgotten tomorrow; make sure that YOU'RE not. Always remember that Hollywood is a "relationship business," so be sure to spend your time and energy building relationships, not destroying them.

CHAPTER FOURTEEN

Contracts:
Watch Your Back!

"Good swiping is an art in itself."
—Jules Pfeiffer

It would be a pleasure if the major concern of the movie and publishing industries was to see that a writer reaches the widest possible audience by writing in the format that is most appropriate to his work. Unfortunately, this is not the case. The concern that dominates both industries is The Deal—negotiating the deal, writing the contract for the deal, and, sometimes, breaking the deal. Throughout this book, I have attempted to offer you advice on how to develop your writing so that its fullest potential—in the appropriate medium—is realized.

Now, let's take a leap of faith: Let's assume you have written a book or screenplay that is generating interest from professionals. While not trying to sound negative, one must be realistic; millions of manuscripts are written each year while only approximately 100,000 books are published. Some manuscripts are immediately left to gather dust in their authors' attics; others make the rounds of agents, publishers, or lawyers without success; a few appear on the marketplace. The numbers are worse for screenplays making the rounds in the film industry.

You might expect this to be the time to sit back and relax and wait for the kudos and financial rewards to start rolling in. NO! As a writer, you are responsible for your work and this, in turn, means you must make sure that your representative negotiates a quality contract for you.

A contract is more than a schedule of potential royalty payments or a way to ensure that you have enough copies of your book to hand out to friends. A contract is the writer's only assurance that his work will reach the public in the form in which he envisioned it. Of course, money is important—as a representative, I'm certainly not going to deny that!—but self-respect is just as important.

In your first deal as an author—whether it is a contract for a magazine article, short story, book, or screenplay—you should not expect that your work will be sold for the optimum price. (You very possibly have already had this experience.) There are exceptions, of course, and stories about those twenty-five-year-old waiters who sell their first scripts for an extraordinary amount of money are well-known. It is much more likely that producers or publishers will try to take advantage of the writer's eagerness to make that first sale. (Indeed, many will attempt to take advantage of the second- or third-time writer, too.) The cardinal rule is to make sure that you emerge from the negotiations with a satisfactory contract. By the same token, once your book or screenplay is a smashing success, don't expect to renegotiate the deal.

CONTRACT DELICACIES

When the delicacies of negotiations come in to play, the prospective earnings of the book must be balanced against the writer's status. Many times, because the producer has acquired a terrific script by a first-time writer for an astoundingly small sum of money, the writer (motivated by his natural desire to make up for the last injustice) is able to command a huge salary for his second script (which may be nowhere near the same high quality). In fact, this is one of the principal reasons why costs in the film industry are skyrocketing: Almost nothing sold is bought on its own merits. Representatives are aware of this situation and will move to take advantage of it; it's not the healthiest course for the industry.

In publishing, certain standard royalties are offered to authors, depending on the type of book that has been written. Usually, hardcover royalties are 10 percent of retail earnings for the first 5,000 copies, and escalate to 15 percent thereafter. However, publishers sometimes lower this percentage rate on books they feel may have problems selling; sometimes, sliding rates are arranged (i.e., 10 percent on the first 15,000 copies; 12.5 percent on the next 10,000; 15 percent thereafter). The permutations are endless.

With simple math, you'll see that these percentages can escalate into thousands of dollars if the book is successful; if the book is not successful, the financial returns are minimal.

The book industry is conservative with its accounting methods. For instance, too many publishers offer a flat 6 or 7.5 percent royalty schedule on trade paperbacks when there might be a more imaginative way for a deal to be structured between author and publisher. One thing I try to do is to negotiate performance bonuses whereas when a book reaches a certain level of success—for example, 25,000, 50,000, 75,000 copies—either the royalties escalate via a negotiated "ladder of escalation" and/ or the author receives a performance bonus as an additional advance against royalties earned.

Naturally, as with any good representative, I always try to negotiate higher royalties for my clients. Representatives and authors have a symbiotic relationship: The representative is the author's employee. Only when the author's book is sold does the representative make any money. If the author's book becomes a bestseller, the representative can expect his commission to swell appreciably the next time he negotiates for that writer.

Book deals are almost never made on the basis of net proceeds (i.e., profits returned after the publisher has deducted its sales discounts on the book) because the success of any given project is so uncertain.

I represented an unauthorized biography of a well-known political figure and this book served as an exception to the net proceeds rule. Time was of the essence in publishing this book, so my client was willing to consider an unprecedented offer in order to time its publication with an important upcoming election. I negotiated a royalty for the author which began at 15 percent on the net proceeds for the first 5,000 copies; 17.5 percent on the next 5,000; 20 percent on everything over that. Because of the unmitigated confidence we had that the book would sell well, we structured this unusual deal; with a less certain project, I would have rejected this contract out of hand. Because the author was flexible and willing to step outside of convention, he earned considerably greater royalties than he would have with a standard publishing deal.

Another practice that is completely outdated yet can still happen is the attempt by publishers to maintain participation in the motion picture or television rights to the books they publish. This is a complicated and often nasty procedure in which the publisher collects a fee from the movie or television sale of one of their properties but then refuse to allow the author's revenue to "flow through" the book until they conduct their biannual accounting. (*Flow-through* occurs when an author's advance payments have been earned and the publisher pays the author his additional subsidiary rights earnings as they are received.) Because of this antiquated process, the author often is deprived of the returns from a legitimate sale of his book for up to six months—simply so the publisher can ensure its 10 percent cut. The system is unfair, but it may still be used.

I often argue for a "flow-through" clause in book contracts; once the author's advance has been paid by royalties from the sale of his book, any revenue received by the publisher should flow through to the author within ten to thirty days of its receipt.

Another common publishing practice is the publisher's attempt to claim as much as 50 percent of the sale of foreign rights of an author's work. A more reasonable standard, and one which I try to negotiate, is 25 percent. A representative can help segregate the ownership of foreign rights from the sale of the U.S. rights (which usually includes Canada), thereby allowing authors to increase their revenue by selling rights to publishers in individual territories, rather than seeing everything sold off in one large deal.

Should you opt not to employ a representative, please use an attorney to negotiate your contracts. Before doing so, however, review the costs involved, as it is possible to build up enormous legal fees (which sometimes would be greater than a representative's commission) for the performance of relatively simple duties.

If you choose to have an agent represent you, it could result in a long-lasting relationship with major benefits for both of you. Besides selling your writing and negotiating the contracts, your representative collects monies owed to you. Book contracts tend to be more standardized than those in the film or television industries, so collecting on royalties is generally not a problem. Film deals are often complicated and messy, especially when net profit participation is included. Studio bookkeeping is quite labyrinthine; the writer usually stands little chance of seeing money from his points in profit participation unless he brings a lawsuit.

A well-known example of collecting—or trying to collect—on net profit participation is the Art Buchwald case against Paramount Pictures. He received a certain percentage of the net profits from the 1988 Eddie Murphy movie *Coming to America* after he filed a lawsuit alleging that his story treatment was used as the premise for the film. After winning the lawsuit, his problem became collecting the money owed him. Despite the fact that *Coming to America* was a huge success, Paramount's books claimed otherwise. It reminds one of an old Hollywood joke:

> *Question:* "Do you know what the difference between gross profit and net profit is in Hollywood?"
>
> *Answer:* "No profit!"

To insure against this sort of accounting sleight-of-hand, I attempt to negotiate for my clients the same level of profit participation as the producer of the project. The purpose is obvious: It's harder to cheat two people out of the monies owed them than it is to cheat one, especially if they have exactly the same deal. This is known as a "Favored Nations" profit participation clause, whereby no one else involved with the production receives a more favorable definition of profits than you. In the process, the structure of the deal encourages honesty.

Any representative who manages that has done his job.

A SAMPLE DEAL MEMO

The following is a short-form deal memo for a rights option agreement on a book property that I negotiated. This kind of memo could be used for a feature film or television property. This was a fair deal for the property this contract was negotiated for.

May 20, 20__

Peter Miller, President
PMA Literary and Film Management, Inc.
P.O. Box 1817
Old Chelsea Station
New York, NY 10113

Re: Ms. Author
     Mr. Author
     "Working Title"

Gentlemen:

This will confirm the agreement for an option to purchase all motion picture and television rights with respect to the book (excluding the story entitled "The New Connection") written by Ms. Author and Mr. Author entitled "Working Title."

Our agreement is as follows:

Ms. Author and Mr. Author have granted Producer an exclusive one year option commencing on May 16, 20__, and continuing through and including May 15, 20__, to purchase the motion picture and television rights to the book, for the total sum of Fifteen Thousand Dollars ($15,000).

"The Company" aka "Producer" shall have the right to extend the exclusive option period for an additional year for the additional sum of Fifteen Thousand Dollars ($15,000).

The purchase price for the motion picture and television rights to this property shall be the sum of One Hundred Twenty-five Thousand Dollars ($125,000). The initial option payment shall be applicable against this purchase price, but the extension payment shall not be. The purchase price shall be paid on exercise of the option, but not photography of the motion picture.

In the event one or more pictures are released as a theatrical motion picture in the United States prior to the initial network broadcast of the pictures, Producer shall pay Authors a theatrical release bonus in the amount of One Hundred Twenty-five Thousand Dollars ($125,000), per such motion picture.

In the event one or more such motion pictures are released as theatrical motion pictures in the United States subsequent to the initial network broadcast of the motion picture or is released as a theatrical motion picture in foreign release (with a bona fide distribution as a theatrical release), or a television sequel is produced based on literary material, Producer shall pay Authors a theatrical releases bonus, or sequel payment, in the amount of Sixty-two Thousand Five Hundred Dollars ($62,500).

Authors shall be employed as technical consultants on each such motion picture for a total fee in the amount of Fifty Thousand Dollars ($50,000). Such fee shall be payable as follows: Ten Thousand Dollars ($10,000) shall be payable during the script development phase of the motion picture, subject to the applicable broadcast network agreeing to recognize such fee as a development cost of the motion picture, but in no event later than during production of the motion picture; and Forty Thousand Dollars ($40,000) shall be payable during production of the motion picture.

In the event that the broadcast network orders an episodic one-hour dramatic prime-time series based on the property, Producer will pay Authors a series sales bonus in the amount of Twenty Thousand Dollars ($20,000) based on an order consisting of twelve (12) episodes, which bonus shall be reducible to a floor of Ten Thousand Dollars ($10,000) on a pro-rata basis if the network orders fewer than twelve (12) episodes.

Authors shall be employed as and shall receive on screen and paid advertising credit as technical consultants on the series for a total fee of Seven Thousand Five Hundred Dollars ($7,500) per episode for the first season and ten percent (10%) cumulative increases each season thereafter.

Producer shall pay a series royalty in the amount of Two Thousand Five Hundred Dollars ($2,500) per episode during the first broadcast season on the series, which royalty shall increase by Five Hundred Dollars ($500) per episode in the second and subsequent broadcast seasons on the series.

In addition to the foregoing, Producer shall pay Authors two and one half percent of one hundred percent (2.5% of 100%) of the net profits attributable to the exhibition of the motion picture(s) and the series episodes (if applicable). Net profits shall be defined, accounted for and paid in accordance with Producer's standard Definition of Net Profits-Motion Picture – Episodic Series, which definition shall be subject to good faith negotiations on a favored nations basis with any executive producers, script writers, or directors.

Producer will pay the Author's advances against the foregoing net profit participation in the amount of Two Thousand Five Hundred Dollars ($2,500) per episode, beginning at the episode number 67 and continuing thereafter, with all such advances retroactive to episode number 1. Advances will be paid at such time as the series is placed into domestic syndication, provided that payment of such advances shall not put Producer in a negative cash flow position, being defined as all actual out-of-pocket production costs (excluding any production fee or overhead charge) plus interest thereon.

All payments made pursuant to the terms of this agreement shall be made to the PMA Literary and Film Management, Inc.,

Federal ID number ##-#######

If the forgoing is in accordance with your understanding of our agreement, I will prepare a formal contract.

Sincerely,

Vice President Business Affairs
Producer

Agreed and accepted:
Peter Miller, President
PMA Literary and Film Management, Inc.

By _____

Peter Miller

By _____

SS# _____

Ms. Author

By _____

SS# _____

Mr. Author

CHAPTER FIFTEEN

Making the Deal
in Hollywood

*"A verbal contract isn't worth the paper it is
written on."*

—Sam Goldwyn

For years, the lowest paid "above the line" talent on motion picture and television productions has more often than not been the author or screenwriter—unless, of course, you are John Grisham, Michael Crichton, or William Goldman. Being properly represented and having a seasoned entertainment attorney in your corner can gain you the footing you need to properly position your career. In the words of the late Rodney Danger-field, "I can't get no respect," and believe me, you won't get any unless you have good representation. It's all about "quotes" in Hollywood, meaning what you are paid. Some screenwriters get "scale" without profit payments and some get a million dollars a script. Which one do you want to be?

CONTRACTS AND RIGHTS

If you are optioning the rights to your book, being hired to adopt the book, or writing a spec screenplay, TV movie, miniseries, treatment, or an episode for a TV series, don't do it unless you have a written contract that was negotiated by an agent or attorney experienced in the business. DO NOT represent yourself.

Assuming that you need representation, that would mean that you've written something that someone wants to buy, like a treatment, a screenplay, a novel, nonfiction book, a published book, or a book that has not yet been published (a manuscript) that you own the rights to. Let's emphasize that last point—*that you own the rights to*. It is essential that the ownership of whatever rights you own have been carefully identified. You will need a copy of the contract with the publisher who you've worked with; or, a copy of the WGA registration for the treatment or screenplay; or, in the case of a work based on a true-life story, you will need a right of privacy release. Basically, you will need copies of any agreement related to the work to be produced.

In order to defend and place your rights—or, really, to have your representative do so—you will need to establish a clear chain of title in identifying whatever rights you have. Assuming that you re-license whatever rights you have to a motion picture or TV company to make a film or television work, the main rights I would suggest you hold on to is the world publishing rights. You should also try to have your attorney or representative negotiate the best possible negotiation in merchandising/ancillary/licensing rights.

NEGOTIATING IN HOLLYWOOD

Typically, your contractual deals—the amounts paid for options, terms and deadlines—will be handled by your manager or agent. But it is always a good idea to keep apprised of the negotiations yourself, in order to have an understanding of how the talks are coming along, and to be able to tell whether the terms are acceptable to you. This will help in two regards: one, it will help to ensure that you are not surprised when the final contracts are drawn up, and two, by staying in touch with your agent or manager, you will have a sense of how good of a job he or she is doing. Many writers' reps sell themselves well over lunch, but only in the middle of negotiations can you truly get a sense of how good they are at their job.

In Hollywood, even more than in the New York publishing industry, producers and executives can be particularly off-putting and hard-nosed. Because there is typically more money at stake in film and television deals, Hollywood upper brass can be difficult and unpleasant to deal with. A new writer with little professional experience will have troubles gaining leverage in negotiations, so it is best to keep in mind that this is a career you are building, not a lottery you just won where you expect to get rich fast. Many writers have to write for years before they can gain the leverage on negotiations that they would prefer. Each project you sell will typically give you more power to exert on the next deal. This takes time, so be patient. Your agent or manager is doing their best, but it's not fair to expect miraculous deals from them early in your career.

DO'S AND DON'TS WHEN DEALING WITH HOLLYWOOD

There are always ups and downs, yeses and nos, and do's and don'ts in any transaction, business or just life in general. Hollywood is a fickle place. I will never forget a conversation I had with a studio executive on one of the biggest film deals I ever made. It went something like this: "Peter, there is no way I am going to give you a million dollars for a first time, unknown novelist."

Well, the author was paid $770,000, so that wasn't too bad. That's the good news! The bad news is that the studio never made the movie. This is why I say Hollyweird is a fickle place.

Do's

1. Write something great! Not good, okay, but absolutely great! Fantastic!
2. Research what is standard in the industry for a similar sale or circumstances to your property. This way, you and your representation can aim your expectations at what could be a slightly higher sale for you that would be considered fair and reasonable. However, if you have something great and several people want it, then go for the gold and God bless! Note: I like making people pay for what they want. That old saying, "Put your money where your mouth is," has always worked for me when negotiating a deal. Truer words were never spoken because you will find a lot of people want a lot for free and don't want to pay for it. That is why I call it Hollyweird.
3. Do a lot of research on who is interested in your work—that is, what have they previously produced and whether or not they have been sued for plagiarism, breach of fiduciary obligation, theft, fraud, or misappropriation of funds. You should also find out whether or not they are litigious and sue other people without good cause. Simply put, know your buyer and make sure they are someone you want to do business with, particularly if they are an independent producer or production company.
4. Secure excellent representation in choosing your agent, manager and/or lawyer. Again, do your research. Making representation choices in managing your career is the most important decision you can make.
5. It is your representative's or lawyer's responsibility to report to you all specific details and deal points during any negotiations. Do negotiate with your representatives about this so you are not left out in the dark.
6. Keep your faith in yourself, and good luck! In Hollywood, you will definitely need it.

Don'ts

1. Do not submit your work or property to anyone unless it is registered with the Writers Guild of America (the eastern or western branch) and/or without having placed a common law copyright on the front pages. (For example, write "Copyright 2006, Author or Company Name, All Rights Reserved" on the title page.) You should also send a copy of the work to yourself via registered mail. This mail will remain unopened unless you ever have to use it as evidence in a court of law to prove when the work was created and by whom.

2. Do not randomly submit your original ideas to people in the industry unless you have carefully researched who they are. Reminder, ideas are stolen everyday and you wouldn't want this to happen to you.

3. Do not adapt another person's story, nonfiction book, or novel without having the rights to do so. (See the section above on contracts and rights.) I have seen many writers come to me with adaptations they have written for works they have no rights to. This is unfortunately a huge waste of time, since the rights may be very difficult or impossible to get, or another writer in Hollywood may have already adapted that work.

4. Do not interfere with your representatives or lawyers during negotiations. While it's a good idea to remain apprised of the negotiations, some overly eager writers make the mistake of calling every day to see what's happened. This is not productive, and only causes tensions. At the same time, DO NOT phone the buyer or their representatives. Let your agent or manager handle all negotiations; you should not be in touch with the buyer until the deal is signed.

In regards to this last point, I have heard stories of buyers
calling the writer during negotiations and trying to get the writer
to agree to certain terms that the agent or manager is negotiating against. Essentially, the buyer in these cases was trying to
trick the writer. Always let your own representative handle these
issues. Remember when I said that Hollywood was a jungle on
another planet? Well, in such a place you always need to have
someone on your side who knows the territory and who will
help you to fight your way through.

PART THREE

Proposals That Get the Deal Done

PROPOSAL

#1	A Biography Proposal
#2	A True-Crime Book Proposal
#3	A Self-Help/Relationship Book Proposal
#4	A Cookbook Proposal
#5	A How-to Book Proposal
#6	A Health Book Proposal
#7	A Fiction Proposal
#8	A Television Series Proposal and Script
#9	A TV Movie and Dramatic Series Proposal and Treatment
#10	A Novel Coverage

A Biography Proposal

The first proposal in this section is for Lee Butcher's *The Accidental Millionaire: The Rise and Fall of Steve Jobs at Apple Computer*, an unauthorized biography of Jobs, the creative force behind the founding of Apple Computers. Butcher was formerly the editor of the *San Jose Business Journal*, which covers events in Silicon Valley, so he was in a unique position to write this book: He witnessed the rift between Steve Jobs and Apple's new executive John Sculley and had plenty of inside information on the power struggle. As an established writer, Butcher created a successful proposal by opening with a complete overview of the story; he then offered a detailed, chapter-by-chapter breakdown of the book. The proposal concluded with his argument on how the book would fit into the current literary marketplace. He also included a brief statement about his work as an editor and about his ability to write the biography.

The book was first published by Paragon House; its trade paperback edition was published a year later. Finally, the mass-market paperback rights were sold to Knightsbridge Publishing, unfortunately a now-defunct company. The motion picture and television rights were optioned to Chessman/Main Films and the project was in development as a feature film for years but unfortunately was never made. If you study Butcher's proposal carefully and if you have the right subject—someone timely and well known—you, too, could create a successfully published biography.

Accidental Millionaire

The Rise and Fall of Steve Jobs

at Apple Computer

A Proposal for an Unauthorized Biography

Approximately 400 pages

Photos Included

By Lee Butcher

THE STORY

You could hardly imagine two personalities that were as disparate as those of Steve Jobs, cofounder of the Apple Computer Company, and John C. Sculley. Jobs, who until the middle of 1985 was Chairman of the Board and head of the elite Macintosh Division of the Cupertino, California, company, has been considered by many as the driving force behind one of the most successful business enterprises in history. He is widely believed to have been responsible for the creation of the first Apple computer, usually taking the spotlight away from Stephen Wozniak, the electronics genius who actually designed and built what was to become a revolutionary device that spurred the development of a multimillion dollar industry.

There are just as many, and perhaps more, who think Jobs bullied his way into Apple and that he was more of a detriment than an asset. Not long after Apple became a public company, he had developed a reputation for being willful, dominating, divisive, arrogant, and mercurial. Apple was in disarray and morale was a shambles when Sculley became president of the company in 1983 and a large part of it was Jobs' doing. Less than three years after Sculley joined Apple, Jobs was stripped of all operating power and eventually resigned as chairman after a bitter fight with Sculley and the Board. Sculley, a traditionalist, was voted chairman in addition to his duties as president.

Even by Silicon Valley standards, where the unusual is often the norm, Jobs was considered quirky. He wore his hair long, went barefoot, and threw himself with almost manic obsession into such things as diets that were supposed to reduce "unhealthy" mucous from the body, fruitarian diets that he thought eliminated the need for bathing, and had a long-lasting flirtation with the mysticism of India. He would fast for days.

"Whatever Steve did, he became obsessed with it," says his acquaintances from the early days before Apple. "He was a fanatic and it was hard to be around him because he was constantly lecturing others."

This facet of Jobs' personality never changed. A stock analyst who watches Apple says: "We had hoped that Steve would grow up with the business, but he never did." He was driven to be the self-appointed expert in whatever enterprise he undertook, and to say that it made him unpopular would be an understatement. Even Wozniak never really liked or trusted him. "He will use everyone to his own advantage," Wozniak says. Jobs' dominating personality manifested itself at an early age. When his adoptive parents were forced to move for economic reasons, Jobs attended an elementary school he didn't like. He told his parents that he would not continue at the school under any circumstances. They gave in to his demands and moved so Jobs could attend an elementary school more to his liking.

He defied them shortly after graduation from high school when he announced that he was going to live with his girlfriend, Nancy Rogers, in the Santa Cruz Mountains for the summer. His parents replied, "No, you're not." Jobs retorted, "Yes, I am," and walked out the door. Jobs was determined to attend Reed College, an expensive, ultra-liberal institution in Portland, Oregon, but his father, an engineer at Hewlett-Packard, argued that his son should attend a more traditional college. Jobs informed his parents that if he couldn't go to Reed, he would not attend any college. The elder Jobs gave in. Once more the parents submitted to the headstrong son over whom they had little, if any, control.

The senior Jobs paid thousands of dollars to support Steve, who soon lost interest in classes and stopped attending. Even on a campus noted for the bizarre, Jobs was considered weird. Before long he dropped out of classes completely and became a "floater," moving from one vacant dormitory room to another. His main interest was in Eastern mysticism and he spent a goodly portion of his time with the Hare Krishnas searching for "enlightenment." He had no idea what he wanted to do with his life.

Wozniak, however, had thrown himself head over heels into the world of electronics and was immersed in a highly illegal activity known as "phone phreaking." He had created a "Blue Box" that allowed him to make telephone calls around the world without the nuisance of paying for them. He had met Jobs a few years earlier and the two teenagers had struck up a guarded friendship. Jobs convinced Wozniak that they should form a partnership to manufacture and sell the Blue Boxes to college students. The illegal venture made the young men edgy and they dropped it after about a year.

Wozniak turned to the world of microcomputers, a field still in its infancy. He was an avid member of the Homebrew Computer Club in California and took great delight in showing his latest creations to other computer hobbyists. He did not meet with instant success but, by ingenious use of microchips, he eventually created a sensation among his peers. Jobs again saw commercial possibilities for the circuit board that Wozniak had designed. He persuaded Wozniak that they could make money if the circuit board was refined. They established a garage work-shop at Jobs' parents' home.

Wozniak had little interest in fame and fortune and had to be constantly prodded by Jobs, who pleaded, begged, and even had weeping fits to keep Wozniak working.

Wozniak was still a full-time engineer at Hewlett-Packard and worked on the computer part-time. Jobs scrounged for parts and became expert at finding them for rock bottom prices. The business was called Apple in remembrance of Jobs' days with the Hare Krishnas where he picked fruit in an orchard. He also scouted for investors to keep the financially strapped business from going under. His appearance, abrasive manner, and lack of experience made it hard. Apple also needed guidance in marketing and advertising, but had no money to pay for professional services.

Jobs was guided by acquaintances at Intel, a company that manufactures semiconductors, to the Regis McKenna Advertising and Public Relations Agency. Frank Burgess had the task of screening potential accounts and was not enthusiastic, but Jobs launched an all-out telephone campaign, leaving stacks of messages, until Burgess decided to pay Jobs and Wozniak a courtesy call. His initial misgivings were compounded when he first met Jobs, who emerged from the kitchen in sandals, jeans, long unwashed hair, and a straggly beard. He thought Jobs was just another Silicon Valley flake until the unkempt young man started talking. The full impact of Jobs' personality hit him like a thunderbolt and he was struck by two thoughts: first, Jobs was smart, and second, he was so smart that Burgess didn't know what in hell Jobs was talking about. Burgess checked further and discovered that the company had the potential to become a moneymaker. The agency agreed to handle all of Apple's marketing for a share of sales revenue, but hedged its bets by saying that the results of Apple's first advertisement should be reviewed before the commitment was carried further.

Considering the phenomenal success of other Silicon Valley companies that had grown from garage enterprises into multimillion-dollar companies, the McKenna agency was not taking much of a risk. A memo concerning Apple noted that the company had experienced little success in selling its computers to end users, even though it had moved a quantity to distributors. Wozniak and Jobs were young and inexperienced, but the memo compared them to Nolan Bushnell who was young when he started Atari and was currently reported to have a net worth of $10 million.

Apple's plans were far greater than its financial resources in 1976. The microcomputer industry as a whole was growing much faster than Apple. The company needed money and marketing guidance and Jobs turned to Bushnell, where he had once worked, for advice on finding investors. Bushnell educated Jobs about the world of venture capitalists, but warned him, "The longer you can do without those guys, the better off you are." The meeting ended with Bushnell giving Jobs the names of three potential investors, one of whom was Don Valentine, who had invested in Atari during its infancy.

Valentine was a hard-nosed venture capitalist who was not likely to be bowled over by a glib teenager like Jobs. He had started his own venture capital firm, Sequoia Ventures, after making a fortune with other successful investments. He was, in almost every way, the antithesis of Jobs. He was a fashionable dresser and was fastidious about his personal appearance, and equally careful about his investments. He had met Jobs briefly when the latter worked at Atari and remarked that Jobs "looked like a refugee from the human race." (When he worked at Atari, Jobs was on the fruit diet, which he believed eliminated the need for bathing. His co-workers did not agree and insisted that something had to be done because he smelled so bad they couldn't stand to be around him. Jobs was eventually shunted off to a private cubicle.)

Valentine's meeting with Jobs and Wozniak did not go well. The two young entrepreneurs were not talking big enough to suit him. They were satisfied with nibbling away at the fringes of the single board computer market, hoping to sell 1,000 units a year. This was guaranteed to turn Valentine away. "If someone wants to be a millionaire, I'm not interested," he said. "If he wants a net worth of $50 million to $100 million, I'm interested. If he talks in terms of billions, I'm interested, because if he even comes close, we'll both make a killing." His assessment of Jobs and Wozniak underlined his lack of enthusiasm for Apple. "Neither of them knew anything about marketing or the size of the potential market," he said. "In short, they weren't thinking big enough."

Although Valentine declined to invest, he suggested three venture capitalists whose interests might mesh with those of Jobs and Wozniak. One of them was Mike Markkula, a thirty-three-year-old millionaire but, in Silicon Valley terms, a "small" millionaire. Markkula was living a luxurious retirement when he agreed to meet with Wozniak and Jobs. His most recent association had been with Intel. In Silicon Valley, where the pursuit of worldly pleasure rivals those of the most exaggerated soap opera, Markkula was a straight arrow. He preferred home to life in the fast lane. At Intel, he had been considered competent and steady, but no one saw him as a person who was going to create thunder and lightning. Markkula borrowed heavily to buy Intel stock and, when the company went public, he became a millionaire overnight.

Markkula's meeting with Wozniak and Jobs marked a major turning point at Apple. He was impressed with the computer Wozniak had built and agreed to help organize the company. After talking it over with his wife, he agreed to invest $250,000 to develop the Apple II and to devote four years of his life to the company.

Markkula's tie with Apple had implications far beyond the money he invested. He brought a steadying influence, knowledge of management and marketing, and experience gained in the rough and tumble world of business and venture capital. He was a moderating influence who helped keep Jobs from running rough-shod over people, a sympathetic audience for Wozniak, who needed constant assurance and praise, and a vision for Apple that far exceeded that of either of the two youngsters. In retrospect, it is fair to say that there would have been no Apple Computer Company if it had not been for Markkula's guiding hand.

Markkula met with Jobs and Wozniak on weekends and in the evenings to discuss Apple's future. Arguments arose over the division of the stock, with Wozniak openly questioning the importance of Jobs to the organization. To Wozniak's surprise, Markkula came to Jobs' defense. "He had a lot of confidence in Steve," Wozniak said later. "He saw him as a future executive, a future Mike Markkula."

Wozniak had little faith in Apple's future and believed that Markkula would lose every dime he had invested. He deliberated over whether to place all of his eggs in one basket or to accept a transfer to Oregon with Hewlett-Packard. Both Wozniak and his first wife liked the security that came with a regular paycheck.

Meanwhile, Markkula and Jobs were trying to decide whether or not Apple could continue without Wozniak and agreed that it could not. They pressured him into a decision by telling him he had to join Apple full-time or he was out. Even then Wozniak dallied. Jobs launched a campaign to convince Wozniak that his future was with Apple. He telephoned Wozniak's friends and asked for their help in persuading him to stay with Apple. As a last resort he visited Wozniak's parents where he begged for their help. Wozniak's parents scolded Jobs, telling him that he was an opportunist who had capitalized on their son's work and that he deserved no part of the company. Jobs left the meeting in tears.

Markkula plotted a more practical approach to entice Wozniak to hitch his star to Apple. He presented a strong argument as to the future prospects for the company and vision. "He started talking about money, about a computer we could sell, and that decided it for me," Wozniak remembers. "I decided to stay with Apple."

Apple Computer Company was officially formed on January 3, 1977. It bought out the partnership that consisted of Jobs, Wozniak and Markkula for $5,308.96. Markkula's most pressing concern then was to find someone to run the company. A man who came to Markkula's mind was Michael Scott, whose career had been interwoven with his own.

Scott, a native of Gainesville, Florida, had attended the California Institute of Technology where he majored in physics. He had worked at Beckman Instruments Systems Division in Southern California where he helped build equipment to check Saturn rockets before lift-off. He was hired by Fairchild Industries, but quickly became disenchanted with corporate politics, and left for National Semiconductor Co. He was overseeing a $30 million production line by the time he was thirty-two. The discomfort he had experienced with corporate life previously continued to plague him and he was also bored by the lack of glamour and excitement in manufacturing semiconductors. He was interested in at least exploring the possibilities when he heard from Markkula.

Wozniak was ecstatic. He said he would be glad to have anyone but Jobs managing production. Jobs, on the other hand, gave the proposal a cool reception, fearing the loss of power. Markkula, accustomed to Jobs by this time, convinced him that a better-managed company, not power, was at stake. Jobs balanced the loss of power with the possible financial gains and agreed to hire Scott as president. He knew that any combination of himself, Wozniak, or Markkula could unseat Scott at anytime. Scott was hired for $20,001 a year, one dollar more than the triumvirate of Jobs, Wozniak, and Markkula, and became their titular boss. Scott's biggest worry was whether or not he could get along with Jobs. It turned out that they were anathema to each other.

The arrival of Scott was disastrous for Jobs, who had been accustomed to doing whatever he wanted. Jobs found himself confronted with unyielding authority for the first time in his life. He bridled. When Apple began growing, Scott issued numbered security passes to designate employees. Because he considered technology to be the most important part of the new company, he issued Wozniak pass Number One. Jobs was beside himself. "Who's Number One?" he demanded. "I want to be Number One." Told that Wozniak had that number, Jobs countered, "Let me be Number Zero." Another time they fought when Jobs wanted to sign a batch of purchase orders. "I got here first," Jobs argued. "I should sign them." Scott replied that he would sign them and, if he didn't, he would quit.

The four had little in common except for an interest in high-technology. Jobs relished money and power and pushed himself into Apple because he had nothing better to do. Wozniak was there because he was the ultimate hobbyist who liked nothing better than showing off the machines he created. Markkula became associated with Apple because he saw it as a way to increase his personal wealth, and Scott wanted to be president of a company that would leave an indelible stamp on high-technology.

The Apple II was introduced at the First West Coast Computer Fair in the spring of 1977. It was a lightweight computer with a new switching system that eliminated the need for a cumbersome and noisy fan to keep it cool. Jobs was always behind the scene, cajoling, pushing, rejecting design and function until he was at least partly satisfied with the computer.

Shows such as the First West Coast Computer Fair were of monumental importance to computer companies. Prospective customers came by the hundreds to see the latest offerings and a start-up company could become successful immediately if its product aroused enough attention. Markkula understood the importance of displaying the computer and Apple employees in the best light possible. He rented a booth and paid to have it look as smart and elegant as he could. He ordered Jobs to "spruce up" and sent him out to buy the first suit he had ever owned. The display made Apple appear much more impressive than it actually was, and it began to receive orders.

Apple had moved out of the Jobs' garage and into a suite in a two-story building on Stevens Creek Boulevard in Cupertino. A plasterboard wall separated a few desks from the laboratory and assembling areas. Scott and Jobs continued to battle. Before Scott, Jobs had done pretty much as he wanted and now he found his responsibilities and power limited. Their arguments continued for years and became known as "The Scotty Wars."

Amid the turmoil and hand-holding, Markkula went about the business of formulating marketing plans. He was helped by a casual acquaintance, John Hall, a group controller for a Palo Alto pharmaceutical firm. They planned a three-pronged assault to hobbyists, physicians, and home users. Hall was asked to join the company, but demurred. "I couldn't afford the risk of joining a screwy company like Apple."

Jobs irritated and alienated almost everyone with whom he came into contact. He angered suppliers, many of whom were much larger than Apple, with his arrogant and headstrong attitude. When Apple began hiring employees, Jobs interviewed those who were to fill key positions. He would throw his dirty feet up on a coffee table in front of them and dumbfound them with a merciless inquisition. When interviews were held over lunch, he often embarrassed prospective employees by sending his food back and loudly proclaiming that it was nothing but garbage. One Apple employee described Jobs' treatment of people: "He would blow up over the smallest things. He was very obnoxious to them. We all wondered, 'How can you treat another human being like that?'"

Five months after the Apple II was introduced, the strife-ridden company almost went belly-up. Apple was gaining a reputation as a company that could not fill its commitments. As inventory piled up and revenues dropped, Apple's thin cushion of cash began to evaporate. Scott and Markkula agreed to underwrite a loan of $250,000 to help keep the company afloat. The tension between Jobs and Scott continued to mount and had a demoralizing effect on the company's employees. On Jobs' twenty-third birthday, Scott sent him a funeral wreath decorated with white roses and bearing the inscription: "R.I.P. Thinking of you."

The enhanced Apple II used a disk drive rather than a tape cassette to record information. It was a triumph of technology. When it was introduced at the Consumer Electronics Show in 1978, it was an instant hit. One engineer who saw it says, "I almost dropped my pants. It was so clever." Apple's orders began to pile up.

Markkula knew that Apple needed reputable investors, not only for cash, but to lend it a respectable sheen. He was looking toward the day when Apple would become a public company and well-known investors would make Apple much more attractive. He found the investors he wanted and when the papers were signed and stock exchanged in January 1978, Apple was valued at $3 million. The company was starting to receive serious attention on Wall Street and in the nation's business press.

By September 1980, three and a half years after the Apple II was introduced, revenues rose from $7.8 million to $ 117.9 million and profits increased from $793,497 to $11.7 million. There were more than 1,000 on Apple's payroll. But for all of its seeming success, the core of Apple was rotting with internal strife. Not only did Jobs constantly harass, humiliate, and berate employees, but Scott's personality seemed to change overnight and he began doing the same thing, possibly because he was in pain from a serious eye infection that doctors feared might cause permanent blindness. The company touted itself as one having high humanistic ideals, but, in practice, it had become a stressful, difficult place to work. Scott issued terse memos and became a heavy-handed disciplinarian. The appearance of either Jobs or Scott at an employee's desk could cause a constriction in the throat and clenching of the stomach muscles. As the lesser of two evils, Scott was fired, a move that threw him into a deep depression. The drapes and curtains at his house remained closed for weeks as he struggled to come to terms with his personal and professional disaster.

There was no one to replace Scott as president except Markkula. Jobs was too young, inexperienced, and mercurial to be trusted to do the job. Markkula, whose four years he had pledged to Apple were drawing to a close, reluctantly became president while Jobs replaced him as Chairman of the Board. Jobs, meanwhile, was having his own personal problems. Nancy Rogers, his boyhood sweetheart with whom he had lived, filed a paternity suit against him. Jobs steadfastly denied that he was the father and refused to pay the $20,000 settlement Rogers sought. Markkula didn't think that was enough and urged Jobs to settle for $80,000. He refused. To the surprise of everyone who knew him, he agreed to a blood test to determine paternity. The results stated that it was 94.4 percent positive that Jobs was the father of Rogers' daughter, Lisa. Jobs chose to look at it another way: "All it shows is that 15.4 percent of all men in America could be her father." He finally agreed to pay $385 a month in child support and to settle $5,856 in public assistance that Rogers had received.

In spite of the turmoil, Apple was thriving. In 1977, the partnership of Jobs, Wozniak, and Apple had been valued at $5,308. On New Year's Day in 1980, three weeks after Apple went public, the company was valued at $1.788 billion, which was more than

Ford Motor Company and four times Lockheed. The public stock offering was one of the most sensational in history and, in the hyperbolic parlance of Silicon Valley, created instant "zillionaires." Jobs' shares were valued at $256.4 million.

As Chairman and operating head of the Macintosh division, Jobs created deep and bitter resentments and rivalries, pitting department against department, division against division. Jobs had more of a penchant for losing friends than for making them. One of the first casualties was Wozniak, who had left Apple totally disillusioned, not only with Jobs but with the corporation Apple had become. He is still bitter. "Even in personal conversations with the guy, you could never really tell what he was thinking," Wozniak says. "Ask him a 'yes or no' question and the answer said 'no' to anyone who heard it, but the answer was 'maybe yes, maybe no.' He puts his own interests ahead of anyone else. Aside from not being able to trust him, he will use anyone to his own advantage."

Apple was being severely hurt by other computer companies and Jobs' unwillingness to conform to the marketplace. Jobs insisted that the end users take what Apple offered and do the conforming. He had also seriously underestimated the entry of IBM into the personal computer market. In fact, when IBM announced that intention, he published an advertisement that read, "Welcome IBM. Seriously." Apple failed to deliver computers on time, further increasing its reputation as a company that could not meet commitments. Jobs dallied, procrastinated, and rejected design after design of an enhanced Macintosh computer to the point that its designers were discouraged and placed little importance on timetables. "It didn't matter when you got it in," one engineer said. "You knew he was going to reject it anyhow."

IBM was able to bite deeply into the personal computer market with a philosophy that was diametrically opposed to that of Jobs. Instead of building a computer to its own expectations, it sent hundreds of representatives into the field to determine what customers wanted, then incorporated those features into its designs. In 1980, Apple had 32 percent of the personal computer market for those in the $1,000 to $5,000 price range. By 1985, Apple's market share had dropped to 24 percent even though the market was blossoming.

Not long after Apple's stock offering, the Board of Directors began looking for a strong president to replace Markkula, who longed to return to his interrupted retirement, millions wealthier than he had been previously. The man who caught the Board's attentions was John C. Sculley, President of the Pepsi-Cola division of PepsiCo. Sculley was credited with breaking Coca-Cola's monopoly at soda fountains across the nation and for developing a market campaign that allowed Pepsi to bite deeply into Coke's market.

Sculley's background was traditional. He had graduated with a degree in architecture, but abandoned that interest in favor of an MBA from the University of Pennsylvania's Wharton School of Business. When Sculley joined PepsiCo in 1967, he was sent straight to the shipping docks to learn the business from the ground up. Although he didn't have to, he spent long hours loading heavy cartons of soft drinks on delivery trucks. He even worked out with weights each night at the YMCA to become stronger so his job performance would improve. "That wasn't required of the job, but he wanted to make good," says Charles V. Mangold, a PepsiCo senior vice president who was Sculley's supervisor at the time. "He wanted a total background." Sculley was married to the daughter of PepsiCo's chairman when he joined the company, but his worth was proven when he was retained after the marriage broke up. Sculley and his former wife's father remained fast friends as well as business associates.

When Apple turned its attention to him, Sculley was a member of the PepsiCo Board of Directors, Keep America Beautiful, and the Soft Drink Association. He also lectured weekly at Wharton. He was considered somewhat of a cold fish with strong ideas about marketing and traditional business management. He was as different from Jobs as night is from day. Sculley had a passing interest in technology but was a babe in the woods when it came to the intricate workings of computers.

Individual Board members at Apple wooed Sculley privately, and then Jobs was given the task of recruiting him. Sculley had misgivings about joining Apple, largely because he was concerned about whether or not he could get along with Jobs, whose reputation had spread far beyond the confines of Silicon Valley. The two men spent hours together chatting, walking through leafy parks on both the East and West Coast. They didn't talk about business or computers, but about poetry, art and Eastern philosophy. Later, Apple's public relations company line was, "They were like brothers, or sometimes like father and son. (Sculley was fifteen years older than Jobs.) They would finish each other's sentences." In retrospect, it appears that the two men may have been more like gladiators circling one another, looking for strengths and weaknesses. Sculley had also been assured privately of the Board's support. Apple offered Sculley a sweet deal. He was guaranteed salary and bonuses of $2 million for his first year and help in buying a $2 million home.

Sculley joined Apple in 1983 as President and soon began a bloodbath of frightening proportions. Sculley, who had pledged to operate Apple in non-traditional ways, went about his job in a distinctly traditional manner. He immediately consolidated five divisions into two and took charge of one division himself to improve sagging company morale. Within a year he had fired more than 1,000 Apple employees and only eight senior executives remained of the fourteen who were there when he was hired. Sculley's arrival in 1983 heralded a banner year for Apple, with stock rising from $22 to $62 per share, increasing Jobs' holdings in the company to $432 million. The Macintosh, long delayed, was finally launched in 1984, selling a record of 70,000 units in just 100 days.

Jobs had finally succeeded in turning the Board against him. Sculley was told that he must get the Macintosh division, which

Jobs headed, in line. He replied, "It's a little hard to do when the division head happens to be the Chairman of the Board." When Jobs heard about this, he began his own campaign to have Sculley fired, but the Board turned a deaf ear. Jobs' arrogance and mismanagement had finally caught up with him and his career at Apple was unraveling. In May 1985, Jobs was stripped of all operational authority even though he remained Chairman of the Board. The full impact did not hit Jobs until later when he found himself isolated within the company and important company papers bypassed his desk. No one bothered to return his telephone calls. The Apple public relations machine, seeking to minimize controversy, issued a statement saying that Jobs would remain as "the soul of Apple." But Jobs knew he had been castrated.

He resigned September 17, 1985, and told Sculley that he was taking a few employees with him to start a company he called "NeXT". He showed Sculley a list of names and vows that Sculley raised no objection. Sculley remembers it differently. "He was taking key people who knew Apple's secrets. The Board was alarmed." Apple filed suit against its former Chairman and cofounder but eventually settled out of court. In the middle of 1986, as a last gesture of defiance, Jobs sold all of his shares in Apple except one.

In less than a decade, Apple had risen from a corner garage business to a multinational company worth $2 billion. The contribution that Jobs made cannot be overlooked, but it has often been exaggerated in the nation's press. He was the visionary who saw a business in Wozniak's ventures as a computer hobbyist and it was he who scrounged for parts and saw the need for outside investors. It is accurate to say that, without Jobs, there would have been no Apple Computer. He is the one who brought Markkula, with his cash and vision, on board, and who kept Wozniak working when the latter showed little faith.

Jobs was only thirty years old when he was ousted from Apple. Nick Arnett, high-technology reporter for the *San Jose Business Journal*, said: "Without Jobs, Apple is just another company. And without Apple, Steve Jobs is just another Silicon Valley millionaire."

OUTLINE

1. Introduction. Jobs in the final days of his career with Apple. He has achieved great wealth and power as cofounder of Apple and Chairman of the Board. Now he sits isolated in his office knowing that he has been usurped by John Sculley. It was not always that way.
2. The Rebel. Jobs was a loner as a youth and not at all popular with his peers. He also was able to dominate his adoptive parents. He was interested in high-technology and attended evening classes offered by Hewlett-Packard. He attends Reed College and drops out for lack of interest and throws himself into Eastern Philosophy, practicing various diets and fasting. He spends time with Hare Krishnas searching for enlightenment. Later he spends time bumming around India, gets scabies, and leaves the country in despair, vowing that Thomas Edison had done more to improve the world than all religious philosophies put together.
3. Jobs meets Stephen Wozniak who is an avid "phone phreak." Wozniak has created a "Blue Box" that allows him to make telephone calls around the world without paying for them. Jobs persuades Wozniak to enter into a partnership to make and sell Blue Boxes to college students, a moderately successful, but illegal venture with risks that soon force them to shut down. The two men have little in common except that they are both interested in high-technology and are loners with few friends.
4. The Homebrew Computer Club. Wozniak and Jobs are members of this club, which is composed of avid computer hobbyists. Wozniak works on various computer boards and eventually created a sensation with a single circuit board. Jobs sees commercial possibilities and they

establish a workshop in Jobs' garage to manufacture and sell the boards. Jobs had to prod Wozniak to improve the board while he scrounges for parts and looks for investors. He is eventually steered to Mike Markkula, a "small" Silicon Valley millionaire who has retired at age thirty-three.

5. Markkula becomes fascinated with Apple and decides to invest $250,000 of his own money to develop the Apple II computer and to devote four years of his life to organize the company. Wozniak has little faith in the venture and predicts that Markkula will lose every penny of his investment. He considers leaving Apple and accepting a transfer to Oregon with Hewlett-Packard, where he works as an engineer. He decides to stay with Apple after an intense campaign by Jobs and Markkula to keep him. Apple Computer Company is formed and buys out the partnership for under $6,000.

6. Markkula begins to organize Apple. He hires Scott to become President of the company. Wozniak is ecstatic because he would prefer anybody heading operations rather than Jobs. Jobs bridles at Scott's arrival because his power is limited now. For the first time in his life he meets with unyielding authority. Scott and Jobs dislike each other from the beginning and a long-running battle between the two eventually becomes known as "The Scotty Wars."

7. Apple begins to have success with the introduction of the enhanced Apple II at the First West Coast Computer Fair. Markkula, through an impressive display booth, makes Apple appear to be a more substantial company than it really is. He orders Jobs to spruce up and sends him out to buy his first suit. The Fair results in a number of orders for Apple and the company moves from the garage into a suite in Cupertino. Jobs and Scott continue feuding as the company starts to grow. Jobs displays an arrogant attitude toward suppliers and employees and divisiveness and confusion is apparent within the company. Apple gains a reputation as a company that can't fulfill its commitments

and almost goes belly up. Markkula and Scott underwrite a $250,000 loan to keep the company afloat.

8. Markkula goes about the business of preparing a business plan as internal strife continues. He knows that the company must have well-known and respected investors to give it cash and credentials. He is already looking forward to the day when Apple will become a public company. Markkula finds the investors he wants and Apple starts to receive attention on Wall Street and in the nation's business press.

9. As Apple becomes more successful, the internal strife intensifies. Scott suffers from an eye infection that doctors fear may cause permanent blindness. He becomes dictatorial and, added to the problems that Jobs causes; there is terror in the ranks of Apple employees. The turmoil causes computers to be shipped too quickly to distributors, often without manuals on how to operate them. There is little software being developed for the Apple computers. Apple's executive board fires Scott, and Markkula reluctantly steps in as president while Jobs becomes Chairman of the Board.

10. Apple goes public in one of the most spectacularly successful stock offerings in history. Jobs' shares are worth $256.4 million. Apple is now worth $1.788 billion, which is more than Ford Motor Company and four times the value of Lockheed. Jobs, in the meantime, is hit with a paternity suit from his boyhood sweetheart and live-in companion. She is willing to settle for $20,000 but Jobs disclaims his responsibility, even though Markkula urges him to pay $80,000 to settle the case. Jobs takes a blood test to determine paternity and results show it is almost certain that he is the father. He is forced to pay $385 a month in child support payments and to settle public assistance debts for the child.

11. Apple has trouble meeting its commitments because of divisiveness within its ranks. Jobs, who is head of the Macintosh division, creates an elite corps that increases

the internal strife. He does not abide by company policies even though he expects others to follow them to the letter. The Macintosh is not completed, as promised, because Jobs rejects design after design. Engineers and technicians in the division pay little attention to timetables because they are convinced Jobs will reject anything they propose.

12. Markkula is anxious to return to his interrupted retirement. The Apple Board privately woos John C. Sculley, a strong marketer and manager who is president of Pepsi Cola. Sculley's major concern is whether or not he can get along with Jobs, whose reputation for arrogance has spread far beyond the confines of Silicon Valley. The two men meet several times and discuss art, poetry, and philosophy. Sculley, assured privately of the Board's support, and offered $2 million a year in salary and bonuses, plus help in buying a $2 million house, joins Apple as president. The Apple public relations machine pumps out the official line that Sculley and Jobs get along like soulmates.

13. Sculley's arrival starts a bloodbath. He had pledged to operate Apple in non-traditional ways, but he goes about his job in a distinctly traditional matter. He consolidates divisions and fires 1,000 employees. A year after his arrival only eight of the fourteen senior executives who were with Apple remain. Sculley's arrival also heralds a banner year for Apple with stock almost tripling in value and Macintosh finally ready to market. More than 70,000 units are sold in the first 100 days.

14. The Board had finally wearied of the turmoil that Jobs causes and his mismanagement of the Macintosh division. Sculley is ordered to shape up the division. He replies that it is hard to do so when the division head is Chairman of the Board. Jobs hears about this and launches a campaign to have Sculley fired, but the Board turned a deaf ear. Jobs is stripped of all operating authority, even though the company says he will remain as "the soul" of Apple and retain his position as

Chairman. Jobs finds himself in exile within the company. He has been thoroughly castrated.

15. Jobs resigns as Chairman to start a new company he calls "NeXT". He shows Sculley a list of people he wants to take with him from Apple and says that Sculley raised no objections. Sculley recalls the incident differently and says that Jobs would denude Apple by taking key employees. Apple files a suit against its cofounder and former Chairman but eventually settles. Jobs, in a final gesture of defiance, sells all of his Apple stock except one share.

16. Epilogue. Jobs played an important part at Apple in its early days by seeing opportunities for the circuit board Wozniak created. Even though he went about it in an abrasive way, he was the one who found parts for Wozniak at prices they could afford, and who brought Markkula on board. There probably would have been no Apple Computer Company without him. At thirty he was worth nearly $500 million and may have reached the pinnacle of his career. It will be hard for him to top his achievement at Apple, even though he is confident that he can, through a blending of computers with education. A business writer in Silicon Valley noted, "Without Jobs, Apple is just another company. Without Apple, Steve Jobs is just another Silicon Valley millionaire."

THE MARKET

Steve Jobs is one of the most fascinating entrepreneurs in the history of American business. He is brusque, abrasive, ingenious, mesmerizing, an enigma of driving ambition coupled with a life-long devotion to the gentle philosophies of the East. Jobs has been the "whiz kid" of America's personal computer industry and has been publicized on the covers of major national magazines, television spots, newspapers, and is the subject of endless fascination. His fight with John Sculley at Apple, which resulted in his being kicked out of the company he helped them form, has brought Jobs even more prominently into the limelight. His story is one of controversy: a hippie who became a "zillionaire" when he was twenty-one; a ruthless businessman who has the heart of a poet-philosopher. This is a type of story that has aroused interest around the world in the past. Jobs already has the status of a hero and is a star in the world of big business; the national publicity concerning his battle with Sculley, and his shocking defeat, make him an ideal subject for a biographical book.

THE AUTHOR

Lee Butcher is a veteran writer and journalist who was editor of the *San Jose Business Journal* in Silicon Valley when the rift developed between Jobs and John Sculley. He was the first to report the conflict to the public. Butcher is intimately familiar with Silicon Valley, Apple, and has contacts in Silicon Valley who have promised to talk with him, either for or not for attribution. Butcher is the author of four nonfiction books and the author or coauthor of four novels. He has written for *Forbes*, *BusinessWeek*, *Barron's* and other national business and general interest magazines, and has been the editor of *Texas Business* and *Florida Trend*, the nation's two leading regional business magazines.

A True-Crime
Book Proposal

True crime is another genre of publishing that has become very popular over the years. Every major crime is first covered in the newspapers, and there often is interest from readers who would like more detailed information, so the crime makes a good and marketable subject for a book. Frequently, books of this type are optioned for a Movie of the Week or miniseries.

Some time ago, I was approached by a writer named Steven Salerno, whose first true crime, *Deadly Blessing*, was successfully published in hardcover by William Morrow and in paperback by St. Martin's Press. He had an idea for a new book, tentatively titled *Fatal Freeway*, about the murder of a college student named Cara Knott by Craig Alan Peyer, a thirty-six-year-old California Highway Patrol Officer, outside San Diego. Salerno developed the seventeen-page proposal that follows. I sent his proposal to twenty publishers interested in true crime. Of these, more than a half dozen wanted to buy it. We auctioned the book to Clarkson N. Potter and it was scheduled for hardcover publication. Furthermore, the television and motion picture rights were optioned to a major Los Angeles-based television production company. Unfortunately, the book was never published nor was the movie made, but the proposal is an excellent example of how to write a true-crime proposal.

Marketing this particular book on true crime was problematic for several reasons:

At the time Salerno and I began soliciting the sale of the book, the case for Cara Knott's murderer had not yet gone to trial. When the case eventually did go to trial, with Peyer as the defendant, no verdict was delivered due to a hung jury. (Peyer was retried later that year and was convicted of first-degree murder; he is now serving his sentence.)

Because Peyer never testified at his own trials, Salerno was faced with the difficult task of writing the book without testimony from the convicted murderer. The structure of any story is the first element to be considered by editors, potential producers, and network executives when they examine new projects. Therefore, a good rule of thumb for gauging the potential success of a true-crime nonfiction book, motion picture, or television project is whether or not the crime has a clear beginning, middle, and end—the standards of drama that make any story accessible.

An excellent illustration of this rule comes from Ernest Hemingway. More than thirty years ago, at the beginning of my career, I had lunch with a well-established newspaper syndicator who told me the following story: Ernest Hemingway was lunching at the Algonquin, sitting at the famous "round table" with several writers, claiming he could write a six-word-long short story. The other writers balked. Hemingway told them to ante up ten dollars each. If he was wrong, he would match it; if he was right, he would keep the pot. He quickly wrote six words on a napkin and passed it around. The words were: "For Sale, Baby Shoes, Never Worn." Papa won the bet: His short story was complete. It had a beginning, a middle, and an end!

However, like all rules, there is an occasional exception. For example, when Claus von Bulow was arrested for the attempted murder of his wife Sunny, the jury could not reach a verdict. Nevertheless, the story was released as a feature film starring Jeremy Irons as Claus and Glenn Close as Sunny (*Reversal of Fortune*, 1990). This scenario did not work for *Fatal Freeway* because a book or movie deal might have been jeopardized if Peyer had not been convicted. For the Knott family, Peyer's late conviction provided the closure they needed.

FATAL FREEWAY

A True-Crime Proposal

By Steve Salerno

Twenty-year-old Cara Knott was the kind of daughter mothers dream about. She was lovely to look at, physically at least, the classic California blonde. But Cara was also bright and articulate, unerringly polite, socially aware, a devoted church-goer who performed volunteer work for several causes around the quiet San Diego suburb in which she lived. In the libertine atmosphere of San Diego State University (ranked by *Playboy* magazine as one of the nation's top ten party schools), Cara had nonetheless established herself as a girl who subscribed to life's traditional values. She had one boyfriend whom she planned to marry in a few years, once both of them were more established. She did not believe in "playing the field." And yet, Cara was not preachy. She was, as a close college friend put it, "someone who always finds the common denominator. With Cara, everybody feels at ease."

Cara's feeling for humanity did not cloud her awareness of the dangers of modern living. Though celebrated for her numerous acts of good Samaritanship, the recent graduate of a police course on self-defense for women knew how to avoid potentially dangerous situations. Her credo being "Better safe than sorry," she was appalled at some of the unnecessary risks her more devil-may-care friends would take during their late-night escapades.

Later, those friends would talk about the irony of tragedy having chosen Cara Knott for a victim.

On December 27, 1986, Cara drove to the North County home of her boyfriend, Wayne Bautista, for an uncharacteristic Friday night visit. Wayne hadn't been feeling well, and they had been unable to spend much time together over Christmas. Although their schedules were such that they ordinarily saw each other only on Saturdays or Sundays, Cara thought a special pre-weekend stopover might be therapeutic.

After spending an hour or so with Wayne, she left his house at about 8:45. As was her custom, she had phoned her parents just before leaving to tell them she was on her way. Cara then pulled into a gas station near a major shopping mall and filled the tank of her white 1968 Volkswagen Beetle. She pumped the gas herself, exchanging a few Yuletide pleasantries with the clerk. He would remember her vivacious manner and her pretty smile.

Several hours later, Cara had still not arrived home, and the uneasiness Joyce and Samuel Knott had unaccountably felt all evening blossomed into full-scale alarm. Their daughter was not the kind of girl to make capricious side-trips. If she called and said she was en route, it meant she was en route. But Cara was long overdue; the trip should have taken twenty-five minutes, a half hour at the outside. No more than that.

At 11 P.M., the Knotts attempted to file a missing person claim but were rebuffed by the San Diego Sheriff's Office. Their daughter had simply not been gone long enough, they were told. An hour later, frustrated with sitting and waiting, the Knotts decided to recruit a search party from among neighbors and nearby relatives. So well-liked was Cara that they had no trouble doing so, despite the lateness of the hour. By 12:30, the ad hoc posse had deployed itself at intervals along the main north-south freeway in an effort to find the girl.

Not until the following morning did their search bear fruit. At 8:30 A.M. Cara's brother-in-law, Bill Weick, spotted her abandoned Volkswagen on an obsolete freeway access road, just off the freeway about midway between Wayne's house and the Knott home. The car looked none the worse for wear. The driver's window was down, and Cara's keys remained in the ignition; Weick turned them and the engine promptly started. Recognizing foul play as a distinct likelihood, the terrified Knotts once again phoned the police.

This time, the response was swift. And the subsequent news, for Joyce and Samuel Knott, was crushing.

A quarter-mile south of the empty Volkswagen, the police found Cara Knott's battered body. She had been strangled and then tossed seventy-five feet from an old bridge to the murky ravine below. There were signs of sexual assault.

Besides sparking a panic among the residents of the quiet neighborhood in which the body was found, Cara Knott's killing mystified investigators. They could not reconcile the apparent circumstances of her murder with the few facts that they had to go on. She had been seen leaving the Chevron station, alone in her car, at about 9 P.M. From there she would have had to drive just a few hundred feet before entering the freeway, followed by a straight run of twenty miles to her home. How had her assailant intercepted her and gained access to her car? Her father assured everyone she wasn't the type of person to knowingly place herself at peril. Pick up a hitchhiker? Cara? To Sam Knott, it was unthinkable.

An investigator summed up the mood at police headquarters: "Right now, we're at a total loss to explain exactly what might have happened out there on the freeway."

Meantime, in quiet and futile acknowledgment of its role in the Knott case, the exit ramp that had taken the girl to her death was hurriedly sealed off. The stretch of road beneath—called, ironically enough, Mercy Road—led nowhere anyway; the highway to which it had once given access had itself long since been closed, and therefore, in the words of a sheepish transportation department spokesman, it presented "too much potential danger for the unwary motorist." The action was seen as a clear admission of official negligence and was expected by some to inspire an immediate lawsuit by Cara's parents. For the time being, however, Sam Knott could only be philosophical.

"It always seems to take a tragedy like this to make people see the things they've overlooked," he said. "We think we've taken all the precautions, and yet we don't realize just how many hidden pitfalls our children face out there." Eventually, Cara's family filed a wrongful death suit for $20 million.

Officer Craig Alan Peyer was a cop's cop. As 1976 drew to a close, Peyer was completing his thirteenth year with the California Highway Patrol, one of the nation's truly venerated law enforcement agencies (owing at least in part to its depiction in such blockbuster TV series as *Highway Patrol* and *CHiPs*). His career with CHP, following a meritorious stint with the Air Force, had been a model of professional dedication and achievement. On several occasions he had been decorated for service above and beyond the call.

At the same time, Peyer was anything but a gung-ho, Clint Eastwood type. He had built a reputation for being low key and helpful, constructively critical rather than harsh in his treatment of errant motorists. Craig Peyer was just not the type to harass drivers "for the hell of it." He even lacked the hard-bitten look of the career cop. Peyer's soft, boyish face was a perfect complement to his bedside manner. In fact, since his earliest days with the force, his colleagues had joked that Peyer should charge the department a fee for his public relations services on its behalf.

So it was not surprising that, a year or so before the Cara Knott case, in the midst of a series of stop-and-go robberies of stranded motorists, Peyer had been called upon by the media to give fearful viewers a primer on how to protect themselves in such situations. Public response was so enthusiastic that KGTV, the local ABC affiliate, has showcased his advice a number of times since. Peyer seemed to welcome the opportunities to share his professional wisdom and concern.

On the evening following Cara Knott's murder, KGTV turned once again to Peyer, who had himself been on duty the night of Cara Knott's disappearance. They wanted him to reassure female drivers, to offer some countermeasures against freeway desperados. As always, Peyer obliged.

Watching Peyer's performance from their respective homes, some of his fellow officers began to lean a bit closer to the TV screen; they were disturbed by what they thought they saw. On his right cheek was a series of small marks. Not shaving cuts, but the kinds of parallel scratches that might have been caused by a hand being raked across his face: a hand with fairly long nails, the length a young woman would wear them. None of Peyer's CHP buddies recalled seeing such marks on his face when he left to go out on his December 27 shift. Nor had Peyer reported a confrontation or anything else out of the ordinary—though come to think of it, he had seemed rather ill-at-ease during his routine call-ins later that night. And now, on the screen, he struck them as being uncharacteristically agitated. This was not the same laid-back guy they had come to know.

The officers began phoning each other. One of them, who had shared a ride with Peyer a few days earlier, recounted an eerie coincidence. As the two of them were driving past the Mercy Road exit, Peyer had gestured toward the bridge in the background and said, "If you ever wanted to dump a body, that would be the ideal place to do it." At the time, Peyer's companion had attached no special significance to the remark. Now he was troubled.

To Craig Peyer's coworkers, the irony was excruciating. "Stay in the vehicle, and lock all doors," they had just heard Peyer tell his viewing audience. "Even if you have to wait all night, it's better to be in the safety of your vehicle than to try to walk and get assistance. Anything can happen. Being a female, you can be raped, robbed, all the way to where you could be killed. Once you get in that other person's car, you're at their mercy. . ."

Was it really possible that their spokesperson and friend, Craig Alan Peyer, had something to do with Cara Knott's death?

Investigators began a piece-by-piece reconstruction of Peyer's activities on the night of the murder. They interviewed a young San Diego resident named Jean-Pierre Gulli. Gulli told them he had been driving on Interstate 15 on the evening of December 27 when he was pulled over by a CHP officer and cited for having an inoperative taillight. Gulli would remember the time as 9:45, "possibly later but definitely no earlier." His recollection was strong because he had planned to be someplace by ten, had gotten a late start to begin with, and was annoyed that the ticket would put him still further behind schedule. Gulli would also recall that the officer acted "wired," and spent an inordinate amount of time in his patrol car before returning with the ticket.

Casually examining the citation as any motorist might, Gulli noticed that an alteration had been made. In the box that said, "time of issuance," the officer had at first written the correct time, 10:20 P.M. Then, for some reason, he had thought better of it, crossed out the original numerals and written over it, 9:20. Looking down, Gulli had read the signature at the bottom of the ticket as that of one "Chris Peyer, CHP."

Over the next few days, the forensics people worked nonstop. They refined their original account of the murder, determining that Cara had probably been strangled with a heavy rope—carried as standard equipment in the trunks of CHP vehicles—and tossed from the bridge while still alive. (Thus, for Cara's family, there was the thought of the incomprehensible horror those last moments must have held for the daughter they so cherished.) Her time of death was fixed at between 9:00 and 9:30 P.M. Fibers found at the scene were compared with those taken from a rough spot on the pocket of a uniform shirt that was surreptitiously removed from Peyer's locker; there was a disturbing similarity. Tire tread analysis seemed to reveal that a CHP car had been adjacent to Knott's on the lonely exit ramp. Blood that matched Peyer's type was found on Cara's shoes and fingernails.

On January 9, Peyer himself was called in for questioning, which he at first considered routine. But the length of the session—some eight hours—and the tone of the investigator's queries left little doubt about what was really happening.

Returning home, he sat his wife down and voiced a shattering prediction. "They're going to arrest me, Karen," he told her. "Maybe not tomorrow or next week, but they're going to arrest me sooner or later for the murder of Cara Knott." Both of them began to cry.

On January 15, Peyer's prophecy was fulfilled. A police caravan roared through the somnolent tree-lined neighborhood in which Peyer and his family lived (no more than five minutes from the site where Cara's body was found). Two of the cars careened into Peyer's driveway, and a virtual strike force of city police and CHP officers handcuffed Peyer in front of his heart-sick wife and frightened children. The Gulli ticket had been the clincher. Interpreted as an attempt to fabricate an alibi, one that would have placed Peyer several miles away at the time Cara Knott died, the ticket had led investigators to the nightmarish conclusion that the killer was, indeed, one of their own.

In the aftermath of Peyer's arrest, stunned friends and neighbors rallied to the officer's defense. Their support went far beyond the usual platitudes about how quiet and friendly the accused was. Convinced, as one neighbor put it, that "time will vindicate Craig Peyer," many of them mortgaged their homes in a successful grassroots campaign to raise Peyer's unprecedented seven-figure bail.

Eventually, Karen Peyer, who with her three children had retreated behind drawn curtains after the arrest, came forward to make a statement about her husband. Briefly she recalled for reporters the circumstances of their courtship and marriage. Less than two years before, Craig had been the boy-next-door when Karen's first marriage collapsed. (Peyer's second marriage had gone sour just a year before that.) She praised her embattled husband for his compassion, said that "without his no-strings support and sincerity" she would have been unable to get through the most trying period of her life. "Craig Peyer is the most loving, affection-ate, and concerned human being I've ever known," she declared tearfully. "Then one day, someone comes along and says he killed a girl. I say someone is playing a terribly cruel joke on us. . . ."

Still, there must have been some doubts. Karen and Craig had been married only a short time, less than eighteen months. In the six years before that, Craig Peyer had gone through two previous marriages.

Despite her steadfast public allegiance to her husband, Karen Peyer must have asked herself, is there a side to this man I know nothing about?

The arrest of a California Highway Patrolman in the Knott case did little to quell the anxiety that had plagued San Diego since the night of the killing. In fact, the city was gripped by a new, and in many ways, more chilling kind of fear. The "man in blue" had become an object of suspicion; CHP's 4,700 traffic officers suddenly found themselves operating under a cloud of dishonor. As one young woman told a reporter for the *San Diego Union*, "It's like being afraid to go to confession because you think the priest might try to rape you!" Women brazenly announced their intentions to ignore police instructions to "pull over." Still others hinted at the possibility of arming themselves in the hopes of getting the drop on any late night CHP assassins. Ad hoc counseling centers had to be set up to help stymied officers deal with the prospect of public intransigence, hostility—or worse.

CHP Chief Ben Killingsworth tried to defuse the tensions: "We don't believe there is any reason for anyone to have any fear during any subsequent contact with any law enforcement agency because of this."

Killingsworth stressed the unique and isolated nature of the occurrence. He reminded everyone that, given the thousands of officers on patrol and the millions of cases of public contact, the CHP record was nothing if not admirable.

The public was unappeased. For one thing, as recently as 1982, there had been a similar unpleasantness. The CHP officer cruising the deserted stretch of road between California and Las Vegas had raped and then killed a vacationing Utah woman. And in 1984, there had been a shooting allegedly precipitated by racial epithets from the mouth of a drunken CHP officer. Was there a laxity in CHP screening procedures? Was there a weakness in the system that prevented the authorities from predicting when Peyer seemingly had it the pre-Christmas weeks of 1986? Newspaper editorialists pondered the question.

Present, too, was a certain fatalism, a cynical outlook on the system and one's chances in the world. San Diego Chief of police Bill Koender understood. "We know what they're thinking," he sighed during a televised press conference. "Right now they're saying, 'Is there anyone left I can trust?'"

As the investigation proceeded, a subplot as bizarre as the murder itself began to emerge.

Over the past six or eight weeks, Craig Peyer had shown an affinity for pulling over young blond women driving Volkswagen Beetles. The pattern seldom varied: citing some trumped up charge, he would make the stop, force his quarry to leave the freeway at a deserted exit ramp, and proceed to engage the women in odd conversations that bore little ostensible relevance to the matter at hand. In one case, he had effectively imprisoned a young lady in his squad car for nearly two hours; only when another motorist pulled over to ask directions did Peyer's captive take the opportunity to return to her car and drive off.

Then, Christmas Eve, just three days before Cara's death, Peyer had behaved strangely in the process of making a stop on a girl who bore a remarkable resemblance to Cara Knott. He had pulled up behind her, flashing his lights, but when she started to pull off onto the freeway shoulder he ordered her to continue down the off ramp to the same deserted stretch of road where Cara Knott's car would be found four days later. Without issuing a ticket, Peyer let the woman go after about fifteen minutes, during which time "he acted really, really friendly, almost flaky," according to the woman. "He just didn't conduct himself like a cop. I started getting chills."

Incredibly, prior to Cara Knott's murder, only one woman thought Peyer's behavior sufficiently disquieting to warrant filing a formal complaint (which suggests that many of the women were perhaps less disturbed by his attentions then they would now like CHP to believe). In that instance, a man named Sigurd Ziglar wrote a letter to CHP on behalf of his wife, Donna. He explained that on December 13, Peyer had pulled over the Ziglar's late-model Volkswagen "evidently in the belief that Donna was alone in the car." Ziglar drew this inference because when Peyer came to the window and Ziglar, who had been sleeping in the passenger seat, suddenly roused, Peyer seemed taken aback. "The officer offered no legitimate explanation for the stop, and essentially told us to go on about our business," wrote Ziglar.

"He seemed flustered. It left us wondering what might have happened if my wife had actually been alone in the car." Ziglar's complaint received no formal reply from CHP.

But the most damning piece of circumstantial evidence emerged from police archives in mid-February. Six years before, on December 28, another blond college coed, Amy Leibing, had disappeared during one of Peyer's evening shifts. No connection was made to the CHP officer at the time, but one fact stood out now that seemed to link the unsolved Leibling disappearance to the present matter.

Like Cara Knott, Amy Leibling had been driving an older model Volkswagen bug.

The question was tantalizing: Was Craig Alan Peyer the "Christmas-week killer-cop?"

Through his attorney, the colorful, locally celebrated Robert Grimes, Craig Peyer had been adamant about his innocence. (Grimes, master of sarcasm and understatements, promises to add a certain comic relief to the tale.) Barring a change of venue—requested but unlikely to be granted—courtroom arguments should begin by early September. Lately, and much to the bemusement of his erstwhile colleagues at CHP, Peyer seemed to be on a "born-again" kick. His occasional statements evince a decided "700 Club" flavor that could only enrich the texture and irony of this case. The deposed officer had been hired by a friend to do backyard swimming pool installations until the beginning of the trial (prompting another public outcry).

The outcome of the trial seems certain, given the mammoth indictment prepared by CHP—the great bulk of which, by the way, has yet to be publicly released. A source who has seen the full text of the warrant says he sees "no way" that Peyer can win acquittal. But journalistically speaking, this is a win-win situation. If Craig Peyer is found guilty, then the book has its expected denouement. If, on the other hand, Peyer is exonerated, three intriguing questions remain to be answered: 1. What was the significance of Peyer's unorthodox behavior out on the freeways? 2. Has there been a grievous miscarriage of justice? And/or 3. Who really killed Cara Knott?

Competing books

None – although the nature of the material would suggest that the project be tackled immediately.

Projected Length

350-400 manuscript pages

Availability

Principals on both sides are cooperating with the media. Attorney Grimes is especially valuable and the Knott family seems ever willing to make public statements. Some of the outraged relatives, and in particular the boyfriend, Wayne Bautista, are especially "good copy."

Also, professional sources have been contacted to help provide some perspective on the larger questions raised by the facts of the case: i.e., How adequate are the screening procedures for law enforcement hiring? What makes someone "snap"? How well do most of us know the people we live with, and what are some of the subtle yet telltale signs of maladjustment.

Projected Market

This is a true-crime book that explores a gripping, universal fear, to wit: What happens when the system breaks down, when the rules that make civilized life possible no longer apply? Is there a more heartbreaking and unexpected way to lose a child than to a symbol of the very institution that is charged with shielding us from such tragedy?

In Southern California, the case has been front page news since the day of the killing. Even now, the most trivial new details are accorded lead-story status on nightly newscasts, and public interest, as judged by letters to the editor and the like, remains voracious.

Besides the sensational crime itself, there is the added depth of how many relationships to be examined (between Cara and the Knotts, between Cara and her fiancé to be, and, perhaps most interestingly, between Craig and Karen Peyer) that will make readers care about the characters and evaluate this story beyond the realm of "just another murder mystery."

Overall, in terms of emotional impact, the proposed book is a cross between *The Onion Field* and *Terms of Endearment*—a moving human drama with a dark, irresistible underside.

About the Author

A San Diego resident, Steve Salerno has written essays and investigative pieces for a wide spectrum of leading publications, including *Harper's*, *New York*, the *New York Times*, *California*, *The New Republic* and many others. His first book, *TNS: The Newest Profession* (Morrow 1985), chronicled the rise of "the new salesmanship" in America.

Due out from Morrow in November is Salerno's first true-crime effort, *Deadly Blessing*. The book is an inquiry into the bizarre circumstances surrounding the death of Price Daniel, Jr., reluctant scion of one of Texas' leading political families.

Several production companies have expressed interest in adapting the book for television.

A Self-Help/Relationship Book Proposal

The next example of a nonfiction book proposal, *Mack Tactics Volume One: The Science of Seduction Meets the Art of Hostage Negotiation* by Rob Wiser and Christopher Curtis, was sought after by many publishers. This is an excellent example of a self-help, personal empowerment, pre-relationship book based on the strategies of a Las Vegas Police Department hostage negotiator. The proposal we submitted attracted the interest of several major New York publishers and was sold to Chamberlain Brothers, a division of Pearson, within two weeks of our putting it in the market. My assistant, Julie Hahn, who originally read it, helped to fine-tune the proposal and the manuscript so that it garnered the authors a terrific deal with an imprint of one of the largest publishers in the world.

M.A.C.K. Tactics:

The Science of Seduction Meets

the Art of Hostage Negotiation

Book proposal by

Rob Wiser and Christopher Curtis

OVERVIEW

Anyone braving the singles scene will tell you, it's a jungle out there. Women complain that all the good men are taken, and that the ones they meet are insensitive and oblivious to their needs. Men complain that women are impossibly complicated, and often assume that the "women of their dreams" are only interested in certain qualities—i.e., Brad Pitt abs and a seven-figure bank account—that they can't possibly offer. It's a vicious cycle that breeds cynicism, compromise, and way too many misleading photos on Internet dating sites.

But now, at long last, the solution has arrived. **M.A.C.K. Tactics: The Science of Seduction Meets the Art of Hostage Negotiation** is the ultimate guide for today's man in his quest to succeed with women. Designed to inspire, empower, and educate, it's a complete course of self-improvement—beginning inward by helping men bolster their self-confidence and recognize their strengths, then working outward to teach the most effective ways to create and build relationships with women.

In order to form a successful relationship with anyone, you must be able to communicate effectively and know how to satisfy their demands as well as yours. This is where *M.A.C.K. Tactics* contains a powerful hook that no other book in its field can match. Christopher Curtis, the co-author of *M.A.C.K. Tactics*, is a former Hostage Negotiator who defused countless "armed and barricaded" situations. *M.A.C.K. Tactics* puts a hip spin on negotiator psychology and strategy and applies it to the dating game, resulting in revolutionary ways to approach women—and life—with greater skill and confidence.

SUMMARY

In urban vernacular, a "Mack" is a man whom women find irresistible. In *M.A.C.K. Tactics*, the word is an acronym that stands for Method, Action, Confidence, and Knowledge. These four

"Pillars of Power" are the keys to achieving your romantic goals. The book also explains how this mindset is the key to reaping rewards in your professional life and in all other personal relationships.

Chapter by chapter, *M.A.C.K. Tactics* breaks down every aspect of dealing with women, while leading the reader on a journey of personal transformation. Every lesson is interconnected. While chapters cover specific topics such as improving your fashion sense and the keys to planning a first date, this type of advice can't yield maximum results unless the man understands the logic behind these actions and has the confidence to back it up. (As the book puts it, "Any house can be superficially improved by a new paint job, but what is it worth if it lacks a solid foundation?") *M.A.C.K. Tactics* transcends other books of its genre by coaching and building each reader as an *individual* rather than offering general tips and advice.

What qualities do women *really* desire in a man? What are the best places to meet the kind of women you want to date? How should you approach her without seeming obtrusive, and what are the "red flags" you need to be aware of? What are the secrets to engaging her attention and sparking a fun, interesting conversation? What's the foolproof way to get a girl's phone number? What's the surefire method for securing a first date, and how do you make it a memorable evening within the constraints of your budget? What are you *truly* looking for in a mate, and how do you distinguish yourself from every other guy on the scene? From opening approaches to Advanced Mack Maneuvers, all of these questions—and many more—are answered in a clear, practical manner, illustrating the difference between "Wack Tactics" and "Mack Tactics."

Written in a hip, humorous style, and packed with information and inspiration, *M.A.C.K. Tactics* covers it all, "from the fashion to the passion." The strategies of hostage negotiation are interwoven throughout the book, incorporating negotiator/military jargon that will become buzzwords among its readership.

Just as the Negotiator builds a bridge of trust with the hostage taker, using "Minimal Encouragers" and "I.O.U.'s" to become their "fellow traveler" and work toward a solution, the Mack understands how to form quick, effective connections with women and guide each encounter toward a victorious outcome.

THE MARKET

One of the goals of M.A.C.K. Tactics is to establish a brand that pervades pop culture, one that is equally accessible to the white collar, blue collar, and urban markets. Unlike most "experts" in the fields of relationships and dating, the authors of M.A.C.K. Tactics, Rob Wiser and Christopher Curtis, are young, hip, single guys who are ready to promote this book to the world.

Their partnership symbolizes the project's crossover appeal. Between Wiser, the NYU-educated hipster writer, and Curtis, the streetwise cop and negotiator (whose charm and flamboyant style earned him the nickname "Hollywood" within his department), you've got a team that crosses color lines and makes them suitable to promote the book in virtually any media outlet.

Wherever there are men, there are potential buyers. This book is designed to appeal to *any* man who wants to improve his relations with women, whether it's a teenager taking his first, hesitant steps toward dating, or a middle-aged man re-entering the singles scene after a divorce. It's as relevant for big-city hipsters on the nightclub scene as it is for someone trying to build a friendship with a coworker into romance. This is information that any man—regardless of age or background—can immediately begin putting into practice. By encouraging readers to be more outgoing, dynamic, and original, and to *listen* rather than trying to dominate conversations, a man schooled in M.A.C.K. Tactics is one whom women will appreciate and enjoy being with.

For men who are nervous around attractive women, the Tactics will break down those self-imposed barriers. For those who have had success with women, the Tactics will take their game to a level they never dreamed possible. And instead of alienating women, the book will be of great interest to them as well since it contains many valuable insights into dating and the way men and women relate to each other. Female readers who are versed in M.A.C.K. Tactics will know whether they're dealing with a confident, mature man, or one who needs to work on his game. And what greater favor could a woman do for a male friend than teaching him some Tactics?

The relationships/dating genre has spawned numerous titles and sold countless books; we live in a culture where everyone wants the quick, easy fix. But the advice these other books contain is generally superficial—the literary equivalent of learning just enough karate to get your butt kicked. M.A.C.K. Tactics does away with the tired notion of "pickup lines" and explains *why* its methods work, *why* women are attracted to certain qualities in men, and *why* the approaches you may have used in the past have been holding you back.

It isn't enough for the Hostage Negotiator to simply memorize the manual; he needs to understand how certain phrases and actions work on a subconscious level, and when to apply them. The same maxim holds true for men when dealing with women. M.A.C.K. Tactics removes these mysteries and presents a road map to success.

AUTHOR BIOS

Rob Wiser

Born in New York City, Rob Wiser is a graduate of New York University, where he majored in film. While a student, he began his professional screenwriting career. He was then hired by producer George Jackson (*New Jack City*, *Sugar Hill*, the *House Party* franchise) to create "Bulletproof Diva," one of the most popular and technically advanced animated shows on the Internet. The dark tale of a female assassin battling demons in a post-apocalyptic future, "Bulletproof Diva" was profiled on a VH-1 special and was the first Internet series to be seen in multiplexes across the country, when its 35mm trailer ran before *The X Men*.

In his early twenties, he became a produced screenwriter with *Snipes*. The urban thriller featured hip-hop superstar Nelly along with Dean Winters (HBO's *Oz*), Sam Jones III (the TV show *Smallville*), Zoe Saldana (*Pirates of the Caribbean, The Terminal*), and Frank Vincent (*Raging Bull, Goodfellas, The Sopranos*). The film was an official selection of the 2001 Toronto film festival and was released theatrically the following year to favorable reviews.

An expert in the gaming industry, Wiser is currently the Managing Editor of *Casino Player* magazine, the industry's top publication. He is a regular contributor and columnist for *VEGAS* magazine as well as other national publications.

Christopher Curtis

Christopher Curtis was born and raised in Queens, NY. At seventeen he joined the Marines and traveled the world, providing security for various foreign embassies. Upon his return to the United States, he earned a degree in Criminal Justice and joined the Las Vegas police force, where he entered the field of Hostage Negotiations.

After graduating from the Basic and Advanced Negotiator Schools and Interview and Interrogation School, Curtis served in over fifty armed and barricaded situations and became an Instructor. He eventually returned to patrolling the streets, where he is now a Field Training Officer and a member of the elite Crisis Intervention Team. He has also specialized in domestic violence cases, undercover work, and community relations. While making the streets of Las Vegas safer, Curtis works as a part-time model and has been featured on episodes of *Cops*.

PROMOTABILITY

In Las Vegas, efforts to promote *M.A.C.K. Tactics* have already begun and the buzz is building. Now, it's a matter of opening the floodgates.

As a writer, **Rob Wiser** is already established on multiple fronts. He is recognized as a screenwriter, having written the film *Snipes* which starred Nelly, one of the hottest stars in popular music. He is a contributor to national magazines including *FHM*, *VEGAS*, *Cigar Aficionado*, and others, while serving as the managing editor of *Casino Player*, the top publication in the global casino/gaming industry. Between these magazines, his writing is read by over one million readers each month.

Utilizing his extensive contacts in the magazine world, Wiser plans to write a series of high profile articles about M.A.C.K. Tactics once the book approaches publication. (The first of these articles can be seen in the November issue of *FHM*.) Wiser has also notched some experience on the media circuit, having appeared on MSNBC's "Countdown with Keith Olbermann" to discuss issues in the gaming industry. He has also been interviewed for stories in the *New York Times*.

Christopher Curtis is a force of nature waiting to be unleashed on the media circuit. His extraordinary charisma and experience make him a natural for speaking engagements and leading M.A.C.K. Tactics seminars. He was a Marine Corps instructor, taught the Hostage Negotiation course to a number of major police departments, and is a certified law enforcement instructor in the state of Nevada. He is looking forward to promoting the project in print, radio, and television, and there is not a question on relationships that he isn't ready to answer. Because of the book's unique subject matter—hip, sexy, and with its fascinating Hostage Negotiator hook—he'd be as suited for an appearance on *Howard Stern* as he would on *Oprah*, as eligible for a segment on MTV as for a profile in *GQ*.

The M.A.C.K. Tactics Web site has already generated a cult following on the Internet. When the book reaches print it will become a forum for all members of the "Mack Militia," an online community where fans can share their personal experiences and exchange advice and tips.

In their adopted hometown of Las Vegas, Wiser and Curtis are extremely well connected, with friends ranging from casino bosses to VIP hosts to owners of the hottest nightclubs. In Las Vegas, the sexiest city on earth, huge promotional events for M.A.C.K. Tactics are a given.

Franchise Opportunities

This book can spawn a number of M.A.C.K. Tactics-related products that will drive book sales. These products can include:

- An audio CD that condenses the lessons of the book and is ideal for the Mack-on-the-go.
- Promotional book signing events can be staged in a seminar format, with Christopher Curtis lecturing on M.A.C.K. Tactics and dispensing one-on-one advice. This can lead to larger seminars held in cities throughout the country.
- A series of instructional DVDs, each devoted to a different aspect of M.A.C.K. Tactics: Confidence Building, Conversation Control, Negotiations, Fashion, Dating, etc.
- A reality TV show, which could be structured in any number of ways. Essentially, each episode would feature a team of Macks coaching a guy through his personal transformation and helping him to achieve his goals with women.
- A feature film based on M.A.C.K. Tactics. As a screenwriter with a theatrically released movie under his belt, Rob Wiser has ideas on how to take this concept to the big screen.
- An ongoing series of M.A.C.K. Tactics books (Volume II, Volume III, and so on) that cover additional topics and more advanced strategies. One of these books could be written expressly for women.

FORMAT

The book is structured chronologically. One of the basic tenets of M.A.C.K. Tactics is that in order to make a lasting transformation, the process must begin inward and work outward.

After laying out the Ten Mack Commandments, the rules that every M.I.T. ("Mack In Training") must live by, the book begins on an introspective note, asking the reader to consider "the man in the mirror" and explore his own strengths. The message is that most men have attractive qualities that they're either unaware of, or don't know how to showcase properly. Identifying these "positives," and learning how to make them work for you, are crucial steps toward building confidence.

Subsequent chapters lead the reader on a progression toward Mack status: topics covered include fashion, home decoration, where to go to meet women, opening approaches, conversational strategies, dating, and so on. A number of chapters deal with topics that have never been covered in print. In "Hypotheticals," we explain the power of hypothetical questions and show they can be used to spark thought-provoking conversations. "Negotiations" is devoted to explaining the close parallels between hostage negotiations and communicating with women. "Bad Boy 101" explores a question that has baffled and frustrated men from all walks of life: what is it about bad boys that women find irresistible? M.A.C.K. Tactics show how nice guys can incorporate a "bad boy edge" into their game, while staying true to themselves. And in "Wingmen" we explain how to coach your buddies to back you up when you approach two or more women, and how to provide support for them when it's time to return the favor.

To make the book more reader-friendly, quick "Mack Quotes" and "Mack Facts" are interspersed throughout the chapters. (Did you know that on average, a human being will have sex more than 3,000 times and spend two weeks kissing in their lifetime? And that's someone who *hasn't* learned the Tactics!)

TABLE OF CONTENTS

Introduction.

The true and amusing origins of M.A.C.K. Tactics. How Rob Wiser, a writer, and Christopher Curtis, a veteran cop and former Hostage Negotiator, formed an unlikely alliance in Las Vegas—and used the hottest nightlife scene on the planet to develop, test, and confirm the arsenal of information contained in this book.

1. What is M.A.C.K. Tactics?

Why this book is a powerful tool for the modern man, and why the Mack mindset is crucial to success in today's dating scene. The system is based upon the four Pillars of Power, which form the acronym M.A.C.K.

- **Method:** The strategies and techniques every Mack must know.
- **Action:** Knowing how to put the lessons of M.A.C.K. Tactics into practice.
- **Confidence:** The most attractive quality a man can possess, crucial to success in all areas of life. M.A.C.K. Tactics shows you how to develop and utilize it.
- **Knowledge:** Understanding the psychology of women and how to gather the necessary Intell: Her availability, her interests, what her previous relationships were like, whether she's right for you, etc. Equally important is knowledge of self—understanding the package that you present to women, and how to showcase your best qualities.

2. The 10 Mack Commandments

Our 10 Mack Commandments, and explanations of each.

- Flee and they will follow. Follow and they will flee.
- Wherever you're at is the place to be.
- Every interaction with a female is an opportunity.
- Guide the conversation.

- Tip and tip well.
- Be original.
- Eye contact leads to body contact.
- 3/4 of macking is listening.
- The first 60 seconds is everything.
- It's not a mystery. It's a science.

3. The Building of a Mack

"The most profound relationship we'll ever have is the one with ourselves."

—Shirley MacLaine

The personal transformation that goes into becoming a Mack, from building self-confidence to becoming a more dynamic, outgoing individual.

- Taking "self inventory" and identifying your own positive qualities.
- Creating your list of Favorites—a crucial conversational tool.
- Why the most important "quality time" a Mack can spend is not with a woman, but with himself. When on his own, the Mack is constantly exploring new subjects and improving himself.
- Creating your Personal Mantra.
- Batting Practice: The importance of constantly interacting with new women and making a positive impression on every woman you encounter.
- Mack Visualization: Envisioning a positive outcome for every encounter and the steps you must take to reach it.
- Knowing Your Goals: Be clear on the type of women you want to meet, and what you hope to achieve.
- The Mack Pack: The essential items a Mack never leaves home without.

4. Mack Style: From the Fashion to the Passion

Fashion tips that never go out of style, and why your clothes should be the best possible reflection of you.

- Fashion Do's and Don'ts.
- Wardrobe Essentials.
- Understanding dress codes, from "Business Casual" to "Black Tie."

5. Conversation Control

"Wise men talk because they have something to say; fools, because they have to say something."

—Plato

How to engage women in creative, stimulating conversations and guide them toward the desired outcome. (Always remember Mack Commandment #8: "3/4 of macking is listening!")

- Mack Intros vs. cliché "pick-up lines."
- The Three-Point Introduction
- The Name Game: Making her remember yours, and recovery techniques in case you forget hers.
- Guiding Force: How to steer the conversation without dominating it. Learn how to highlight your attractive qualities while prompting her to open up about herself.
- Creative Phrasing: Putting an original spin on the questions you ask, and the responses you give.
- Jobs: The Mack way to tell her what you do for a living.
- Conversational Wack Tactics vs. Mack Tactics
- Humor: Use your sense of humor wisely. Don't overdo it.
- Minimal Encouragers: A negotiator technique used to keep the dialogue flowing.
- Mood Killers: The subjects no Mack should discuss.
- Articulate Avoidance: How to maneuver the conversation away from uncomfortable topics.

- Polite Interruptions: A clever technique for closing the physical gap during conversation.
- Baiting Questions: How to deflect questions she might ask in an attempt to expose character flaws.
- The 20 Minute Convo Rule: The significance of passing the 20-minute mark.
- Comfort Zones: How to put her in a relaxed, comfortable state of mind.
- Gathering Intell: Questions and statements that will prompt her to reveal key details about herself.
- The 70/30 Rule: An Advanced Mack Maneuver used to isolate her from a group of friends.

6. Hypotheticals

How to pose clever Hypothetical Questions during conversation, in order to reveal aspects of her personality and reinforce your own positive qualities. Once you understand the importance of Hypotheticals, you can create your own.

Examples we give include:

- The Dinner Date
- Cops at the Door
- The Million Dollar House
- Age Is Just a Number
- The Five Senses
- The Voyeur

7. Negotiations

"A mind troubled by doubt cannot focus on the course to victory."

—Arthur Golden

Explaining the parallels between Macking and Hostage Negotiations. Once mastered, these strategies can be used not only with women, but to advance your professional career.

- Applying the Negotiator Mindset
- Overcoming Barriers
- There Is No Such Thing as Rejection
- I.O.U.'s: Making even minor efforts seem like special favors.
- Setting Precedents: Establish the parameters of your relationship, and the things you are willing and unwilling to do.
- Life Applications: How negotiator strategies can be used in your workplace and beyond.
- Gifts: The correct way to approach gift-giving.
- Demands: Understanding how many of her requests are, in reality, polite demands. Learn to identify and deal with them.
- Approach Parameters: How to approach women in a way that makes her comfortable and receptive.
- Getting Past No: Leading her down the path to "yes" instead of creating opportunities for her to say "no."
- Pre-Emptive Actions: Laying the necessary groundwork to eliminate her doubts or concerns.
- The Five Step Negotiator Model: The step-by-step process that Hostage Negotiators use, and how it correlates to Macking.

8. The Ex Factor

The type of men she's dated in the past will help you to better understand her, and how you can win her over to your side.

- The general categories of negative ex-boyfriends/husbands: The Stalker, the Cheater, the Loser, and the Commitaphobe.
- What these past relationships suggest about her, and how they should factor into your strategy.
- Protect Your Past: How to respond when she inquires about *your* "exes." Build a bridge toward a romantic future; never dwell on the past.

9. Target Rich Environments

Places for meeting new women, and how to modify your strategy depending on the environment.

- Thinking outside the box, beyond the standard "singles" environments (bars, nightclubs, etc.).
- Tips for striking up conversations in bookstores, clothing stores, supermarkets, etc.
- The Walk-Away: An Advanced Mack Maneuver that involves making the introduction, then politely excusing yourself…and waiting until later to engage her in conversation. It's the sure sign of a confident Mack.

10. Women to Be Wary Of

"It takes a woman twenty years to make a man of her son, and another woman twenty minutes to make a fool of him."

—Helen Rowland

Don't allow yourself to be blinded by her beauty; be aware of "red flags" before you commit your time and money. How to identify and deal with certain categories of women, such as:

- The Money Chick
- The One-Night Stand Chick
- The Rebound Chick
- Drama Queens
- Man-Haters
- Consumers

11. Phone Control

"I was ordering dessert when they were eating dinner. When they were having coffee, I was asking for a check. *I had business.*"

—Ray Liotta, *Goodfellas*

Once you've swapped digits, how to play the "phone game" and keep the ball in your court at all times.

- When you should call her
- If she calls you first
- Phone Fundamentals: Etiquette, setting time limits on the conversation, making plans, using phrasing to get optimal results

12. Bad Boy 101

Why do so many women prefer bad boys to nice guys? If you fall under the latter category, you'll learn how to work bad boy elements into your game.

- Understanding why some women are attracted to bad boys.
- Examples of famous bad boys, and understanding their appeal.
- The top three characteristics that bad boys share with Macks.
- How to add a bad boy edge to your personality, while remaining true to yourself.

13. Wingmen

"When the character of a man is not clear to you, look at his friends."

—Japanese proverb

Sometimes the woman you're interested in meeting will be accompanied by friends. This is why behind every great Mack is a great Wingman. Learn how to incorporate support personnel into your next Mack mission, and how to return the favor when one of your buddies needs backup.

- Wingman Scenarios: When to use one, and how to formulate and execute a two-on-two strategy.
- Why you should never use an untrained Wingman—don't risk a "friendly fire incident."
- What a Wingman should and should not say.

- Using cues to communicate with your Wingman.
- If things go south, knowing when and how to abort the mission.

14. Closing the Deal

"Anyone who's a great kisser I'm always interested in."

—Cher

Now that you've built a connection, here's how to achieve your end goal—whether it's getting her phone number, or taking her home tonight.

- Reading signals, and knowing when and how to capitalize.
- Probing Questions: Gathering Intell about her to determine where this encounter is headed.
- Body Contact: How to establish it, and gradually escalate it.
- Talking Dirty: Why the Mack doesn't need to use overtly sexual language to get her in a sensual frame of mind.
- Neutral Corners: Extracting her from challenging environments (i.e. a crowded party) so that you can spend one-on-one time with her.
- Blame It On the Rain ("The Milli Vanilli Principle"): Creating an atmosphere of spontaneity, the sense that anything can happen tonight.
- The First Kiss: Knowing when to make your move, and how to virtually eliminate your chances of rejection.

15. Mi Casa, Mack Casa

Home improvement tips. Inexpensive, simple ways to turn your house or apartment into a Mack Pad.

- Why the Mack must maintain a home that is conducive to having women over.
- What is an acceptable living situation, with respect to your age.
- The Do's and Don'ts of home decoration.

- Mack Etiquette for hosting female company.
- The importance of lighting and music.
- Wine Fundamentals.
- Setting a Mack Mood.

16. First Dates
Pull off a memorable first date without blowing your bankroll.

- The three "first date places" that average guys think are acceptable—but Macks avoid.
- When picking her up, how to put yourself in the driver's seat in more ways than one.
- Dinner Dates: Choosing the right restaurant, proper manners, tipping, etc.
- Advanced Mack Maneuver: "Taste Tests." How sampling each other's food can create an intimate connection.
- Just Desserts: The importance of dessert, and why it should always cap off the meal.
- Original Date Ideas: Daytime activities, and how they can work to your advantage.
- Cancellations: When you're not in your optimal Mack Mindset, why *you* should reschedule the date.

17. Wolves
Dealing with other men who want what you're after.

- A Friend To All: Creating male allies, instead of viewing other men as threats.
- Recognizing Wolf-Heavy Environments.
- Safe Zones: Identifying areas within the environment where you can separate her from Wolves on the prowl.
- Advanced Mack Maneuver: "Ex Marks the Spot." Why you want female friends to accompany you whenever you go out on the town.

18. The World Is Yours

Welcome to the Mack Militia. Now that you're armed with the Tactics, a world of new possibilities are yours.

- A summary of the road you've traveled, and the different attitude you now take toward women—and life.
- The Michael Jordan principle: Why the Mack constantly seeks to improve his game.
- A brief word on M.A.C.K. Tactics: Volume II, the next stage in your Mack evolution.

<u>M.A.C.K. TACTICS sample chapter</u>

Chapter 1: What are M.A.C.K. Tactics?

Picture a house at the end of a dead-end street. A police helicopter hovers overhead, bathing the scene in a spotlight. An army of cops is massed on the perimeter. A heavily armed SWAT team has their guns trained on the house, waiting for the command to unleash hell.

A man is holed up inside, sweating bullets, clutching a gun. His ex-wife and kids are huddled in the corner. He screams his demands out the window: a taxi to the airport and a fueled-up plane going straight to Cuba. If these demands aren't met, there's going to be bloodshed.

Then a car rolls up to the scene—not the requested taxi, but an unmarked sedan. Out steps a man. Though average in size, he radiates an aura of total control and confidence. He coolly walks around to the back of his car, pops the trunk, and dons a bulletproof vest. From his calm expression, you'd think this is just another day at the office.

For this highly skilled Hostage Negotiator, it is. He has seen and conquered this situation a hundred times before. The circumstances vary, but the rules of the game are always the same. And this is a game he has mastered.

The Negotiator begins to converse with the hostage taker: for the release of the hostages, and eventually for his peaceful surrender. It might take hours, even days, but the Negotiator's focus and discipline never waver. Everything he says, every phrase he uses, is part of a strategy to build a bridge of trust. For everything the hostage taker says, and every demand he makes, the Negotiator has a response that steers the encounter in the direction he wants it to go. He can already envision how this situation is going to end; now, it's simply a matter of guiding it there. Like a world-class chess player, he's always thinking several moves ahead.

The Negotiator is confident, highly trained, and commands respect from his fellow man. He is a force to be reckoned with— on and off the job.

In other words, you might say he's a Mack.

Creating the System

This parallel, between hostage negotiation and the science of succeeding with women, is what spawned M.A.C.K. Tactics. Christopher Curtis, the co-author of this book, comes from a law enforcement background and served as an actual Hostage Negotiator. He was the guy they called in when some maniac had taken his wife and kids hostage and was waving a gun around making demands, or when some sad soul had given up on life and was ready to end it all.

Time after time, Christopher was able to "talk down" these troubled individuals. He succeeded by applying specific principles and psychological techniques he'd learned through his training, and many hours spent in the field dealing with these situations.

He operated from a playbook which he had drilled into his brain. For anything the hostage taker said or did, Christopher was ready with the correct response. He was patient and disciplined. He kept his cool, formed a bond of trust with the hostage taker, and negotiated until the situation was defused.

But the work was physically and emotionally grueling. When his shift would end, he would often hit a nightclub or a bar to unwind and decompress. Living in Las Vegas, there was never any shortage of options.

Something interesting began to happen during these late-night excursions. When he met women at the clubs and bars, instead of engaging them in the usual small talk he would subconsciously slip into "Negotiator" mode—drawing upon his training and using those same principles and techniques in his conversations. He would deal with women in the way that would be most effective in a hostage scenario. Instead of talking about himself, he would listen and earn their trust. Instead of giving them reasons to say "no," he gave them reasons to say "yes."

His success rate boosted his confidence. Soon, he was throwing caution to the wind and approaching gorgeous women that he was once intimidated by. It didn't matter how guarded they normally were toward men; once he started applying his strategy, the walls came down. Meeting new women every day became an adventure to look forward to, instead of being frustrating and stressful as it was for many of his friends.

Christopher also began to discover parallels between hostage takers and the typical single woman. Both were jaded by past negative experiences and tended to be non-trusting. With women, this attitude was often a result of the way they had been treated by men, whether it was their father or an ex-boyfriend. But by establishing a bond with them, and gaining their confidence, Christopher was able to knock down those barriers and connect with them on an intimate level. In the process, he formed a belief that just as no encounter with a woman is arbitrary, every encounter with a woman must be viewed as a negotiation—the difference being instead of coaxing them off rooftops, he was coaxing them into romance.

The M.A.C.K. Tactics system was derived from these core strategies and principles. It's time to shed the doubts, anxiety, and all the other self-imposed handicaps that have held you back from achieving your full potential. Stop living in mediocrity, and start living as a Mack.

Defining the Mack

Before we go further, it's important that we state our definition of a Mack. To some, the word conjures up images of a slick pimp in a fur coat and wide-brimmed hat, using his silver-tongued rap to get women to do his bidding. To others, the word suggests a sleazy pick-up artist, forever on the prowl for his next conquest.

We define the modern Mack as a far more impressive and powerful individual. He is a man who possesses confidence, charisma, and style. He has a keen understanding of women: what makes them tick, and what they truly want from men—not what society and the media have led us to believe they want. (There is actually a vast difference between the two.) The Mack knows how to engage and stimulate women, mentally and sexually, and establish a connection with them through words and body language. The Mack doesn't need to use lies or deception. Confidence, knowledge, and a strong mindset are his greatest assets.

More importantly, the Mack has knowledge of self. He's in tune with his own strengths and vulnerabilities. He knows his strong qualities and how to highlight and capitalize on them. Conversely, he's aware of the areas that can be improved, and works on bettering his game on a daily basis. And while even the most gifted Mack gets rejected on occasion, he never lets it faze him. Blows that would crush an average man's confidence simply ricochet off the Mack's armor. In fact, they make him stronger, since every encounter with a female yields valuable lessons.

While the Mack's abilities make him intriguing to women, he uses these skills to great effect with men as well. The Mack understands that life is a never-ending series of negotiations, whether you're purchasing a car, asking for a raise, or dealing with a difficult coworker or family member. While routine daily challenges result in stress, frustration, and depression for the average man, the Mack's attitude and interpersonal skills enable him to navigate these obstacles and achieve the desired results.

For the Mack, there are no such things as problems. There are only challenges, which he enjoys tackling.

Also be aware that Mack status doesn't necessarily mean you're young, buff, or born with traditionally handsome looks. Donald Trump? Mack. Bill Clinton? Ultra-Mack. Tony Soprano? Without question, a Mack—not a traditionally handsome guy, but you'd be surprised how many women find his hyper-masculine onscreen persona incredibly sexy. Even without the wealth and fame, guys like these would be highly successful with women. We'll show you how to incorporate some of their winning qualities into your game.

Playing To Win

Though the primary purpose of this book is to teach you how to succeed with the opposite sex, mastering M.A.C.K. Tactics can start you on a path to success in all areas of life. Getting ahead in business has a lot to do with relationships—how well you connect with people, and how much they respect you. Which man is more likely to thrive in his career: the one who is desperate, willing to settle for any girl who responds to him, or the one who is able to charm and establish a connection with every woman who crosses his path? Chances are, the man who can achieve success with highly desirable women has the confidence necessary to negotiate his way to a promotion, a raise, or the best possible deal when buying a car or a home.

If you're taking the time to read this book, you've already demonstrated that you're in it to win it. Now it's time for us hold up our end of the bargain. If you commit to this journey and begin applying these lessons in your daily life, the M.A.C.K. Tactics system is going to take your game to a level you never dreamed possible.

Desperate Times, Drastic Measures
"We are a society of men raised by women."
— Brad Pitt, *Fight Club*

The situation has reached a crisis point for the modern man. Let's be brutally honest: The male species is weaker and softer than ever, and it's only getting worse. If you want proof of this trend, just check out an episode of *Queer Eye for the Straight Guy*, which was the hottest thing on television back when we started writing this book. It's got some clever little tips, and the so-called "Fab Five" do know how to deck out an apartment. It's the underlying message that we find troubling: that the average man is so pathetic, so clueless, that without the "feminine touch" he is doomed to a life of loneliness.

We're getting bombarded with this type of propaganda from all directions. In this day and age, we're not allowed to follow our primal instincts and behave like the powerful, masculine figures we were born to be. Consumer culture tells the modern man how he needs to dress, what he needs to own, and how he's supposed to act in order to be desirable to women. We base our self-worth on the job we work and the car we drive. We're taught to follow the script and play by society's rules, in the belief that if we do so, we'll ultimately march down the aisle and settle down with a wife—not necessarily the "woman of our dreams," but someone who placates our loneliness and saves us from the frustration and rejection we face on the singles scene.

Most men follow this script because they're afraid to go after what they truly desire. They play around on the singles scene for a while, suffer too much rejection, or figure it's time to "get serious" with their life, then cash in their chips and allow a woman to lock them down. Sometimes it's to the first female who's willing to give them sex on a regular basis. Of course they'd rather be involved with a beautiful, dynamic woman (maybe more than one at a time), the kind that cause other men to stare in envy.

But these men have created rationalizations and excuses for their inability to land a dream girl. They invent excuses: that beautiful women are all gold-diggers, or that they're interested in "bad boys" instead of nice guys.

Make no mistake: Gold-diggers and other types of negative women are certainly out there. M.A.C.K. Tactics shows you how to identify these categories of females so that you don't waste your time on them. You'll also learn effective ways to identify the ones that *are* worth your efforts, whether your goal is to take home the hottest girl at the nightclub every Saturday night or to form a romantic relationship with a woman you've long admired. Whatever your circumstances may be, with M.A.C.K. Tactics you're no longer going to wait on the sidelines for opportunity to come knocking—because it probably never will. These tools will encourage you to get assertive and motivated.

Becoming successful with women is about much more than wearing the right clothes or using the right "lines." It starts by looking inward and creating a solid foundation. It means developing the correct mental attitude, changing the way you view women and yourself. Then M.A.C.K. Tactics works outward, helping you to revise your personal style and teaching techniques that will help you approach women, engage them in effective conversations, and build connections that distinguish you from every other guy that has ever come her way.

Start within, and build outward. That's the only way to make a powerful, lasting transformation.

Pillars of Power

Every one of the techniques and strategies contained in this book is for real. It's not about corny "pick-up lines" or trying to fool women into believing you're something you're not. And it's not about the "numbers game" that your buddies at the bar might consider a viable strategy, hitting on a dozen women a night in the hopes that one will be receptive.

It is about mastering a system that is founded upon a rock-solid foundation. The foundation of the average American male is shaky at best, and that is why M.A.C.K. Tactics is based on four powerful pillars: Method, Action, Confidence, and Knowledge. Applied correctly, they will support you through even the most turbulent circumstances.

Method. Pat Benatar said it best when she sang "Love Is a Battlefield." Before you deploy in the combat zone, you'd better have the right training and tools for the job. There is no universal strategy for macking women. Though all women share certain fundamental traits, each has different quirks that you need to be able to pick up on. M.A.C.K. Tactics teaches you how to recognize the different categories of females and how to employ the correct strategy. These strategies are often rooted in the same techniques employed by Hostage Negotiators. M.A.C.K. Tactics is the first system of its kind to incorporate this information.

Action. Nothing happens until you choose to take action. (He who hesitates, masturbates.) When it comes to women, more is lost by indecision than by bad decisions. But before you start making moves, it is imperative that you develop and hone the backbone of your personality. Which leads us to…

Confidence. This is the single greatest weapon you can possess in life, whether in the business world or in your personal relationships. The average guy views confidence as a trait that some were blessed with and others will never possess. This is false. Anyone can achieve self-confidence, and it doesn't require spending endless hours in the gym or making millions of dollars. What it does require is knowing yourself, and learning to showcase your good qualities instead of burying them under insecurities and nervous habits.

We were all born with an amazing, even foolhardy willingness to take risks. Remember how carefree you were as a little kid? You didn't think twice about climbing a tree. Our parents had to keep an eye on us, since we wouldn't think twice about jumping in the deep end of the pool before we even knew how to swim. Nothing fazed us. If we fell down and skinned our knee, we might bawl for a minute, but then we jumped right back in the game.

Unfortunately, confidence and self-esteem are worn down with the passage of time. Failure, rejection, and disappointment have a cumulative effect. Some of us hold up pretty well over time, and exceptional individuals might even be strengthened by rejection—hey, it took Thomas Edison over 6,000 tries to invent the light bulb. But the sad truth is that most guys, by the time they reach adulthood, have been scarred by all the rejection they've had to endure. Rather than risk any further blows to their egos, they play it safe. This is why they wind up in relationships and careers that are unfulfilling.

Confidence is the #1 characteristic that women respond to. This doesn't mean swaggering around with your shoulders flexed; that's usually the mark of an insecure man who's trying to cover up his deficiencies. Confidence means being comfortable in your own skin, and maintaining the mindset that you are in control of every encounter. Most women are willing to follow a confident man's lead. But you *must* take the lead.

Knowledge. When it comes to dealing with women, there are rules and principles to follow. And as complicated as they may seem, you *can* learn what makes them tick. With M.A.C.K. Tactics you will develop a thorough knowledge of female psychology. Equally as important, you will develop a strong knowledge of self. You need to understand the package you are presenting every time you introduce yourself: your strengths, your interests, and your attractive qualities.

Gathering Intell is one of the cornerstones of Knowledge. From the moment he notices an attractive woman, the Mack is registering details about her that will factor into his strategy. How is she dressed? Who is she with? What does her body language suggest about her personality—and her availability?

Once the conversation begins, the Mack says things to her that elicit further Intell. He doesn't ask point-blank questions;

instead, he uses subtle phrasing to prompt her to divulge details. Is she single? How long has it been since her last relationship? What are her favorite activities and types of food, in case this leads to a date? Are there any "red flags" you need to be aware of? Is she in the market for a serious relationship, or is she looking to have fun tonight—no strings attached? It's all Intell, and knowing how to acquire it makes you a stronger Mack.

Trust the System

A final note: In order to successfully learn M.A.C.K. Tactics, you need to place your trust in this system. Some of the lessons in this book may contradict the way you've normally done things with women. Some of the approaches we teach may even be painful at first. For instance, when you meet a girl you like, your instinct might be to call her every day, try to take her on a fancy date, and state your feelings to her. As you will learn, this is a direct violation of Mack Commandment #1 ("Flee and they will follow, follow and they flee").

These methods have been proven to work, and the principles work hand-in-hand. If you ignore certain steps, others won't work correctly. It is the overall system that produces great results, not the individual rules and techniques.

Christopher Curtis tells a story to illustrate the importance of this system. When he entered the Marine Corps, he was one of the top recruits in his class but one of the weakest swimmers. (As a kid growing up in Queens, New York, the closest he ever got to swimming was splashing around in a busted fire hydrant.) He failed every swimming test miserably. He was embarrassed and frustrated, until one day an instructor coached him one-on-one. He showed Christopher exactly how he needed to use his arms and legs to swim effectively. Precise, powerful strokes, with all four limbs moving in sync. Over and over, he told Christopher to believe in the system.

At first, trying to swim that way, Christopher struggled and gasped for air. But he found that if he focused, and followed through with the strokes exactly how the instructor had shown him, he began to swim with speed and grace.

The analogy makes sense. A lot of guys, when trying to interact with females, feel like they're drowning. Instead of using smooth, confident strokes, they struggle and flail. They look for things to cling to in social situations, such as drinking excessively or surrounding themselves with their buddies. When talking to women, they lie about their job and tell jokes instead of establishing real connections. After dozens, perhaps hundreds of failed encounters, they still can't figure out where they've been going wrong.

Let M.A.C.K. Tactics be your life preserver. Hold on tight, stick with the system, and you will start operating with power and confidence. You'll reach the other end of the pool in no time.

Fellas, it's time for us to take back the power. To put the Mack down. To put the four core principles to work: Method, Action, Confidence, and Knowledge. Your game will never be the same.

A Cookbook Proposal

The following book proposal is for Roy Guste's *New Orleans Creole Cookery: The Definitive Work on its History and Development*. This is a good example of a nonfiction book sold on the basis of its proposal. The story of this book's sale should encourage you to believe in your work and to find an aggressive representative who believes in you, too. And, it should help you understand that, ultimately, it takes only one publisher/editor for your book to find a home.

Chef Roy F. Guste Jr. sent a copy of one of his previously published cookbooks to me, along with an invitation to join him for a meal at his family-owned restaurant in New Orleans, Antoine's. I had been invited to speak at the New Orleans Writers Conference, and Roy and I arranged to meet. Little did I know that Roy was anxious to meet every agent or representative attending the conference, six in all, and every editor or publisher attending; he had probably contacted them all! During our meal, Roy told me about his book, a complete and fascinating history of Creole cooking. He went on to say how fortunate any rep would be to have him as a client. He assured me that he had a wealth of literary properties and that cookbooks were not his only area of expertise. He explained that every representative attending the conference wanted to represent him. He didn't particularly like the other reps, and so I should tell him what could I do for him that the others couldn't. I had already fallen in love with the project and Roy's personal explanation of it left a lasting impression. (So lasting, in fact, that I used much of his sales pitch to me when I later went to sell it to publishers!) After much discussion and, after getting to know Roy better, he asked that my company and I represent him. The first publisher I contacted found the project exciting and agreed to publish it, but only if it contained lavish illustrations (at least 100 color photographs and 200 black-and-white illustrations). The publishing house also disclosed that, despite their enthusiasm, they couldn't make us a firm offer for at least six weeks. I used those weeks to explore other possibilities, but I found that other publishers were more wary of the property; most felt the market was glutted with books on this topic. Furthermore, the cookbook industry is noted for having either big winners or big losers; some editors didn't think Roy's book was a safe enough bet. Viking Studio Books—the original house that was interested—invited Roy to New York to make a presentation. It was one of the best I have ever seen! Roy's belief in his work, combined with his vast knowledge of the subject and juxtaposed against his charismatic style (bow tie included) completely won them over.

NEW ORLEANS CREOLE COOKERY

THE DEFINITIVE WORK ON ITS HISTORY

AND DEVELOPMENT

A Proposal

By Roy F. Guste Jr.

To understand and define the area of cookery that is New Orleans Creole, we must first follow the etymology of the word back to the Latin *creare*, which means "to create or beget." Creare was Franglicized into the *cria*, meaning "a slave brought up in his master's house." The word "Creole" is the diminutive of cria.

The appellation "Creole" developed to be used in many more expansive ways. In the West Indies, the Spanish areas of South America, and the French settlements of North America the word "Creole" means "an individual of native birth but of European descent." The word "Creole" also applies to "the white descendants of early French and sometimes Spanish settlers of the Gulf states who have preserved a characteristic form of French speech and cultures." Also, the word "Creole" is used to denote "a person of mixed French and Negro or Spanish and Negro descent speaking a dialect of French or Spanish," used especially in Mississippi, Alabama, and Florida.

This volume is restricted to the cuisine developed by the Creoles of New Orleans and their descendants, both white and black. It is this cookery that is "New Orleans Creole cookery."

TABLE OF CONTENTS

Introduction
   1. Notes on Illustrations and Photography
   2. What is "New Orleans Creole"?
   3. History of New Orleans
   4. Cultural Influences/Food Development
   5. Principal Practitioners/Early Restaurants
   6. Early Writers/Early Books
   7. Black Creole Cookery
   8. Creole Feasts
   9. Contemporary New Orleans Creole Restaurants
  10. Recipes: Classic Creole, Black Creole, Haute Creole, Contemporary Creole, Dietary Creole
Index

CULTURAL INFLUENCE ON
THE DEVELOPMENT OF THE CUISINE

New Orleans Creole Cookery is the original indigenous American cuisine developed in and around New Orleans from the time of the city's founding in 1718. Its growth continues today.

FRENCH AND FRENCH CANADIANS: The people who came to Louisiana and founded the first settlement of New Orleans were a mixture of French, French Canadian, slaves, and captured Indians. This founding group, headed by Jean-Baptiste le Moyne, Sieur de Bienville, first began clearing away the canebreaks at the banks of the Saint Louis River, now called the Mississippi after the Indian tribe Meschachebi. The cooking of that group was probably done by men who used their knowledge of French cookery and any improvisations they had learned in Canada. They were a group who knew how to utilize the natural products of the region.

LOUISIANA INDIANS: The founding group also included some hostile Indians who were captured and enslaved. The most useful culinary knowledge to Bienville was that of these Indians who already had a cuisine based on the plant and animal life of the area. These Indians were the first to introduce such basic products as corn to the settlers. They used particular roots and nuts to form the basis of their cuisine. Corn, beans, hominy, rice, smilax root (sarsaparilla), sagamite, groundnuts (peanuts), hickory nuts, chestnuts, pecans, acorns, wild sweet potatoes, arrowhead (sagittaria), and Jerusalem artichokes were the bases of their fare. They taught the settlers varying preparations from gruels and breads to beverages and smoked and dried foods. One tribe, the Natchez, had over forty different preparations of corn alone. They were well acquainted with the wildlife of the area and knew many ways of hunting yet unknown to the Frenchmen. When the colony was returned to the possession of the French Crown by Scotsman John Law in 1731, it became more acceptable for the French to begin migrating to the new land and a far more affluent and sophisticated group began to come to the colony.

SPANISH: By 1762 the port had not developed economically for France although the community was thriving well. With the Treaty of Paris in 1763, France agreed to cede the Louisiana Territory west of the Mississippi and the city of New Orleans to the Spanish. The cession brought an influx of Spaniards to the municipality and also a strong infusion of Spanish culture and cuisine.

AFRICANS AND CARIBBEAN: Throughout the entire history of the development, from the very beginning when those first few men began clearing away the canebreaks along the Mississippi for the settlement of New Orleans, slaves from both Africa and the Caribbean were a vital part of the development of New Orleans Creole Cookery.

PRINCIPAL PRACTITIONERS

By the time of the Civil War, New Orleans was a major American city. The first opera house in America existed here, where the elite of European artists come to perform. Mardi Gras, a traditional Catholic celebration, became a citywide festival for the occasion for the visit of the Grand Duke Alexis of Russia, who was himself in the city following the path of the exalted Jenny Lind (1772).

New Orleans was home to several of the grandest hotels in the world and certainly some of the most sophisticated restaurants that existed anywhere. One of the grand New Orleans restaurants that existed in the 1860s and still exists today is Antoine's. It was in houses like Antoine's, Monsieur Victor's, and in the dining rooms of the Saint Charles and Saint Louis Hotels that the cookery of New Orleans, Creole cookery, was served forth to travelers and citizens, where that simple art reached new heights of perfection, where Creole became Haute Creole. The legendary Madame Begue practiced the art in her tiny single table restaurant in the French Market and gained world renown. The Crescent City had become the culinary mecca of the new world.

WRITERS AND COOKBOOKS

It was not until the 1880s that the concern for recording the existing art of Creole cookery grew into several volumes of recipes. Writers Lafcadio Hearn and Celestine Eustis, The Christian Women's Exchange organization, and a local newspaper, The Picayune, all presented their first volumes between 1885 and 1895. Even then, although Creole cookery was soundly flourishing, there began to develop some concern for the preservation of this important legacy. Each of those works imports an aspect of Creole cookery that is peculiar to the writer and all must be taken together for one to attain comprehensive knowledge of that which had by then developed.

ILLUSTRATIONS

The illustrations for the work will be drawn from the most prestigious local collections: The Louisiana State Museum in New Orleans, The Historic New Orleans Collection, The New Orleans Public Library, the libraries of Tulane and Loyola Universities, and private collections. The graphics will include paintings, drawings, engravings, maps, historical photographs, and original color photography. I am anticipating close to 300 graphic elements: 150 in black and white and 150 in color.

There is a resurgence of interest in New Orleans Creole cookery both locally and nationally. In our city, restaurateurs are busy filling their menus with items from the cuisine that first made us the culinary mecca of the New World. Visitors to the city are now looking more and more for the true cuisine of New Orleans, instead of Nouvelle or Cajun. There are more and more cookbooks on the subject appearing on shelves, yet none come close to the work that we are discussing.

This tome is about the development not only of a form of cookery but of the most expansive, indigenous American cuisine. We are talking about a cuisine that brought the city of New Orleans through the regimes of the French and Spanish and finally to the United States. We are talking about cookery as history and culture, not as mere sustenance.

There is no work that covers the entire history of our city as it relates to our cuisine. There is no book that discusses the culture that built this region through their respective, and subsequently common, cuisine. This is the work—this is a major American cultural contribution.

This is a book that is a necessary part of every library's cookery and food history section, along with being a history of the development of the city of New Orleans through food. This is a work that will become an integral part of the personal libraries of every student of the culinary arts, of every chef, of every lover of food and cookery.

ABOUT THE AUTHOR

Roy F. Guste Jr. was the general manager of Antoine's Restaurant in New Orleans, and is a fifth-generation member of the family that owns that establishment. He is the author of *The Antoine's Restaurant Cookbook, The Restaurants of New Orleans Cookbook, The 100 Greatest Dishes of Louisiana Cookery,* and *Louisiana Light* (all published by W.W. Norton).

A How-to
Book Proposal

Years ago, I met a talented speech writer named Joan Detz, who wanted to write a how-to book on speech making. She wrote a brief proposal for a book called *How to Write and Give Great Speeches! A Practical Guide for Executives.* Her proposal did not meet my usual requirements for nonfiction proposals (and, it was only three pages long!). But we sold the book to the first (and only) publisher that saw it, St. Martin's Press. To Detz's credit, her proposal (short as it was) was well written and illustrated her professionalism. In addition, she was able to find a niche in an area of publishing (the self-help or how-to genre), of which the public never seems to tire. *How to Write and Give Great Speeches!* was first published in 1984, and has been updated and reprinted several times. After reading Detz's brief proposal, consider if your own area of expertise is appropriate for a book in the how-to genre.

HOW TO WRITE AND GIVE A SPEECH

A Practical Guide for Executives

A Proposal

By Joan Detz

The proposed book will tell everything I know about the practical business of writing and giving speeches. When people read it, they will learn in a few hours what took me God-only-knows-how-many speech writing assignments to learn the hard way. Lucky readers!

THE TARGET AUDIENCE

*Primary–Business Executives

The United States has about <u>17 million professional and technical employees</u>, plus about <u>7 million managers and administrators</u>. These middle- and upper-level employees are regularly asked to speak at sales conferences, trade associations, professional organizations, industry conventions, public events.

Most of these people are totally unprepared to give a speech. They didn't learn the necessary skills in high school, college, or even MBA programs.

Of course, the presidents and senior officers of major corporations hire people to do their speech writing. But studies show that <u>most</u> executives—more than 90 percent, in fact—must prepare their own speeches. They are, essentially, flying blind.

*Secondary – Politicians

Everybody knows that the President of the United States hires his own speech writers. So do governors, senators, and other top politicians.

But what about the <u>300,000 lower-level public officials</u>—county officials, mayors, township supervisors, local council members? These elected people can't afford to pay for expensive speech writing services. They, too, are flying blind.

THE NEED

The need for speech making skills is increasing. A survey of 500 U.S. executives found that almost 80 percent are making more speeches now than they were a year ago. About half say they "dread" the task.

Unfortunately, their "dread" shows. <u>A million-plus corporate speeches are delivered each year; only a few are remembered for more than 24 hours.</u>

Why do so many speeches fail? People don't know how to write speeches that <u>get a message across</u>, that <u>make an impression</u>, that are <u>quotable.</u>

They stumble through speeches that sound contrived. And then they wonder why nobody listens.

THE COMPETITION

There are already some good books on the market that tell people how to <u>deliver</u> speeches. But, these books don't offer the specific information that an executive needs to <u>write</u> a memorable speech.

For example, almost all the books say, "Keep it short and simple," but they don't tell the readers HOW to keep their writing short and simple. If the readers knew exactly how to do that, they wouldn't need any book—they could be professional speech writers.

THE BENEFIT

Every product must have a benefit.

Here's what my book offers.

Readers will learn hundreds of <u>specific</u> techniques to make their speeches short and simple. They will learn <u>proven</u> ways to make their speeches lively, interesting, and memorable. They will sound more real, more human, and more credible—and their audiences will be more likely to believe them.

So, for all those readers who can't afford to hire me as their personal speech writer, now there's a book that tells everything I know . . . and the readers can do it on their own.

A Health Book Proposal

The next example of a successful nonfiction proposal is Dr. Albert Marchetti's proposal for *Beating the Odds*. After reading Marchetti's first proposal, I sent it back to him with some suggestions for improvement. Because of its topic and the potential for complex language, the proposal included a detailed definition of the book idea, plus a description of all components, including:

- A description of the book
- Why this book was necessary
- The book's intended audience
- The book's chief competition
- The style and tone of the book
- The author's credentials
- The author's marketability
- A Table of Contents page
- A paragraph describing each of the chapters in the book
- "A Closing Word"

After he revised the proposal, we submitted it to several publishers, successfully placing the book with Contemporary Books, Inc. It was later published in paperback by St. Martin's Press.

As with the other proposals in this book, the impact of a highly professional, accurate, and well-conceived proposal may well be the difference between getting published or not.

SPONTANEOUS REMISSIONS/
BEATING THE ODDS

A Proposal

By
Albert Marchetti, M.D.

The complete proposal for the book includes this summary, a book/author sheet, a table of contents, a chapter by chapter outline, sample chapters, and supplementary material on Dr. Marchetti, including previous articles, interviews, and other pertinent biographical information.

DESCRIPTION OF THE BOOK:

The words "spontaneous remission" are utilized within the medical professions to signify the automatic and complete recovery from cancer, a sometimes unexplainable and mysterious event. The same words title Dr. Marchetti's latest book which focuses on the incredible phenomenon and employs numerous amazing real life examples to simultaneously enlighten the reader and inspire an attempt to achieve a personal remission. But more than this, Spontaneous Remissions logically moves the reader through an understanding of the ultimate cause of cancer and an acceptance of the ultimate cure. All information and case studies are well supported by four years of exhaustive research and an ongoing review of the world literature.

WHY THIS BOOK IS NECESSARY:

Cancer is the second worst medical killer in this country, striking new victims with each passing day. One out of every four will fall prey to this most horrifying illness and over 1.5 million new cases will develop this year alone. Even more astonishing is the thought that 40 million already carry the illness in one form or another and that about half a million sufferers will die within the year. All of these people need direction and help. More importantly, they need hope. Spontaneous Remissions inspirationally fills these needs.

THE INTENDED AUDIENCE:

We see three primary audiences for this book:

1. The individual who carries the diagnosis of cancer and who is searching for a successful and lasting cure.
2. The patient's family and friends who wish to help as much as possible yet lack the knowledge to do so.
3. Health conscious people who desire to educate themselves and initiate or augment a sound holistic approach to cancer prevention.

Although the audience is quite broad, it is well-defined; encompassing primarily mature adults who are direct or indirect cancer victims or otherwise generally interested in cancer prevention and cure. Consequently, the most apparent advertising media are health magazines, such as <u>Prevention</u>, <u>Your Health</u>, etc., plus other publication that cater to a health-conscious or health-crazed readership, for example, the <u>Enquirer</u> and the <u>Star.</u> In addition, health-oriented talk shows, on television and radio provide a great means of promotion with which Dr. Marchetti is already familiar. Further, it is important to note that the many individuals who have seen portions of this book, people with and without cancer, believe that the book offers a powerful and self-applicable approach to cancer therapy. Inevitably they all wanted to read more and were very excited about the medical drama that unfolds from page to page.

THE COMPETITION:

Of course there are several cancer books on the market and some are worthy of note. These include: <u>The Indispensable Cancer Handbook</u>, by Kathryn H. Salsbury and Eleanor Liebman Johnson; <u>Getting Well Again</u>, by O. Carl Simonton, Stephanie Matthews-Simonton, and James L. Creighton; <u>Recalled by Life</u>, by Anthony Sattilaro; and <u>Choices</u>, by Marion Morra and Eve Potts.

Far and away, the best of the group is <u>Getting Well Again</u> by the Simontons. This book is not only authoritative and well documented, it verges on the leading edge of medical knowledge, combining conventional treatments with the most vanguard of the adjunct therapies, visualization. The Simontons are to be congratulated for a job well done. Still, there are problems with the text. It can drag and occasionally bogs down in wordy passages that tend to distract rather than stimulate the reader. To put it simply, the book is dry, from the title, <u>Getting Well Again</u>, to the text itself. In addition, the main thrust of the book is to present and promote the technique of visualization in the treatment of cancer—a very worthwhile endeavor but one that is somewhat limited in practice. Although the technique is effective for those who can master it, it simply is not for every one. Certainly a choice, but not a panacea.

My main criticism of Satillaro's book is that it is primarily restricted to one man's experiences, his own. And while it makes interesting reading, it is too narrow in scope. Like the Simontons, Satillaro expounds on a single treatment modality, the macrobiotic diet to which he attributes his cure. Sure, macrobiotics have a solid place in adjunct therapy, but once again, is a choice, not a cure-all.

<u>The Indispensable Cancer Handbook</u> is actually a comprehensive guide to the latest and best diagnosis, treatment, and supportive services for cancer patients. It is quite different from <u>Spontaneous Remissions</u> since it serves more as a compendium of cancers, tests, therapies, and institutions; a reference book, not a readable work designed to enlighten the inquisitive.

<u>Choices</u> is very much the same sort of book. Its own description is a "handbook designed to cover all the down-to-earth questions people have about doctors and hospitals, diagnosis and tests, treatments and their side-effects, and the many options available."

In contrast, <u>Spontaneous Remissions</u> is about the total and sometimes unexplainable cure of cancer. Through numerous dramatically presented case studies, it proves that natural healing is a definite component in cancer recovery—at times, the only possible explanation for the cure. For people who have cancer, it is a book that offers a direct understanding into personal involvement in therapy and, therefore, a higher chance for total recovery. For people who don't have cancer, it is an exciting examination of a dreaded disease and proof-positive that cancer, like all other illnesses, can be prevented. Collectively, <u>Spontaneous Remissions</u> is a revelation about "turning on" the natural defense system that each of us possesses.

<u>STYLE AND TONE OF THE BOOK:</u>

From the first chapters on, the style and tone of the book become immediately evident. It is a popular treatment, not one intended to impress medical authorities and cancer experts. It is written for the general public, specifically the cancer victim who desperately needs the knowledge, encouragement, and inspiration it provides. It is filled with incredible case studies that pique the reader's interest and flows easily and logically from one topic to another. It is written in the most concise and stimulating manner possible, because cancer victims, like any other critically ill individuals, don't have the time, patience, or energy to plod through a long, dull book about their illness, regardless of how desperate they may be.

The subject matter that is presented is also very exciting. From the concept of spontaneous remission to the discussion of experiments on DNA, interferon, natural killer cells and natural cancer defense, each topic carries the reader further down the road of understanding and culminates in the best means of promoting a spontaneous remission in each individual case. Macrobiotics and visualization are certainly not overlooked, but there are a host of other catalysts, and they are all presented so that the reader can tailor a specific program from the widest selection of alternatives to be used in conjunction with established medical treatments.

But most importantly, the book is inspirational in tone and style. Each case study provides not only knowledge but also hope. Each topic proves that we all naturally possess the substances, cells, and elements needed to bring on a remission. Even the vocabulary, the very words used to describe the incredible phenomenon of cancer defense, exhilarates and motivates the reader. The ultimate purpose of the book is to assist in the cure, so the tone and style are positive and uplifting.

THE AUTHOR'S CREDENTIALS:

Following a Magna Cum Laude graduation and a Bachelor Degree in biology from Providence College, Dr. Marchetti entered the New Jersey College of Medicine and obtained his medical degree in 1973. His postgraduate training took place at Tampa General Hospital where he studied and practiced pathology. In 1977, he was awarded a fellowship to the American Cancer Society and spent the following year compiling cancer data and lecturing to health care professionals, predominantly Tampa-based surgeons, on a variety of cancer topics.

In 1979, Dr. Marchetti's first book, Common Cures For Common Ailments, was published by Stein & Day and made regional bestseller lists around the country, following a two-month, twenty-city, talk show tour made by the author. His second book, Dr. Marchetti's Walking Book, was released in 1981 and was undoubtedly responsible for much of the current interest in walking for good health.

Dr. Marchetti has continued to write (contributing to Cosmopolitan, Forum, Science Digest, Boca Raton Magazine, Atlantic City Magazine, and Florida Style), and for the past three years has amassed a wealth of information on cancer therapy and cure, currently being compiled into his third book, Spontaneous Remissions.

DR. MARCHETTI'S MARKETABILITY:

Dr. Marchetti has appeared on regional television and radio talk shows in every major market around the country. (A copy of his last itinerary is enclosed with this proposal.) In addition, he has given numerous printed interviews for the best newspapers in the United States and has contributed to several popular national and local magazines. He is personable, intelligent, and articulate, and intends to be actively involved in the promotion of the book.

SPONTANEOUS REGRESSION OF
LIVER CANCER IN A FIVE-MONTH-OLD CHILD

Twenty-five years after the diagnosis of liver cancer was made, the patient seemed to have beaten all the odds against his survival and was reported to be "in good health and gainfully employed." His case had been reviewed in a "follow-up" study which was conducted and reported by William J. McSweeny, M.D., Keven E. Bover, M.D., and James MacAdams, M.D. from the Departments of Radiology, Pathology and Pediatrics at the University of Cincinnati College of Medicine. Although these fine physicians all agreed that the child did, indeed, have a tumor, they disagreed with the initial diagnosis of hepatoma type liver cancer, made when the child was first examined twenty-five years previously. Instead, they favored hemangioendothelioma: a blood vessel tumor that developed within the liver.

In this particular case it is extremely important to note that the diagnoses are significantly different. With hepatoma, children usually die. With hemangioendothelioma, they generally live. Regardless, the tumor was not treated because the child was considered a hopeless case at the time. Surprisingly, twenty-five years later the five-month-old baby boy who had been dismissed from the hospital as a terminal cancer patient, was a grown man, tumor free, "in good health and gainfully employed."
WHY?

SPONTANEOUS REGRESSION OF STOMACH CANCER THAT HAD SPREAD TO THE LIVER

At the age of fifty-one, the patient was admitted to Peter Bent Brigham Hospital in Boston. He had been drinking heavily—three- or four-fifths of whiskey each week—and was troubled by stomach problems, weight loss, and fatigue. A full investigation was begun and when the patient finally went to exploratory surgery, his doctors discovered and removed a stomach tumor that was described as "fist size." In addition, they removed enlarged lymph glands around the stomach and also biopsied abnormal nodules in the liver. The diagnosis was confirmed by the Pathology Department—the tumor was an adenocarcinoma of the stomach—or simply, stomach cancer.

And although the lymph glands did not have cancer within them, a microscopic study of the liver biopsy was positive for adenocarcinoma, just like the cancer removed from the stomach. Obviously, the cancer had already spread and now occupied the liver.

In 1956, when this case occurred, removing the cancer from the stomach was considered difficult although surgically possible.

Removing the cancer from the liver was known to be virtually impossible since the more advanced techniques of radio and chemotherapies were virtually unknown back then. Therefore, at the time the diagnosis was made, the prognosis was extremely grave, and the case was considered terminal. Then, unexpectedly, on the tenth hospital day after surgery, the patient developed an infection within his abdomen and underwent a second operation to drain an abscess that had sprung from the stomach incision where the cancer had been cut away. The good news: The infection quickly cleared and the patient left the hospital. The bad news: Although both surgeries were successful, the patient was still doomed to die because he still had cancer in his liver.

BUT THE PATIENT DIDN'T DIE!

Five months after his discharge from the hospital, he had gained twenty pounds and had returned to work symptom-free, a hopeful sign. Three years later, however, he developed a small mass in his neck and returned to the hospital for an evaluation. Although his doctors believed that the mass represented a further manifestation of the cancer, nothing was done. The case was already considered terminal because of the liver metastases, so why put the patient through unnecessary discomfort in his last few days.

The circumstances began to change. Two years after the neck mass developed, it mysteriously and spontaneously disappeared. Later, in 1968, twelve years after the double surgeries, the patient seemed totally cured. While undergoing unrelated gall bladder surgery for gallstones, the patient was completely re-examined inside and out and was found to be totally free of cancer. No nodules in the liver! No recurrent cancer in the stomach! No cancer in the neck! No cancer whatsoever was discovered!

After reviewing the case and examining all the reports, slides, lab work, and X-rays, M.D.s Steven A. Rosenberg, Edward Fox, and Winthroup H. Churchill of the National Cancer Institute in Bethesda, Maryland, submitted their report to <u>Cancer Magazine</u>. It was published in February of 1972. They concluded "that the patient provide evidence that the regression of hepatic metastases from stomach cancer can occur without therapy." Then they added that "the cause of such regression is unknown."

WHY?

REGRESSION OF CANCER FOLLOWING MEASLES INFECTION

In this case the patient was an eight-year-old African boy who entered Mulago Hospital on December 1, 1970, with a form of cancer known as Burkitts Lymphoma: a malignant condition of the lymph glands.

The case was reported in the July 10, 1971, issue of The Lancet, a highly respected British medical journal. And the work was supported by contract number PH 43-67-1343 and PH 43-6767 from the National Cancer Institute in Bethesda, Maryland.

The case is extremely well documented and very often cited. At the time of admission, the lymphoma tumor was growing behind the child's right eye, causing displacement, blindness, and paralysis of the eye. A biopsy of the tumor was performed and when the abnormal tissue was prepared and examined under a microscope it was described as Burkitts Lymphoma, a horrible form of cancer.

Luckily for the child, on December 13, before any kind of therapy could be initiated, he caught the measles. Also recorded on that same day, his doctors noted that the tumor behind his eye began reducing in size. After just two weeks of recovery, not only has the measles cleared, but the tumor had totally disappeared. Completely and without any form of therapy, the child was totally cured.

Apparently there was a connection between the infection and the disappearance of the tumor. Did the measles virus attack the tumor cells? Did the body's reaction to the measles also provoke a reaction to the tumor? Was it fever, antibodies, interferon, or steroids produced and released from the adrenal glands?

Z. Blumberg and John L. Zeigler who reported this case from the Uganda Cancer Institute at Kampala, Uganda, were uncertain about the relationship between the measles and the tumor but they were convinced that they child was totally free of cancer.

WHY?

CONTENTS

Preface
Acknowledgements
Introduction
The Spontaneous
Remission of Cancer

I. HOW HEALING WORKS
   The Process of Healing
   Conventional Therapy
   What You Need to Know About Cancer
   The Natural Defense System
   The Link Between the Mind and the Body

II. YOUR BODY HEALER
   Macrobiotics and the Remission of Cancer
   Exercise and the Remission of Cancer

III. YOUR MENTAL HEALER
   Meditation and the Remission of Cancer
   Visualization and the Remission of Cancer
   Hypnosis and the Remission of Cancer

IV. COMBINING THERAPIES
   Metabolic Therapies and the Remission of Cancer
   Crossing the Finish Line
   Another Winner

Bibliography
Index

A Fiction Proposal

The following essay was originally published by *Atlantic City Magazine* and was used to propose a concept for a fiction trilogy that was successfully placed with Lynx Books. The author wrote the first novel (his writing style was compared to that of Anne Rice, Richard Condon, and Nathaniel West). Unfortunately, Lynx Books filed for bankruptcy and the novel was not published.

THE JERSEY DEVIL

An Essay

By Christopher Cook Gilmore

MEET THE JERSEY DEVIL

At last, the real story about the wayward son
who ate his family.

DO NOT BE ALARMED. The only person who knows the
whole truth about the Jersey Devil, his mother, has been dead
for almost 200 years. She has nothing to say. She is dead and the
Devil lives, and the rest is lies.

Mother Leeds was not her real name. It was Tatiwawarunu,
or Head of Stone, and she was a full-blooded Leni-Lenape
Indian. When she was fourteen her parents were found roasted
alive in an old, abandoned Indian roaster near Batsto. Blamed
for the tragedy and banished from her tribe, she slept in the
pines until a family of early settlers named Leeds took her in
and married her to one of their men, Zebedee Leeds, sixty-five,
a widower and a deaf-mute. They all lived on Leeds Point in the
Pine Barrens, a very weird place in 1778.

New Jersey is easily the weirdest state in the Union, and
back then the Leeds people were definitely the weirdest in the
state. They were pure Piney, crazy enough, but on top of that
they lived for generations on remote parts of Great Bay so thick
with rats, gnats, flies, and mosquitoes it could drive anyone
mad. Methane gas rotted their brains, while poverty, inbreeding,
and bad whiskey finished off their souls. No wonder that one of
them, sooner or later, would spawn a devil.

The legend is that Mother Leeds, as she came to be called,
was a witch, which she was, and that her husband was a war-
lock, which is a lie. Zebedee Leeds never knew what was going
on. Blinded by lightning on his wedding night, he lived another
fifteen years, long enough to father a dozen children. He was
drowned in the bay and consumed by spider crabs. A year later
his widow gave birth to her thirteenth child. She swore on the
Leeds Bible that Satan had come to her in the night in the form
of an animal, a big flatfish, and seduced her. Because she was the

daughter of a medicine man, she was believed. The baby was a boy, and she called him Son.

The story goes that on his thirteenth birthday, in the middle of a griddle-cake party, Son ate his mother. He then ate his twelve brothers and sisters. Appetite appeased, he sprouted wings, horns, and a tail, flew up the chimney and took off for the pines. He is seen to this day running around the treetops with his feet on fire and howling from the pain. He is blamed for everything that goes wrong: barnyard mutants, vegetable freaks, chain-saw malfunctions, anything at all. Son Leeds, goes the story, never leaves New Jersey. He can't stand the climate, and that is why they call him the Jersey Devil.

The truth is that Mother Leeds and her first twelve children all died natural deaths, mostly by fire, flood, or quicksand. A few of their descendants still live on the marshes, but most of them moved back to the pines. They go to church and can read and write. Today the Devil has no more interest in them than he has in anyone else. Son Leeds, whose real father was a deserter from the British Army, was strikingly handsome and extremely intelligent. A skilled angler, he spent most of his life drifting for flounder on the bay. Son was no demon, but he certainly was a devil with the ladies. A bachelor till he died, he had ninety-two girlfriends, all of them with gentle natures and wonderful figures. Son's amorous exploits became legendary, which is probably at the bottom of everything. Some say Son's spirit passed into future generations, and that this spirit, which exists in many a Jersey boy, is the Jersey Devil. Jersey girls say he comes to them at night, usually in nightclubs, and asks them to dance. They say it's their sweet selves he wants, not their souls, and that what he likes most is to take them fishing. Some girls say he looks like an old yellow dog, some like a wildcat.

And some say he looks a lot like me.

A Television Series
Proposal and Script

This proposal was written for a syndicated television series that was optioned to Atlantic Kushner-Locke. The option lapsed after a year; the project was reoptioned to King World. My partner, Vince Bugliosi, and I wrote the accompanying presentation script, hoping it would increase our chances of selling the series. After King World's option lapsed, the project was optioned to The Ventura Entertainment Group. Currently, we are working on this project.

THE FIRST RUN
SYNDICATED OR NETWORK
TELEVISION SERIES
AND PRESENTATION SCRIPT

TRUE MURDER MYSTERIES

A HALF-HOUR, OR HOUR TELEVISION DRAMA
COMPILED FROM TRUE MURDER MYSTERIES

To be narrated by Vincent T. Bugliosi

Created by:
Vincent T. Bugliosi and Peter Miller

Executive Producers:
Vincent T. Bugliosi and Peter Miller

PRODUCTION NOTES

Each episode will examine one of the most famous, colorful, and significant murder cases in the annals of American crime, ones where an element of mystery, to this very day, endures. The producers have done extensive research as to which murders qualify for this programming, and include a few dozen examples of suggested cases hereafter.

INTRODUCTION

Each show will begin with an introduction by Vincent Bugliosi, in a courtroom setting, giving a brief summary of the case, including its cast of characters, i.e., the accused, the victim, the witnesses, etc. Where possible, the actual scene of the crime will be shown, and film footage and/or interviews with those involved will be incorporated into the segment.

THE ACCUSED

Basing his account on official records and all other available information, Mr. Bugliosi will then give background of the accused, including a psychological portrait of him and his relationship, if any, with the victim. This background and portrait will help the viewer form an opinion as to whether the accused did, in fact, commit the murder, and if so, what his motive was. Photographs and film footage of the accused, where available, will be shown during the segment.

THE MURDER

Next, each show will dramatically recreate the murder (including the known events leading up to and following the murder), allowing the audience to become an eyewitness to the crime. At the end of this scene, Mr. Bugliosi will appear at the scene of the crime ("breaking walls"), and will then reveal the events leading up to the arrest of the accused murderer.

THE EVIDENCE
[PHYSICAL AND SCIENTIFIC]

We will then proceed with an examination of the evidence in the case. Where available, the actual murder weapon will be revealed to the viewing audience. In this segment, Mr. Bugliosi will analyze the key evidence, such as fingerprints, firearm identification (popularly but erroneously referred to as ballistics), blood and hair comparisons, etc. In examining this evidence, Mr. Bugliosi will utilize the official investigative documents in the case, such as police and autopsy reports.

THE TRIAL

Highlights of the trial will then be recreated. This segment may consist of the direct examination, cross-examination, and final summation, utilizing excerpts from the actual trial transcript.

SUMMATION

We will close each program with a summation by Mr. Bugliosi in which he sets forth the results of the trial and the sentence of the accused (if there was a conviction). In the event any new evidence surfaced subsequent to the trial, Mr. Bugliosi will detail how such evidence might have affected the verdict if it had been offered at the trial. He will close his presentation with thought-provoking observations about the case and the evidence and, finally, will render his own verdict as to whether . . . Justice Has Been Served.

OPENING SHOT:

EXT: STREET--DAY
It is the scene of a crime. Police and medics are all busy with their various tasks. As the body is placed in the ambulance and the door is slammed, VINCENT T. BUGLIOSI walks into the scene. He looks down at the chalk outline of a body and then up at the camera.

BUGLIOSI
"Thou Shalt Not Kill." The Fifth Commandment. Murder has, throughout man's history, been viewed as the most heinous crime of all, the one act by another human being we all fear the most. Yet paradoxically, despite its horror, we are endlessly fascinated by it, particularly when there's an element of mystery. Perhaps it's because of the innate desire we all have to play the part of the detective. Or perhaps the reason is that most important element of murder, death, is itself shrouded in mystery! In our never-ended effort to solve the mystery of death, we are inescapably attracted to it.

Mr. Bugliosi walks off screen.

EXT: L.A. COUNTY COURTHOUSE--DAY
Mr. Bugliosi walks onto the scene.

BUGLIOSI
In the past, men looked to primitive codes of justice to provide the solutions to crimes. Today, we have a vast and impressive legal system which we rely on to bring criminals to justice. Yet, it is an imperfect system and not every case can be solved completely and satisfactorily.

Mr. Bugliosi begins walking up the stairs.

BUGLIOSI

Come with me now as I investigate some of the most mysterious murder cases of our time and ask the fundamental question:

Mr. Bugliosi pauses at the door.

BUGLIOSI

Are we satisfied beyond a reasonable doubt that we know the truth?

Mr. Bugliosi walking into the building.

Credits role. . . TMM theme music plays.

    XYZ Production Company Presents

    TRUE MURDER MYSTERIES

    Hosted By

    Vincent T. Bugliosi

    Created By

    Vincent T. Bugliosi

    &

    Peter Miller

Mr. Bugliosi enters the courtroom, puts his coat down at the prosecutor's table, walks up to the Judge's bench and stands.

BUGLIOSI

Hello, I'm Vincent Bugliosi. Some of you may know me as the Deputy District Attorney of Los Angeles County who prosecuted Charles Manson and members of his family for the infamous Tate-LaBianca murders. Or you may have read my book about that case called *Helter Skelter*. In that particular case I was able to clearly prove Manson's guilt beyond all reasonable doubt even though Manson didn't personally commit any of the murders for which he was convicted. In other trials the outcome, whether guilty or not guilty, is not always clear. For instance, I'm sure you've all heard of Lizzie Borden. The well-known limerick about her goes:

Lizzie Borden took an axe,
And gave her mother forty whacks.
When she saw what she had done,
She gave her father forty-one.

But, how many of you know that actually she was found not guilty, despite strong, circumstantial evidence against her? Why is this? In TRUE MURDER MYSTERIES we will see that an explanation for at least some of such cases is that the alternate legal issue at a criminal trial is not whether or not the accused committed the crime, but whether the prosecution was able to prove that he did beyond a reasonable doubt. In American jurisprudence, then, a verdict of "Not Guilty" is not always synonymous with "Innocence."

Mr. Bugliosi walks around to the witness chair and takes a seat.

BUGLIOSI
Or look at the case of Claus von Bulow, the man who was charged, in 1981, with the attempted murder of his wife, Sunny. After an initial conviction he was later acquitted in another trial despite the existence of evidence which had proven him guilty at the first trial. How did two juries hearing the same case arrive at two completely different conclusions?

Mr. Bugliosi stands and walks up to a series of enlarged newsprint type black & white photographs and headlines of the Lizzie Borden case, the Lindbergh case, the von Bulow trial, and an even larger spread for the Kennedy assassination.

[Note: A well lit and carefully designed, durable presentation of famous murders can be designed for this production, and also used for other presentation purposes, i.e., N.A.P.T.E.]

BUGLIOSI

The Murders that we will choose to examine in our series, TRUE MURDER MYSTERIES, will all have a specific element of mystery surrounding them, which endures to this very day. Since there is a vast library of fascinating cases from which to choose, we'll have an inexhaustible supply of murder mysteries. Some of the cases we will explore in our show have been well publicized. Many have not. All will captivate you, the viewer.

With each one-hour presentation, I will begin by giving a brief summary of the case, including sharing photographs and, where available, film footage of the cast of characters, that is, the accused, the victim, the witnesses, etc. . . . Where possible, the actual scene of the crime will be shown to the viewing audience.

Based on official records and all other available information, I will then give the background of the accused, including a psychological portrait of him and his relationship, if any, with the victim. This background and portrait will help the viewer form an opinion as to whether or not the accused did, in fact, commit the murder, and if so, what his motive was.

Next, each show will dramatically recreate the murder, including the known events immediately leading up to and following the murder, thereby allowing the audience to become an eyewitness to the crime.

We will then proceed with an examination of the evidence in the case. Where available, the actual murder weapon will be shown to the viewing audience. In this segment, from the official investigative document in the case, I will analyze the key evidence, such as fingerprints, firearm identification, blood and hair comparisons, incriminating statements and conduct, etc . . .

At this point I will discuss questions and mysteries in the case that to this day remain unanswered, and evidence, some of it new, which cries out for a second look. TRUE MURDER MYSTERIES will give the viewers the opportunity to examine all of the evidence themselves and draw their own conclusions.

The next segment will be a capsulated recreation of the trial. It will consist of the highlights of the direct examination, cross-examination and final summation, utilizing excerpts from the actual trial transcripts.

Finally, in each drama I will give a summation in which I set forth results of the trial and the sentence of the accused if there was a conviction. I will then discuss how the new evidence, if any, and the enduring mysteries about the case, if answered, might have affected the verdict. I will close the presentation with thought-provoking observations about the case and the evidence.

INT: LIBRARY--DAY [Note: either a home library or public]

Mr. Bugliosi enters the scene and takes a seat in a comfortable armchair. From a table by the chair he picks up a book. Behind him the walls are lined with hundreds of books on crime, e.g., *Helter Skelter*, *In Cold Blood*, *Fatal Vision*, *Murder At The Met*, *A Cast Of Killers*, etc.

BUGLIOSI
When I first became fascinated with the concept of creating TRUE MURDER MYSTERIES, I realized that even though other crime anthology programming exists on television, no series has ever dealt specifically with the myriad of true murder mysteries of twentieth-century North American history. Another plus for TRUE MURDER MYSTERIES is the fact that murder mysteries are a major staple in our nation's entertainment industries...from books like *In Cold Blood* and *Presumed Innocent*, to TV miniseries like *The Nutcracker* and *The Billionaire Boys Club*, and major feature films like *The Jagged Edge* and *Suspect*. So there's obviously a large audience for this type of story, most of which are fictional. If fictional murder mysteries have a mass appeal, then TRUE

MURDER MYSTERIES will prove to be that much more intriguing to the viewing public. The incredible nature of many of the murder mysteries we will examine in our series will prove once again that real life is, indeed, stranger than fiction.

Mr. Bugliosi stands and puts his book back on the shelf.

BUGLIOSI
Now, ladies and gentlemen, I will offer a sampling of some of the murder cases.

INT: MIAMI BEACH MANSION–DAY

Mr. Bugliosi walks into a posh foyer and pauses on the stairwell.

BUGLIOSI
On June 30, 1964, multimillionaire Jacques Mossler was bludgeoned to death in his mansion in Miami. Oddly enough, Mossler's wife, Candy, had gone out driving at 1:00 a.m. with their four children. By the time she returned at 4:30 a.m., her husband was dead. Later, investigators discovered that Candy's nephew, Melvin, had flown from Houston to Florida and back within 24 hours of the murder. Then, Melvin was linked to the murder weapon, and his palm print was discovered on the kitchen-counter. The State even produced two ex-cons who claimed that Candy and Melvin had offered them money to kill Mossler. All of this circumstantial evidence was enough to warrant a trial for Candy and Melvin, but it wasn't enough to convict them. What had seemed like a convincing case evaporated under the heat of the defense's brutal attack on Mr. Mossler's character, and the allegation that there were others who had a motive and opportunity for killing Mossler. Candy and Melvin were acquitted.

INT: ELLIS ISLAND. THE EMPTY HALLS OF THE WELCOME CENTER–DAY

Mr. Bugliosi walks through the rooms, the New York skyline or the Statue of Liberty seen through the windows.

BUGLIOSI

On August 23, 1927, two Italian immigrants who had been convicted of murder were electrocuted in Massachusetts seven years after what is still one of the most controversial trials in history: the trial of Sacco and Vanzetti. They were charged in the shooting death and robbery of two couriers who were transferring $16,000. The evidence against the men was slim at the outset, but witnesses' memories mysteriously improved during the year prior to the trial when Sacco and Vanzetti's radical politics surfaced. At the time, the U.S. Attorney General and the immigration service were engaged in a campaign to rid America of all immigrants who held "subversive" political beliefs. Webster Phair, the presiding judge, made no effort to conceal his distaste for the immigrants, repeatedly referring to them out of court as "wops" and "dagos."

Sacco and Vanzetti were found guilty and subsequently electrocuted. But how much of a role did political and racial bias play in the determination of their guilt and innocence? Ten years ago, the Commonwealth of Massachusetts, in an unusual move, formally acknowledged that Sacco and Vanzetti "did not receive a fair trial." This was not, however, a concession of their innocence. Were they, in fact, guilty?

EXT: OPEN FIELD, New Brunswick, N.J.–DAY

Mr. Bugliosi stands near an apple tree. It is September 14, 1922. Some period 1920s cars drive by. Under the tree, a man and a woman are dead.

BUGLIOSI

A little over two years after the killing we just discussed occurred, a murder took place in New Brunswick, New Jersey, which was so fascinating that in 1950, a special issue of LIFE MAGAZINE labeled the Hall-Mills murder the "Crime of the Half Century." On the morning of September 14, 1922, the dead bodies of Reverend Edward Wheeler Hall of St. John the Evangelist Church and his lover, Eleanor Mills, a married member of the church choir, were discovered neatly arranged under a tree, with Eleanor's head resting on the minister's right arm. Edward's genitalia were placed in his mouth, and several love letters were strewn around on the ground. Despite a lengthy and highly controversial trial in which the Reverend's wife and his lover's two brothers were charged with the murders, the case was never solved, all the defendants being found not guilty. To this very day, theories abound as to who the real murderer, or murderers, are. Yet another mystery in the annals of American crime history.

NOTE: We can add other murder descriptions here, depending on how long the presentation tape will be. Those murders could include Charles Lindbergh's baby, John F. Kennedy, Martin Luther King Jr., the Dr. Sam Shepard case, etc.. Also note that we now need specific directions, i.e.: What is the budget? How long is it going to be? Hour? Half-hour?

INT: COURTROOM–DAY

Mr. Bugliosi is back at the counsel's table.

BUGLIOSI

Ladies and gentlemen, thank you for viewing this brief presentation. I hope I've piqued your interest about what I believe to be a ready-made marketability of TRUE MURDER MYSTERIES, a provocative, perceptive, and yes, educational examination of the most intriguing cases in the annals of American crime.

Vince gathers up some legal books.

FADE OUT:

THE END

TRUE MURDER MYSTERIES

Suggested Case List

1. THE BORDEN MURDER MYSTERY (Fall River, Mass., 1892). Ax murders of Borden's father and stepmother. Borden acquitted despite strong evidence.

2. THE DEATH OF STANFORD WHITE (New York, 1906). Eminent architect shot by Harry Thaw, the pathologically jealous husband of a former lover.

3. THE POLITICS AND DEATH OF SACCO AND VANZETTI (South Braintree, Mass., 1920). Italian immigrants found guilty and electrocuted for murder of two payroll couriers.

4. FATTY ARBUCKLE: A CRUSH ON A GIRL (San Francisco, 1921). Weighty screen comic legend Arbuckle accused of crushing starlet Virginia Rappe as he raped her. Arbuckle was acquitted.

5. THE HOLLYWOOD MYSTERY (Los Angeles, 1922). Unsolved slaying of a respected actor and film director.

6. LEOPOLD AND LOEB: THRILL KILL (Chicago, 1924). Rich youths murder a boy for the adrenalin thrill of killing.

7. THE BUNGLING LOVERS MYSTERY (Long Island, 1927). Two lovers clumsily bludgeon a husband to death, each blaming the other in court.

8. THE HAWAIIAN HOMICIDE (Honolulu, 1931). One of a group of Japanese-Hawaiians accused of raping Thalia Massie is executed in racially motivated vengeance.

9. THE LINDBERGH BABY MYSTERY (New Jersey, 1932). Aviator's son is stolen from his crib and murdered, then ransomed by Bruno Hauptmann.

10. THE QUESTION OF DR. SAM SHEPARD (Cleveland, 1954). While blaming an unknown killer, a doctor is found guilty of murdering his wife. Newspaper sensationalism leads to retrial and acquittal.

11. JUDGE, JURY, AND EXECUTIONER (Florida, 1955). Fearing that his corruption will be exposed, Judge Joseph Peel arranges the death of a noted colleague.

12. PERRY SMITH & RICHARD HICKOCK: KILLERS "IN COLD BLOOD" (Holcomb, Kansas, 1959). Ex-cons butcher a farmer and his family, thinking money is hidden in the house. Basis for the book and film *In Cold Blood*.

13. DEATH AND THE SWINGING DOCTOR (Los Angeles, 1959). Dr. Bernard Finch and his lover murder the doctor's wife.

14. THE BOSTON STRANGLER MYSTERY (Boston, 1962). Albert DeSalvo confesses to the sex slayings of thirteen Boston women.

15. CANDY AND MELVIN (Florida, 1964). Blonde bombshell conspires with her boyfriend to murder her husband. Brilliant defense leads to her acquittal.

16. THE ALICE CRIMINS CASE (New York, 1965). Two small children are murdered by their mother, who claims it was the work of kidnappers.

17. THE RICHARD SPECK MASS MURDERS (Chicago, 1966). Psychopath murders eight nurses in a single night in a Chicago hotel.

18. JAMES EARL RAY: THE MARTIN LUTHER KING ASSASSINATION (Memphis, 1968). Ray fires a rifle shot that kills black civil rights leader, Martin Luther King, Jr.

19. SIRHAN SIRHAN: THE ARAB FANATIC (Los Angeles, 1968). Sirhan guns down Robert Kennedy in a hotel kitchen on the night he wins the California presidential primary.

20. DEATH IN HOUSTON HIGH SOCIETY (Houston, 1969-72) A wealthy socialite is ostensibly poisoned by her doctor husband who, in turn, is shot by a paid killer.

21. MANSON (Los Angeles, 1969). Charismatic guru leads a group of followers to vicious murders. Basis for the book *Helter Skelter*.

22. THE GREEN BERET MURDERS (Ft. Bragg, North Carolina, 1971). A doctor claims hippies broke into his house and stabbed his wife and daughters. Convicted nine years later.

23. THE MYSTERY OF THE MURDERED MIGRANTS (Yuba City, California, 1971). Over a period of weeks in the early spring, Juan Corona slaughters twenty-five migrant workers, burying them in shallow graves.

24. THE HOPE MASTERS CASE (California, 1972). After murdering her lover, a charming killer persuades a woman to fall in love with him.

25. THE MYSTERY OF THE MURDERED MOTHER (Connecticut, 1973). Wrongly convicted of killing his mother, a boy wins his freedom with the help of dedicated neighbors.

26. THE "MAN IN BLACK" MYSTERY (Ft. Worth, Texas, 1976). A "man in black" murders millionaire Cullen Davis' stepdaughter and wife's lover. Davis was acquitted.

27. QUESTIONS ABOUT BUDDY (New York, 1978). In a fit of jealousy, a noted horse trainer murders his ex-girlfriend's new lover.

28. AN EVIL WITHIN: THE REINERT MYSTERY (Pennsylvania, 1979). A rich schoolteacher and her children are killed, both for revenge and for their insurance money.

29. THE DEATH OF JOHN SINGER (Utah, 1979). A man making a moral stand by keeping his children from school is shot by sheriff's deputies.

30. THE ENIGMA OF JEAN HARRIS (Purchase, New York, 1980). Dr. Herman Tarnower is shot by his mistress, who claims the shooting occurred when Tarnower tried to prevent suicide.

31. DARK DAYS FOR SUNNY (Rhode Island, 1980). An heiress falls into a coma, presumably after a murderous injection is administered by her husband.

32. TRANSEXUAL TROUBLE (New York, 1981). After a sex change operation, a woman is murdered at the hands of two former lovers: one gay, one heterosexual.

33. THE BLACK MASK MURDER (New York, 1985). An apparent desire for necrophiliac homosexual sex leads to the murder of a Norwegian male model.

34. THE BENSON BOMB MURDERS (Naples, Florida, 1985). Heir to a tobacco fortune plants two pipe bombs in the family car, killing his mother and another family member.

35. THE MORMON MYSTERY (Salt Lake City, Utah, 1985). Master forger of historic Mormon archives murders two people to avoid exposure.

A TV Movie and Dramatic Series Proposal and Treatment

The following proposal and treatment is for a network television movie of the week (MOW) and one-hour dramatic series. This presentation is presently being offered to producers and networks in the hopes of making a development deal for the movie and/or the series production. Often movies of this kind are referred to as "back-door pilots" in that they serve first as an MOW and then as a vehicle for defining the cast of an eventual series.

THE INSIDE MAN

By Jerry Schmetterer

A Proposal for a Television Movie

There is a problem inside Attica. And Dave Lewis knows that if he doesn't solve it, soon, New York State will lose control of its toughest prison.

For months Lewis, Inspector General of the State Department of Correction, has been getting letters from an Attica inmate named Lester Osborne, a three time loser serving a life sentence without possibility of parole for the murder of a schoolteacher. In his letters Osborne tells Lewis of a new gang inside the prison. Osborne says the gang is not like the others that are common in all prisons: gangs of black, Hispanics, Indians, bikers, or homosexuals, banded together for protection against their natural enemies. Instead, Osborne hints strongly that this new gang is a gang of white supremacists, not unusual in Southern or Western prisons but so far unknown in New York's system. But Osborne insists that there is something about this gang that makes it more dangerous than any other—it is made up of the correction officers themselves. The guards have become a criminal entity. Osborne says he will tell more if Lewis can help him get his sentence changed; he wants a chance at parole.

Osborne's letters are not unusual. Inmates often try to help Lewis—who is responsible for the honesty and integrity of the civil servants who run the system (similar to the internal affairs of a police department) in exchange for some special treatment.

Lewis is in charge of a very small department comprising only a dozen or so investigators and clerks. His position is really a political appointment, made traditionally by governors in order to keep prison reformers off their backs. Lewis has neither the staff nor the time to act quickly on things, but Osborne's letters strike an alarming note; they send up a red flag in Lewis' mind.

Lewis is most bothered by the possibility that prison guards have joined together in a conspiracy. This could be a very dangerous situation. It would mean that the guards, not the state department of prisons, were running the institution. There is no doubt in Lewis' mind that this could happen—it had happened in the past, always with devastating results to the penal system. The lowest guards always really knew more about the goings-on inside the prison walls than the warden. If they decided to walk on the other side of the law, guards could in effect turn the prison over to the most powerful inmates. They could smuggle drugs for them, aid in escape, run criminal errands outside the walls—guards had even committed murder at the order of prisoners they worked for.

What made this case so potentially dangerous was Osborne's discussion of the guard's white supremacist motives. The Aryan Brotherhood had long existed among prison inmates throughout the country. Comprised mainly of white, violent inmates, it was ostensibly a means of white prisoners protecting themselves from the black and Latino gangs. In reality, the Aryan Brotherhood was as violent and aggressive as any of the black or Latino groups. Their literature and their prison yard recruiting speeches called for the annihilation of minorities and their goal was an Aryan civilization, with Brotherhood leaders running things.

Clashes between Aryan, black, and Latino gangs had started full-scale riots in prisons from California to Maine. Many inmates, often innocent bystanders trying to avoid prison politics, were killed in these riots and millions of dollars had been spent to repair the facilities. But most of the murder was done without riot. Black prisoners were found hanged in their cells, Latinos were set on fire while they lay in their bunks, whites were found stabbed in showers.

The possibility that the Aryan Brotherhood was now operating among the guards was frightening to Lewis. He knew it was possible and he knew it would have to be stopped.

So Lewis gives the Osborne letters the highest priority within the circumstances of his limited resources. He files the Osborne letters with a note to himself to interview the inmate on his next trip to Attica during which he plans to investigate the suspicious deaths of three inmates. Lewis suspects guards may have helped smuggle in the poisoned drugs responsible, because following the death of the first inmate the warden tightened visiting and mail privileges and was able to virtually rule out those possibilities as a way the next inmates got the poisoned drugs. Lewis was a little mad at himself for not interceding in that investigation, but he had to let the warden try to solve matters himself. Furthermore, Lewis was not really responsible for stopping crime inside the prison. As Inspector General he was primarily concerned with official corruption, e.g., guards' involvement in the murders.

Lewis retrieves the files when he notices Osborne's name on an unusual occurrence report: Osborne has been found hanged in his cell. Preliminary reports indicate suicide. No one is knocking himself out investigating the case.

Lewis calls the warden at Attica and asks if he might be concerned that Osborne was murdered. The warden is not concerned at all. He is sure Osborne, whom he describes as a withdrawn, sullen prisoner, succumbed to lifer's disease. The warden has ordered a review of cell check procedures because Osborne had apparently been overlooked by a guard on a pass through his cell block; perhaps that guard could have saved the inmate's life by cutting him down in time. Perhaps not.

Lewis is not happy with George Prisco's response. The warden of Attica, selected for his toughness, is in charge of the state's most desperate inmates. Not known for his sensitivity to the inmates' problems or fears, he looks at the suicide as available cell space. Lewis thinks the warden would look at an Aryan alliance among his guards as good fraternal fun.

Before the phone is in the cradle, Lewis has decided on his next move. He decides to turn to two men who have helped him solve crimes inside prisons before: Jeff Ford and Dick Walla. Ford is an ex-convict who worked undercover for police and the correction department while doing his time, not so much for the special treatment it got him but because he is that rare individual who enjoys risking his life; he is most alive when at risk. In four years Ford broke up drug-smuggling rings run by guards, solved a murder, and helped convict a warden who was selling weapons and sex to inmates. Walla, on the other hand, is a former guard who was a member of New York City's elite prison SWAT team and handled many investigations for Lewis. Walla was assigned to assist Ford in one of his investigations, and the two became close friends. Ford, a tall, black, streetwise adventure lover, came to look at the middle-aged typical-cop-type, Walla, as a surrogate father. When Ford was released from prison, Walla retired from the department and the two opened a private detective agency specializing in undercover operations.

Ford and Walla quickly gained a reputation as a reliable team willing to take risks and capable of the most sophisticated assignments. They took on jobs in defense plants for the FBI, in foreign embassies for the CIA, and inside prisons all over the world for correction departments. In one of their cases Ford obtained a job inside an aircraft manufacturing plant involved in building the Stealth Bomber. The FBI and CIA felt a KGB spy was working inside and needed to bait him but were afraid to use one of their own counter-intelligence representatives because if it truly was a KGB operation in the plant, an agent might be identified; counter-intelligence is really a small community.

So Ford and Walla got the assignment. Ford was given a job in the top secret area of the plant and Walla was made a security guard. After a short time Ford's reputation grew, with the help of company technicians, and as the budding genius of the company he was approached by the Russian spy. The bait was offered and taken and the trap was set. The CIA got its man and Ford and Walla's reputation grew.

Lewis shares his suspicions about Attica with Walla and they agree on a plan.

One month after Osborne's "suicide," Jeff Ford is in the back of an ambulance pulling up to the infirmary at Attica Prison, wrapped from head to toe in bandages. The medical charts in his file explain that Ford was seriously burned in an accident at another prison hundreds of miles away. He is being transferred to Attica because the chief doctor there is an expert on treating these injuries. Without much notice, the usually outgoing Ford penetrates the prison.

For six weeks, with the doctors' cooperation, Ford "recovers" in the infirmary. Meanwhile, Walla has entered the prison in the guise of an engineer studying the installation of a completely new plumbing system. He has disguised himself slightly in case he runs into a guard or prisoner he knows from his own days in the department. However, he considers this a slight chance because Walla worked almost exclusively for thirty years in prisons in New York City. Dave Lewis is the only person in the Department of Correction who knows the mission the two detectives are on.

Ford is released from the infirmary and joins the general population. Using his genial personality and a dimwit act which hides his natural con man's brain, he quickly makes friends among the inmates and begins to zero in on Osborne's friends. He learns that they believe Osborne was murdered by the guards. They are not so sure about Osborne's Aryan Nation theory, but they do confirm that the guards are usually sadistic and clearly racist. Every day Walla finds an excuse to be near Ford so he can get his report. When he leaves the prison each night, Walla reports to Lewis by telephone.

Ford learns that one of the guard ringleaders, Ralph Easter, needs a porter to work in his office. None of the black inmates want the job because they fear Easter. When Ford volunteers, the other inmates tell him he's crazy. However, since he's playing the role of dimwit, he can pretend he doesn't understand their fears.

Ford gets the job and throws himself at Easter's feet. He plays at being too dumb to even understand why the floor has to be swept, and he profusely thanks Easter for every grungy job he gives him. He becomes the butt of Easter's racial jokes and the other guards join in the belief that Ford is some kind of retard.

Soon Ford becomes part of the furniture. The guards talk freely around him and leave important papers concerning the Aryan gang's intelligence reports and meeting summaries around the office. At great risk Walla slips Ford a mini-camera and tape recorder and Ford begins gathering evidence. On more than one occasion a guard suspects Ford is up to something, but the detective's great acting ability always helps him cover up. At one point he even lets a sadistic member of the group beat him over a spilled cup of coffee, but he never drops his act.

When Easter or another guard curses a black man, Ford joins in. When they talk about how great a man Hitler was, Ford jumps up and clicks his heels in the Nazi salute. The guards think Ford is a total imbecile—just what they would expect from a black inmate.

Ford gathers a lot of information about the guards' illegal activities but they never mention Osborne. Finally, Lewis decides he must put some pressure on. He tells the Attica warden that he has an undercover agent inside the prison working on the Osborne case. But he does not tell the warden who the agent is or who the leading suspects are.

The warden is furious that Lewis would operate so deviously behind his back. He complains to the Commissioner of Corrections and the Commissioner in turn admonishes Lewis and warns him he better be right about the Aryan gang or his job is at stake.

But Lewis' gamble pays off. One of Easter's thugs, working in the warden's office, overhears a telephone conversation and mentions it during a coffee break in Easter's office. The two guards talk about the murder of Osborne and Easter concedes that he ordered it, and another guard is mentioned as the actual killer. Osborne was killed because he had uncovered a plot by the Aryan guards to smuggle in poisoned drugs to sell to black inmates. The guards would actually make money while achieving their goals of genocide against non-whites. Osborne, apparently tired of waiting for help from Lewis, decided to try to blackmail the guards; it was a fatal decision. Luckily, Ford has been washing the floor at the guard's feet and captures the entire conversation on tape.

Now totally paranoid, the Aryan guards make life hell for the inmates. Cells are repeatedly searched as they hunt for the informant. While Ford remains their mascot, he knows he has to get both his tape and himself out of the jail. His tape recorder and camera are hidden in his mattress when the guards begin an unannounced search of his cell block. Ford realizes he needs Walla immediately, so he decides to flood his toilet. Using the tape recorder to stuff up the commode, Ford soon has his way; the cell block is awash and everyone in the building calls for a plumber. Walla is in a maintenance office and realizes the trouble is coming from Ford's cell block. He goes with the repair crew, rushing past them into the cell as soon as he sees it is Ford's commode. Ford puts on his fool act and grabs Walla, saying he's the only guy who can fix the flood.

Walla reaches into the toilet and retrieves the tape recorder. The cleanup job has distracted the guards, and when Walla returns to the cell, Ford tells him he's got to get out now.

Walla immediately calls Lewis and Ford is secreted out of the prison the same way he came in.

In the commissioner's office the next day, Lewis plays the tape and the arrest of Easter and his gang is ordered.

Walla and Ford return to their office in New York to await their next assignment.

WALLA-FORD

Concept for a television series

Based on the characters from

The Inside Man

By Jerry Schmetterer

There is a remarkable man named Jeff Ford. He is six-foot-seven-inches tall, looks like Eddie Murphy, and has no peers among the fast-talking con artists of the world.

When he was in his early twenties, Ford decided to use his steel nerves and fondness for danger to become a professional armed robber. He specialized in sticking up cab drivers. And he got caught.

He was facing forty years in prison when a detective named Ed Weiss realized that Jeff Ford was not your average stick-up man. He was too smart, too brave, and too willing to risk his own skin, to let waste away in prison. The detective thought that Ford was the right man to do him a very special favor. He asked Ford to make friends with an ex-cop in the same cell block who was being held on charges that he murdered his wife. This ex-cop was wise to the ways of law enforcement. He knew the cops would only have a solid case against him if he confessed, and so far that was something he declined to do. But Weiss thought that if Jeff Ford could gain the man's confidence then maybe, just maybe, he could get some kind of confession or admission of guilt out of him. And, according to the plan, his confession would be recorded on a secret tape recorder Jeff Ford would be wearing.

In return for this help the detective would pay him $50 a week and try to get Ford's sentence reduced.

Ford was successful. Over a period of weeks, he subtly gained the ex-cop's confidence. Both were avid checkers players and Ford, who considers himself one of the best in the world, let the murder suspect win. He let him win and he let him talk.

Ford pretended he was not the least interested in whatever his checker opponent had to say. Finally, the day came when the killer mentioned why he was in prison. And then Ford began his prodding; off-handedly asking questions until the moment came when the killer told Ford what he had done and bragged about how he would never be convicted. Ford recorded the whole thing and the ex-cop was eventually convicted on murder charges.

Ford got his reward—he was eventually sentenced to only four years in prison—and got a new start in life. He spent his entire prison stretch working undercover for the Department of Correction helping to nab crooked and even murderous prison guards, getting confessions and intelligence and all the while receiving his $50 a week salary—plus room and board of course.

During one of his assignments, the Department of Correction thought that Ford's life was in extreme danger and so assigned Correction Officer Dick Walla to keep a close eye on Ford to make sure that if he got in trouble he could be rescued.

Dick Walla is a recruiting poster image of a cop. He looks, acts, talks, and thinks exactly like the teachers in the police academy want their students to be.

To be exact, though, he is actually a Corrections Officer—prison guard-first cousin to a cop. He deals with criminals after the police have put them away.

Walla is as honest as the day is long, as truthful as he can be without hurting your feelings, and as dedicated to the basic values of the Constitution as is humanly possible. Though a little rumpled and weighty around the middle as he approaches fifty, he remains a man's man, father of the year, no nonsense guy. This is the guy you want to be in a foxhole with.

For twenty years Walla worked inside New York's prisons. He was a member of the elite CERT unit—Correction Emergency Response Team—called on for help when a jail was about to explode in riot. If you were a prisoner in a New York jail and you got out of hand, you had to deal with Dick Walla and his CERT buddies. Good luck.

When Walla retired, he, like so many ex-law-enforcement professionals, opened his own private detective agency. His desire: to continue to respond to trouble and solve problems, this time for big bucks.

He did the usual, hired a secretary, got an inexpensive office, and hired a bunch of people he could trust as uniformed security men. His bread and butter would come from that kind of service. But Walla had a trick up his sleeve. He knew he would be able to perform a service offered by no other agency and perhaps not available anywhere short of government intelligence services. He was bringing Jeff Ford, the inmate who had done so much brave and valuable undercover work inside New York's prisons, into his agency.

The two had worked together a few times and a trusting, father-son type relationship had developed between them. It would be the Walla–Ford Agency.

Walla and Ford became a fearless team. Ford went undercover in a variety of disguises and characters. One time they busted a ring of drug-dealing prison guards in Arizona. Another case found them cleaning up a notorious welfare hotel. They developed a reputation as a courageous, totally honest detective team. Their twist: only Walla is aware that Ford is an undercover agent. Walla watches everything from a distance, ready to come to his colleague's rescue if necessary. Usually they wind up their cases without even the client knowing an undercover detective was used. It is this method that enables Ford to survive.

He has come a long way from his days as a $50 a week undercover prison inmate, but without precise planning and split-second timing—and of course the complete dedication of Dick Walla—everything could end for Jeff Ford, very quickly.

A Novel Coverage

You will not be surprised to learn (I hope) that producers and other Hollywood executives don't actually read every word of all those books that they might be considering turning into film and TV properties. They rely on other readers to produce *coverage*, which is a summary of the book that provides the information needed to evaluate its screen potential.

The following is an example of film industry coverage of a novel. Fortunately, as you will see, this is excellent coverage and a movie deal was made based on it. Unfortunately, the movie has not been made yet, but my company is still working on it.

SAMPLE NOVEL COVERAGE

A MAJOR AGENCY

STORY DEPARTMENT COVERAGE

TITLE: THE BLACK MARIAH
AUTHOR: JAY BONANSINGA
GENRE: SUPERNATURAL SUSPENSE
TYPE/PAGES: NOVEL/463 PGS.
TIME/LOCALE: MID-1990'S/SOUTHERN AND MIDWEST U.S.,
    LOS ANGELES

SUBMITTED BY: PETER MILLER
STUDIO/NETWORK: N/A
PRODUCTION COMPANY: N/A
PUBLISHER: WARNER BOOKS, INC.

SUBMITTED FOR: PACKAGING

PRODUCER: N/A
DIRECTOR: N/A
TALENT: N/A
PROJECT STATUS: N/A

COVERAGE REQUESTED BY: A MAJOR AGENT

DATE: 5/3/93

READER: A PROFESSIONAL READER AT A MAJOR AGENCY

CONCEPT:

An African-American truck driver and his white, female partner go against their better judgment and help out a disturbed man on the road who claims he's been "cursed." After failing to save the man's life (moving along the freeway is the only way to stay alive), they desperately fight for their own lives as it seems that they've inherited the man's ailments. As they search for a spell to beat the curse they stay alive by continuing to move across the country at any cost.

SYNOPSIS

THE BLACK MARIAH: By Jay Bonansinga

LUCAS HYDE (late 30s, tall, handsome) a well-built African-American truck driver is driving across rural Georgia at night with his partner, SOPHIE COHEN (petite, darkly pretty, Jewish, mid-30s). They're driving Lucas' state-of-the-art truck called THE BLACK MARIAH on the front end of a delivery, and they don't have a job for their ride back to their homes in Los Angeles. It seems to be an ordinary night for the platonic partners when they hear a desperate voice calling himself MELVILLE BENOIT (African-American male, late 20s) on a CB radio. Melville tells the pair that he has been cursed by an elderly, racist witch, VANESSA DEGEAUX (89), who disapproved of his engagement to her white niece. His fiancée has been kidnapped, and not only is he looking for her, he has to keep driving because if he stops then the curse takes effect. Apparently, when he stops he feels excruciatingly burning pains. Thus, he asks Lucas and Sophie for a ludicrous favor: to fill up his gas tank while both vehicles are still moving. The disbelieving Lucas balks at first but after Sophie plays to weakness for betting and wages $200, he agrees.

They stop and get fuel at a truck stop and there they befriend ANGEL FIGUEROA (a disfigured Hispanic teenager), the only person who will give them a gas can that's perfect for their dangerous stunt. Angel, who has been listening to their bizarre conversation on the CB, offers Lucas his help. They accept. They're amusingly shocked when tens of other truckers cheer them and take bets as the gutsy trio exit the truck stop. Meanwhile, Deputy DELBERT MORRISON (late 20s), a thin, freckled, gung-ho cop, calls his boss SHERIFF DICK BAUM (40s, squat man, racist redneck), and tells him about the stunt that he's heard on the CB that's going to take place. On his way to the scene Baum sees a 1927 Rolls Royce limousine but then it disappears.

With Sophie driving, Angel and Lucas in the trailer manning the gas, and fellow truckers and police looking on, they attempt to pour gas into Melville's tank. They manage to get a little in before he speeds off and they get drenched with gasoline. After they find Melville on the side of the road a few miles ahead, they are shocked to see him combust right in front of their eyes on the woodside road. Among the fast food containers and the urine and feces in Melville's car, Lucas sees and grabs a shriveled, black hand. As Sheriff Baum approaches, Lucas sees and scares an elderly chauffeur, who races back into the woods.

Baum arrests Lucas, et al. but then releases them, against Delbert's warnings, because he's too lazy to do all the paperwork needed for the manslaughter charge he thinks they're guilty of. Meanwhile, ERIC KELSINGER (72, bad health, lanky), the chauffeur Lucas saw and the driver for Vanessa, has to tell her that he couldn't find the black hand that Lucas grabbed. Because she's too weak to talk, Vanessa expresses her rage at his failure to grab the talisman, the black hand that spreads the curse, by typing works onto a screen for Eric to see.

Angel, in the meantime, goes home to his UNCLE FLACO (72, tiny Hispanic man, gray-black hair, deeply lined face), who keeps a Catholic shrine to his late wife LOUISA. After the devout Catholic has a heart seizure, he recovers and notices that Jesus' left arm in the shrine has turned black. After Angel tells Flaco of his wild night and of Lucas' possession of the black hand, the good-hearted pair take Flaco's bus and try to catch Lucas and Sophie.

While driving west into Illinois, the chain smoking Sophie notices the eerie black hand that Lucas pilfered from Melville's car and asks Lucas to get rid of it. A believer in the unexplained since her friendship began with a hap, mystical RABBI MILO KLEIN in Berkeley, Sophie rightfully believes that the hand is a luck (good or bad?) charm of some sort. The no-nonsense Lucas, who has recurring nightmares about evil chauffeur drivers, refuses to believe. They pull off and decide to sell the hand at a pawn shop.

After doing some research, Delbert flies to the DeGeaux Estate in Alabama to verify any part of Lucas' and Melville's wild story. There the obese caretaker shows the deputy/amateur detective the DeGeaux family tomb, but they're shocked to find Vanessa's dead father's (MAURICE) tomb semi-open. Delbert's convinced the place is evil when he sees Maurice's right arm missing from his decayed body.

Vanessa bloodily kills a man after he attempts to steal the limo in the same town that she and Eric have followed Lucas to. After Lucas unsuccessfully tries to sell the hand in a small Illinois town, the curse takes its effect on the unsuspecting truck drivers. They double over in excruciating pain, act irrationally, vomit bile and feel as if their stomachs are on fire. They barely make it out on the road after Angel and Flaco show up and help them fill their gas. Just as the late Melville Benoit described, once they get back on the road their ailments go away. They contact Angel and Flaco on the CB and Flaco earns their trust when he tells them that he had a visionary warning about the curse before Angel told him of it. To everybody's chagrin, Lucas loses his temper and throws the black hand out the window.

Speaking in a deliberate, priest-like manner Flaco tells the truckers that he thinks they are in a battle against The Beast (Devil) and that the only way to fight it is with your heart. Lucas and Sophie need gas so they stop and Lucas sprints to fill the tank. The pain is worse and sparks and smoke emanate from the large trucker. With Angel's help they fill the tank but not before the gas station catches on fire and explodes. They get back on the highway but Lucas' hands are burned, his temples pound, and his lungs are "roasted." Taking illegal pills to kill the pain and stay awake, Lucas and Sophie continue driving.

Flaco and Angel put gas into a can and offer the couple to repeat their earlier stunt of gassing up while both vehicles move. The couple agrees to it, but when Angel slips and falls on the gas, Lucas grabs him and saves his life. However, by touching the cursed one—Lucas—Angel is now cursed himself.

Sheriff Baum, in the meantime, falsely believes that Lucas and Sophie are guilty of all the strange happenings in the last few days: the vandalized DeGeaux tomb, Melville's death, the gas station exploding. Baum and the federal police track down The Black Mariah and the long bus trailing it. Baum tells them over his P.A. system that they're under arrest and need to pull over. Lucas tries to tell the cop that he can't stop.

Baum calls Lucas a racist slur and gives way to the Feds. Flaco, however, uses his bus as interference and bumps the Fed's car when they start shooting bullets at the cursed trio. This MAD MAX scenario continues until Lucas sees a road block ahead that he goes right through. Before the Feds rain down bullets on Flaco and kill him, he crashed into them and the two cars explode. The Black Mariah jackknifes and crashes, and the other police cars are also damaged. The limo carrying Eric and Vanessa is the final part of this violent pileup; Eric is killed while Vanessa survives.

Lucas, Sophie, and Angel leave their truck behind, steal Baum's damaged police car, and keep moving westward. Though she is an invalid and her driver is dead, Vanessa is empowered by the Devil's hate and continues to drive after Lucas, et al. to torment them. Convinced that they have to find a cure for their ailment, Sophie uses the car phone and calls Rabbi Klein in Berkeley for advice. He is supportive and tells them about the vast resources of Jewish mysticism that he's drawing on for his advice. He tells them that a sacrifice is usually necessary to rid oneself of an evil curse.

A ghost in the demonic limo takes on all forms of beings as it taps into the fears of each cursed person. Then it magically disappears. As they cross from Missouri to Kansas they decide to try and hop into a moving train while driving the cop car. They drop Angel off at a rural train station and he kidnaps the good-natured conductor of a freight train and has him take a specific route that he and Lucas planned on. When they get there Lucas and Sophie dangerously, yet successfully, jump aboard. After Lucas and Sophie finally admit that they're attracted to each other, Lucas givers her some pills to sleep on. Angel, who's been keeping the conductor honest by putting a shotgun in his back, alerts Lucas to the fact that Vanessa is driving alongside the train. Lucas, tired of running his whole life and willing to make the <u>sacrifice</u> of his life to rid the curse, jumps into the caboose car and separates it from the rest of the train. He's inviting the demonic old woman to take him on. True to form, she inexplicably jumps into the slowing down caboose and physically torments him. While writhing from pain he wakes up and finds himself mysteriously lying in a rural southern field at night. There the ghost of MAURICE DEGEAUX (Vanessa's father) appears and beats Vanessa like he did on the day that he paralyzed her for kissing a little black boy. Apparently, Vanessa torments African-American males to this day for that reason.

Unlike the little boy that day, Lucas does not run away. Instead, he walks up to the ghost and screams at him to leave Vanessa alone and to go away. This breaks the curse and the ghost goes away. Lucas wakes up and finds himself in the burning caboose. Lucas, an ex-football player, athletically jumps out of the caboose. Just as it burst into flames, he sees a finally happy Vanessa (or possibly her ghost) dancing gaily on it. He lands hard on the ground but is alright. His hands and wounds are healed. Angel and Sophie stop the train and Lucas and Sophie embrace lovingly.

Angel, Sophie, and Lucas then turn themselves into the Colorado state authorities and with a plea of bargaining and a willingness to forget their outrageous story they were spared doing any prison time. They settle in Nevada where they have a son (who they name Flaco) and get married. They own a gas station which employs Angel and both Lucas and Sophie live happily in their new home with their newfound peace of mind. Lucas has finally stopped running.

EVALUATION

THE BLACK MARIAH: By Jay Bonansinga

COMMENTS: This novel entitled THE BLACK MARIAH reads like the truck it is named after. Once it gets going it's hard to stop, as this action-packed suspense story lumbers along with increasing speed and thrills. It has that rare distinction of possessing both lots of quick-paced, violent action and compelling subplots involving deeply textured characters.

These are characters that the reader can sink his/her teeth into; they are vividly—yet concisely—drawn, and hero and villain alike has a depth and three-dimensionality that is all-too-rare in fiction. Much of the characters' mettle, courage, hopes and, especially fears are illustrated through dialogue that is always believable and further serves to heighten the tension. Even at 463 pages, this story reads like a taut thriller that highly entertains while reflecting upon the different faces of America. Indeed, there is a large multicultural theme present, with the three main protagonists (one disfigured Hispanic, one African-American male, one Jewish woman) representing the U.S. diversity as much as the story's various settings and terrains (from L.A. to rural Georgia) do. All of this occurs in a scenario which contains a mixture of elements that recalls Spielberg's DUEL and more recently, THE ROAD WARRIOR.

Furthermore, THE BLACK MARIAH works on many levels. While the action entertains, the more esoteric issues of responsibility, conquering one's own fears, and peace of mind are explored. And while the novel's bizarre denouement depicting the disabled white woman tormenting Lucas stretches plausibility of taut dramatic tension to make a compelling drama with definite cinematic possibilities.

	Excellent	Good	Fair	Pass
Dialogue	X			
Characterization	X			
Plot Line	X			
Story Structure	X			

Recommend __X__   Consider _____   Pass _____

KEY LEADS

THE BLACK MARIAH: By Jay Bonansinga

LUCAS HIDE- late 30s, goatee, handsome African-American male, big man, a truck driver with a good heart, intelligent, nearing bankruptcy, expert on black R&B music, attracted to his female, Jewish partner.

SOPHIE COHEN- Jewish, liberal, woman, mid-30s, pretty, dark hair, brown eyes, from rich parents, college educated, independent, tomboyish, smart.

MELVILLE BENOIT- late 20s, African-American who's been cursed to keep moving or die, desperate, fell in love with white girl whose racist aunt put curse on him.

VANESSA DEGEAUX- a racist witch (literally), 89, paralyzed from abuse from her Satan worshipping father, puts curse on Melville and Lucas, puts curse on black men, speaks with CompuTalk machine while being chauffeured around in an old limousine, deformed looking.

SHERIFF DICK BAUM- squat little man, no neck, square jawed redneck, mid 40s, chews tobacco, Sheriff of Pennington County gets killed when his roadblock of Lucas' runaway truck goes awry.

ANGEL FIGUEROA- Hispanic, works at a truck stop, 19, has deformed face from a congenital birth defect, has intelligence and passion, abused by most because of his face, Lucas and Sophie befriend him.

ERIC KELSINGER- over 6 feet tall, 72, lanky and big-boned, drives Vanessa round in the limo, has doubts about his evil chores for the witch.

DELBERT MORRISON- late 20s, gung ho Deputy to Sheriff Baum, rail thin, freckled, too earnest, amateur detective.

FLACO FIGUEROA- 72, Angel's uncle, tiny man, dark hair dusted with gray, deeply lined face, devout Catholic, has a shrine of his late wife Louisa in his "house" (a school bus), follows Lucas across the Midwest freeway to help beat the "devil" that's cursed him.

Appendixes

Book Publishing Glossary
Film Industry Glossary
Resources

Book Publishing Glossary

Advance:

> A payment made by a publisher to an author upon the signing of a contract and/or delivery of a manuscript. It is a payment against the author's royalties that will be recouped by the publisher out of sales earnings. After the advance "earns out" (a term defined below), additional royalties are paid to the author according to a publisher's royalty payment schedule, usually on a biannual basis.

Amazon blast:

> A technique where the author or publisher arranges for a promotional company to organize an e-mail campaign about a book that will go out in a short period to as many as one million people, and often to specially targeted audiences. This is intended to propel sales of the book up to the number one or two slot on the Amazon.com charts for a day or two. Being able to say that the book achieved such a high ranking can then be used to further promote the book and the author's career.

Advance reading copy (ARC) / Bound galley:

> A promotional copy of the book by the publisher, sometimes with cover art and/or quotes about the author and his work, and sometimes plain. If the ARC is for a book by a famous author, it will likely become a collectible.

Auction:

This occurs when a representative orchestrates the presentation of an author's work to a group of publishers and arranges a bid war. This is what an author—and his or her representative—dreams of.

Basketed accounting / Joint accounting:

An accounting practice by publishers in which more than one book is joined in one account. When books are basketed, if one does really well and the other does really poorly it can prevent the author from getting earnings, even from a successful book.

Bells and whistles / Bonuses / Performance bonuses:

These are terms for deal points in the author's favor that can be added to a contract during a successful negotiation. An agent or other type of representative who is doing his or her job well can negotiate such things as a bonus for making a *New York Times* bestseller list, or an escalation of royalties as book sales increase. Other terms might retain large-print rights, or negotiate better splits in the author's favor such as book clubs. The best possible author terms are those called "bells and whistles."

Blurbs / Endorsements:

These are quotes or notices that other authors and various famous (and not so famous) people write to praise a book. They are usually found on publishers' catalogue pages, on book jackets, on the first few pages of a book, and in book ads.

Copyright:

The U.S. Copyright Office is located in Washington, D.C., and it is the government agency where nearly all books are registered and afforded a copyright registration number to protect the author or other rightful owner of a book.

As discussed in Chapter 15, authors should take steps to protect the copyright of their manuscripts (at a minimum, writing the word "Copyright," the year, and your name on the first page). When a book is about to be published, its publisher will usually be responsible for applying for an official copyright.

Earn out:

The situation where the amount of royalties due to an author from sales revenues or subsidiary rights reaches the level of the advance paid by a publisher. It is only after this point that the author will be sent further royalties. All authors' books should earn out their advances, though this is certainly not always the case.

First proceeds:

A term used in a publishing contract whereby if the book is not accepted by the first publishing company, then the author has the right to resell to another publisher and repay the first publisher with the first proceeds on the sale of the book to the other publisher.

Floor:

When a publisher negotiates with an author the privilege to have the beginning bid in an eventual auction to publish a future book, or books. Terms and conditions vary based on the particular negotiation, and such negotiations can include closing, or topping, terms.

Flow-through:

When certain subsidiary rights are licensed on a book and the author's advance has earned out, an author's representative may be able to negotiate the right to have any such subsidiary rights income "flow through" to the author faster than waiting for a normal biannual accounting from the publisher.

Freight pass-through:
> A contractual term where the publisher has the right to deduct no more than five percent of the retail sale price from sales of the book to "pass through" shipping charges of the book.

Genre fiction:
> Novels that are primarily plot-driven and fall into one of several recognized categories, such as romance, mystery, horror, etc. These works seek only to provide entertainment, generally follow familiar conventions, and have well-established markets.

Literary fiction:
> Novels that are primarily character-driven and distinguished by writing of extremely high quality. These books do not necessarily fall into recognized categories, and they often explore complex themes, with the intention not only of entertaining the reader, but also of providing insight into the human condition.

Marketing plan:
> A developed strategy that shows the variety of ways that an author or publisher can promote a book. Most marketing plans include a comparison to similar books already on the market and an analysis of the demographics of the expected audience. Marketing plans have been normally required for nonfiction proposals, but fiction authors are also starting to include them when pitching their book(s).

Net royalty:
> This is the royalty that is calculated by publishers on what is called the "net amount," after they deduct any discount that they may give to certain buyers of the book such as Barnes and Noble, Amazon.com, wholesalers, or discount stores such as Sam's Club or Costco.

New York Times bestseller list:
There are roughly 3,300 bookstores in America that report to *New York Times* Bestseller List. Each bookstore calculates the number of books being sold versus the velocity at which they sell, and adding these factors determines how a book is positioned on the list. This is the most important list in the publishing world, and once a book gets on the list it usually stays on for a long time.

Option:
When the publisher keeps the rights to offer to publish the author's next book under terms of "negotiation in good faith." Sometimes this can be good for the author's career, though sometimes it is better to work with other publishers on different projects.

Platform:
An author's platform is the measure of how established he or she is in the media. Examples of a platform are a magazine or newspaper column, a radio or television show, e-zines, Web journalism, newsletters, speaking and lecture circuit presence, and celebrity. More often than not, publishers are now insisting that authors have a platform, particularly on nonfiction books.

Pitch letter:
A letter or e-mail that a representative sends out to publishers to sell a book. A pitch letter will include a brief synopsis, author biography, and the book's marketability. Pitch "letters" can also happen over the phone.

Pre-empt:
When a publisher aggressively pursues a book, offering a deal that is too good to pass up. This prevents the book from going out to other publishers and causes a contract to be agreed to "in a pre-empt."

Pseudonym / Nom de plume:

When an author chooses to write a book under a different name, such as Samuel Clemens, who wrote under the name Mark Twain. Many authors have chosen to use different or false names throughout their careers, such as John le Carre, whose real name is David Cornwell. Some authors publish only certain of their books under a pseudonym, usually either for books in a genre outside what they usually write, or because they simply are writing too many books for the market to handle. An example of the latter is Stephen King, who has published several novels under the name Richard Bachman.

Reserve against returns:

This is a way for publishers to ensure that they don't overpay an author for all books sold on commission to a bookstore. Bookstores return any books that are not selling to publishers, and an author would then be overpaid if he or she had already been paid royalties for such books. Publishers keep reserve against returns to prevent this from happening. Different publishers have different policies on this practice.

Retail royalty:

This is a royalty calculated on the retail sale price of the book. Sometimes royalties can be calculated after no more than 5 percent of the freight pass through (defined above) is deducted. Retail royalties are usually paid on hardcover and trade paper, on mass market and variety copies depending on the kind of publisher, and, depending on the contract terms, they can often go up with an increase in the volume of the sale of the book.

Right of first refusal:

When a publisher maintains the exclusive right to look at an author's next work before any other publisher has. This is similar to an option, and the terms and conditions are negotiated.

Royalty escalation / Royalty ladder:

There are three kinds of royalties: Hardcover/Cloth, Trade Paperback, and Mass Market. Usually royalties are divided into two categories, Retail or Net. When a good representative is negotiating for an author, he or she will attempt to escalate the royalties. For example, standard hardcover royalties may begin at 10 percent for the first 5,000 copies, 12.5 percent for the next 5,000 copies, and then 15 percent thereafter. From my own experience, I just negotiate a straight 15 percent deal and eliminate a royalty ladder. Trade Paperback usually begins at 7.5 percent, but some publishers will allow a representative to negotiate an escalation. A 10 percent royalty in Trade Paperback is excellent. Mass Market royalties typically begin at 8 percent on the first 150,000 copies and 10 percent thereafter. However, some publishers will go as high as 12.5 percent.

Special sales clause:

When the publisher has the right to reduce the royalty to the author on sales of high discount, sometimes up to 60 percent of the retail price of the book at places such as Sam's Club, Costco, and other large company and department stores.

Subsidiary rights:

Any rights that are licensed by a publisher. These rights include UK rights and other foreign/translation rights; audio, motion picture, television and dramatic rights; e-book, electronic/multimedia; large print; book club; first and second serial rights; and others.

Topping:

When a publisher who has suggested a floor (defined above) has the right to top other offers by beating pre-negotiators by paying a greater amount (perhaps 5 to 10 percent higher) of their bid.

Two book / Three book / Series deal:
A situation where a publisher wants to guarantee its future with a particular author and negotiates a multiple book deal.

Viral marketing:
A style of Internet marketing that spreads throughout the World Wide Web. This can be done with e-mail blasts, banners, Web sites, and press releases.

Film Industry Glossary

Above the line:
> *See* Below the line

AFTRA:
> The American Federation of Television and Radio Artists, the union that represents performers for work in radio and television.

Adjusted Gross Profit (AGP):
> This is a type of profit definition that can be negotiated. Such negotiations will detail and limit the deductions, if any, that a studio, network, production company, or distributor can make that will reduce any artist's profits. The success of such negotiations is contingent on the status of the artist.

Adjusted Net Profit (ANP):
> Like AGP, this is a type of profit definition that is negotiated and details the deductions a studio, network, production company, or distributor can make and reduce any artist's profits. Gross, or AGP, are the best definitions of profits to have in an artist's contract.

Agency vs. Manager:
> The main difference between an agent and a manager in Hollywood terms is that an agent can't produce, while a manager can. Also, literary managers can legally negotiate contracts for their clients, but talent managers are not supposed to.

American Film Market (AFM):

The AFM is a consortium of film distributors, studios, and film sales reps that meet annually at the AFM convention in Santa Monica, California.

Art director:

The person who designs the sets on a film or television production.

Back end:

A situation in which there is a profit participation for an artist. Frequently, prominent actors and directors will take less money up front and more on the back end.

Below the line:

There is a (sometimes) imaginary line on the first page of a film budget, separating the artistic elements of the budget from the technical elements. The artistic elements (writer, producer, director, actors) are listed above the line and the technical elements (crew, equipment costs, etc.) are listed below it. For the sake of brevity, expenses are often referred to as "above-the-line" or "below-the-line."

Blocking:

Working out the physical movements of performers and/or the camera in a scene.

Breakdown:

A list of all roles in a production, from largest to smallest, with a description of each character. This includes, for the smaller roles, how many scenes and lines each character has.

Call:

The exact time at which an actor or crew member is to report to a set.

Camera left / Camera right:

Directions given from the camera's point of view. Opposite of STAGE LEFT and STAGE RIGHT, which are given from the actor's point of view. May also be called LEFT FRAME and RIGHT FRAME.

Character arc:

This is when a certain character's role is expanded and developed; it is particularly used in television series. The story line then develops other characters and creates arcs for them as well.

Character-driven:

A quality of a script where the protagonists and antagonists are larger than life and drive the story line more than the plot does.

Close-up:

A person or object, or any part of a person or object, that is seen at close range and framed tightly. As camera directions, EXTREME CLOSE-UP (ECU) is from the bottom of the chin to the hairline (also called a 'cowboy close-up'). CLOSE-UP (CU) is head-and-shoulders. MEDIUM CLOSE-UP (MCU) is below the shoulders to above the head. Also called a "TWO-T" shot.

Commencement of principal photography:

The specific date when a film actually goes into production and cameras start rolling. This date triggers major payments to authors whose work has been optioned, and usually purchase price payments are triggered with commencement. This date is also meaningful to the director, producers, and almost everyone involved with a production because this is when everyone goes on the payroll.

Continuity:

A very important part of film making, this is the process of ensuring that the visual aspects of a production are consistent from one take to the next. The continuity person often takes Polaroid snapshots of principals and featured extras in a scene in order to check later for inconsistencies.

Cover:

To photograph a scene from many angles (*coverage*). Or, to get between another actor and the camera (*covering*).

Crew:

The technicians in a production. Typically everyone but the producer, director, and actors.

Cue:

The actions or words that precede an actor's words or actions. "Pick up your cues," means to perform the action quicker after receiving your cue.

Dailies:

Also called "rushes," these are the previous day's scenes, processed overnight by the lab and screened after work the next day by the producer, director, and crew heads. Actors are not generally invited to view dailies.

Development hell:

I unfortunately have been in this hell too often. This is when a studio or network prolongs the development process for a film production.

Dialogue director:

The person who reviews lines with actors to ensure memorization, interpretation, and/or dialect. May be called a Dialogue Coach if that is his or her only function. A Dialogue Director is a comparatively rare position.

Director:
The person responsible to the producer for translating the screenplay into images and sounds. He or she directs the cast and crew from pre- through post-production.

Director of photography:
The DP is responsible to the director for achieving the optimum image on film. He or she selects the camera and lighting equipment and supervises camera and lighting crews for each shot.

Directors Guild of America (DGA):
The union that represents directors, assistant directors, and production managers.

Dissolve:
A scene that slowly fades to the next scene. If a scene is planned to dissolve, the actor may be asked to hold the last look.

Dolly:
A four-wheeled camera support that can move on the ground or on tracks. The word is also used as a verb, meaning to move the camera on a dolly. The dolly can be a sophisticated piece of equipment or something as mundane as a wheelchair.

Dubbing:
Also called "looping," this is recording a voice in synch with a film image. Generally, "dubbing" refers to using a different voice, as an actor dubbing English onto a foreign film, and "looping" refers to an actor re-doing his own voice due to poor sound quality on the original.

Establishing shot:
Usually a long shot orienting the audience to a new location, such as a shot of a building before cutting to the interior.

Executive producer:

If there is one, this person is usually responsible for the financing on feature films—either he or she puts up their own money or else finds the investors. In television, the Executive Producer is usually the most important producer on the production.

Fade in / Fade up / Fade out:

Going from black to picture and vice-versa.

Foreground:

Whatever is between the camera and the subject of the picture.

Frame:

The viewing area as seen by the camera.

Follow shot:

A shot in which the camera moves to follow the action.

Green-light:

The point at which a studio, network, production company, or distributor authorizes a film production to move immediately forward. Sometimes, films are green-lit, cast or star contingent, meaning that the studio is ready to move forward once they approve the star.

Gross profits (GP):

A profit definition that begins with *all* profits. Only major stars like Jack Nicholson, Mel Gibson, Tom Cruise, Clint Eastwood, Julia Roberts, Sandra Bullock, John Travolta, or directors like Steven Spielberg, Ridley Scott, George Lucas, or James Cameron can command this kind of participation from dollar one of gross box office.

Guild scale:

Certain guilds, like the WGA (Writers Guild of America), the DGA (Directors Guild of America), and SAG (Screen Actors

Guild), have minimal payments that are due to artists, and these are stipulated in their underlying basic agreements. Most major studios, networks, and productions companies are signatories to these organizations.

High concept:
Films like *Top Gun* or *The Terminator* or even TV series like *CSI* are perfect examples of high concept. It is when the basic premise is usually filled with action, and is the opposite of character driven.

Housekeeping deal:
When a producer, production company, actor, or director is afforded a certain deal with a studio or network where specific terms are negotiated for eventual productions; in many cases, certain overhead costs are paid for by the network or studio.

In the can:
A scene that has been filmed to the satisfaction of the director and is therefore considered to be complete.

Indie:
Companies, such as producers or distributors, that are not part of a major entertainment conglomerate like Warners/NewLine, Disney, Paramount/Viacom, Sony, Fox/NewsCorp, et al.

Letter of commitment:
This is when a studio, network, or production company makes a legal commitment to proceed with an acquisition of a property or the securing of an artist's services.

Location:
The overall working area where filming is taking place. See *Set*.

Looping:
See *Dubbing*.

Low concept:

This is normally the opposite of high concept and relates to more character-driven material.

Names attached:

This is when an actor or other talent such as a director or composer allows their name to be used in packaging or financing.

Net profits (NP):

This is a definition of profits that is rarely negotiated; it details the laundry list of all deductions a studio, network, production company, or distributor can make and reduce any and all of an artist's chance of profits.

Note: The difference between "gross profit" and "net profit" is "no profit."

Network deal:

When a production company or a television production division of a studio has a pre-negotiated deal in place with a network to supply a certain amount of programming to the network.

No profits:

When an artist only works for a fee and has no profit participation, not even a generally meaningless net profit.

Option to purchase:

When a buyer advances a certain amount of money against the purchase price of a literary property for a certain amount of time to develop the property. The property can be a book, script, treatment, newspaper or magazine article, short story, song, life rights or group of life rights, or any combination of any of these.

Output deal / Put deal:

This is when a studio, network, production company, or distributor has guaranteed a production company a certain amount of productions; no matter what happens, they are obligated to pay for productions or at least pay the producing and artists fees that have been guaranteed. Companies often do this to secure the exclusive right to work with artists.

Packaging / Attaching talent, etc., to a script:
This is when one or more talent or financing elements are added to a property. This could be an actor, director, producer, or a pre-sale on financial investment. A common question in Hollywood is "What is the package?"

Pay and play:
When a studio, network, production company, or distributor guarantees payment of fees and credit on a production.

Pay or play:
When a studio, network, production company, or distributor guarantees payment of fees but does not have to guarantee credit on a production if they do not require the artist's services on the actual production.

Pitch meeting:
This is when an agent or manager arranges for a writer and/ or producer to present an idea by way of a verbal pitch of a film to a buyer. This meeting could be followed with a treatment, script, or manuscript, or a deal could be concluded just based on the success of the meeting.

Pitch season:
Networks have certain periods of time when new series concepts can be pitched. This usually occurs after the pilots for an upcoming season have already been ordered. A good time to pitch is June, as all the fall pilots have already been ordered.

Points:
This refers to actual percentage points that an artist earns vis-à-vis their negotiated profit participation.

Production company vs. Studio (umbrella deal):

Many production companies are independent of studios; they make movies independently and then license them to a studio for distribution. Studios may produce and distribute films that are made by production companies with a studio deal in place.

Pre-sales:

This is when certain territories, as in foreign markets, DVD, TV, or cable rights, are licensed prior to a production in order to help fund it.

Pre-production start date:

This is the official date that a studio, network, production company, or distributor authorizes the commencement of pre-production, which is the amount of time necessary to ready a film production. The size and scope of the production will dictate the length of time this phase will take. In the instance of a movie made for TV, for example, it may be as little as a month. Frequently, studios have already scouted the locations and decided on a budget for a picture before they announce pre-production.

Producer:

The person in overall command of the production from pre- through post-production and release. He hires everyone, and has ultimate creative and budgetary control over the project.

Production designer:

The person who establishes the "look" of the production. He or she conceives, plans, and supervises the overall visual design of the production.

Production manager:

The person who assembles the budget, organizes the shooting schedule, and authorizes expenditures. He or she may have an assistant and several secretaries.

Property master:
Responsible for the inventory and maintenance of all properties (props).

Readers:
These people evaluate material for producers, studios, networks, or production companies. If they have actual jobs at a company and are not freelance, they are referred to as "D" people, or development employees.

Rushes:
See *Dailies.*

Scene:
A portion of a script that has been given its own number.

Screen Actors Guild (SAG):
The union that represents actors for film, television, and commercials.

Script supervisor:
This person takes detailed notes, recorded in the script, of all production information; this includes the scene and take number, camera position, performance continuity, dialogue changes, and running time of each shot.

Set:
The location where filming takes place, either indoors or outdoors. The set is where the camera is, as opposed to the "location," which is the overall working area. There may be several "sets" at one "location."

Set-up:
Each new camera angle, especially when lighting must be moved.

SFX:
Special effects, sometimes called "FX."

Shot:

Whatever the camera is seeing. In a script, LONG SHOT (LS) is anything shot from a distance with a wide field of vision (head-to-toe of a person). MEDIUM SHOT (MS) is waist-up. TWO SHOT is generally a medium or closer shot of two people.

Slate:

A flat board, previously a chalkboard but now a digital clock with a writing surface, containing letters and numbers identifying the production and scene. Also called *sticks, clapboard,* and *marker.* The two sticks fastened to the top of the slate are snapped together at the top of each take, and the "click" is used to synchronize the audio and the video. *Second sticks* are called for whenever the camera or sound misses the marker the first time. Occasionally, the slate is put at the end of the scene (a *tail slate*) and the marker is turned upside-down.

Sound mixer:

Selects and operates the recording equipment. He or she mixes (balances) the various microphones for optimum dialogue reproduction. Also keeps the paperwork.

Story board:

A series of sketches showing each shot of a scene or film in order, with dialogue and scene number underneath. Used to plot the shooting economically.

Studio deal:

When a production company has a pre-negotiated deal in place with a studio. Different deals have different terms where the studios may pay certain overhead expenses and/or salaries and additionally allow the company certain monies for financing the development of films.

Talent:

A term that refers to all above-the-line personnel, but specifically to the actors. Sometimes this term is used by agents and casting directors to mean "actors."

Tilt:

Vertical camera movement.

Trades:

The newspapers that address the film industry.

Trailer:

A preview of coming attractions (not everything in the trailer is necessarily in the film). A trailer is sometimes used as a selling tool to raise funding for a feature film.

Treatment:

A synopsis of a film idea, relating most details of the story through present-tense action and no dialogue. A treatment is usually five to thirty pages in length, and it can be copyrighted.

Voice-on-camera (VOC):

A scene in which an actor speaks a line while the camera is on him.

Voice-over (VO):

A scene where an actor speaks a line while the camera is not on him. Commercials, both radio and television, often utilize voice-overs.

Video:

The picture portion of a production. In film it's actually called *picture*.

Wrap:

The completion of a workday, or of work at a particular location, or of work on the whole production. A *wrap party* is a party celebrating completion of a production. You could say that this definition serves as the "wrap" for this glossary.

Resources

BOOKS

Adventures in the Screen Trade by William Goldman (Warner)

Making a Good Script Great by Linda Seger (Samuel French)

The Writer's Journey: Mythic Structure for Writers by Christopher Vogler (Michael Wiese Productions)

The following guides and directories are all updated regularly:

Literary Market Place (LMP) (Information Today). A hefty volume that is the standard directory for the publishing industry. As it costs about 300 bucks, you can look at a copy at your local library.

Jeff Herman's Guide to Book Publishers, Editors, & Literary Agents (Writer, Inc.)

Guide to Literary Agents by Katie Brogan (Writer's Digest Books)

Writer's Market (Writer's Digest Books)

Hollywood Creative Directory This directory of entertainment industry professionals is known as "the phone book of Hollywood." An online subscription version is available at *www.hcdonline.com.*

PUBLICATIONS

PublishersLunch. This daily e-mail newsletter gives summaries and links for stories on books and book publishing from throughout the media. It also provides a widely read listing each week of deals made in the book industry (including the names and sometimes the e-mail addresses of the agents and editors involved). You can subscribe to this newsletter at the PublishersMarketplace Web site *(www.publishersmarketplace.com)*. Signing up for a paid subscription gives you access to broader and more detailed content.

Publishers Weekly. This weekly magazine covers the book industry from the perspective of publishers and editors. Its back section carries numerous reviews of upcoming books in all genres. On the Web at *www.publishersweekly.com*.

Writer's Digest. This monthly magazine has articles, tips, and listings of various markets to sell your work. Their Web site is at *www.writersdigest.com*.

Variety. This show business bible has daily, weekly, and online versions that you can subscribe to at *www.variety.com*.

The Hollywood Reporter. This daily entertainment trade publication also has a subscription-based Web site at *www.thehollywoodreporter.com*.

WEB SITES

The Book Standard—*www.thebookstandard.com*
This Web site contains numerous articles with the latest news on the book publishing industry; it also includes resources and reviews. A subscription is required to access some material.

Amazon.com—*www.amazon.com*

Barnes & Noble—*www.barnesandnoble.com*

These bookselling sites can be very useful in your research to find what books are already out there on your chosen topic.

U.S. Copyright Office—*www.copyright.gov*

Index

A

above-the-line costs, 106
Accidental Millionaire, The
  (Butchner), proposal for,
  141–63
Acevedo, Mario, 27–28
adjusted gross profit (AGP), 287
adjusted net profit (ANP), 287
advance reading copies (ARCs),
  279
advances, 279
agents/managers
  agents vs. managers, 29, 287
  vs. attorneys, 87–88
  choosing between, xx, 29–30
  contracts with, 39
  for fiction, 61–62
  for film and television
    industries, 84–87
  finding, 23–29
  gaining attention of, 13
  Hollywood, 36, 79–80
  negotiations by, 125–28
  New York, 36
  query letters to, 9–10
  relationship between authors
    and, 33–34, 40–41, 51
  researching, 86
  ways to meet, 26–28
  working with, 31–41
Amazon blast, 279
American Federation of
  Television and Radio Artists
  (AFTRA), 287
American Film Market (AFM),
  288
art directors, 288
attorneys, 87–88, 127
auctions, 7, 280
authors
  See also writers
  becoming a successful,
    xvi–xxii
  confidence needed by, xviii,
    7–8
  dealing with criticism, 62–67
  editors and, 34
  financial rewards for, 6
  platforms of, 5, 283
  relationship between agent
    and, 33–34, 40–41, 51

B

back-door pilots, 255
back end, 288
basketed accounting, 280
Beating the Odds (Marchetti),
  proposal for, 223–34
bells and whistles, 280
below-the-line financing, 106,
  288
biographies, 53–54
biography proposal (sample),
  141–63
Black Mariah, The (Bonansinga),
  novel coverage for, 267–76
blocking, 288
blurbs, 280

305

bonuses, 280
book business. *See* publishing industry
book ideas, evaluating, 12–15
book proposals. *See* proposals
books
    See also fiction; nonfiction books
    entertainment value of, 13–14
    with film potential, 58
    optioned but not made into films, 103
    optioning rights to, 133–34
    promotion of, 6–7
    publishers' decision about publishing, 5–6
bound galleys, 279
breakdown, 288
Bugliosi, Vincent, 120, 239
business books, 53
Butcher, Lee, 141, 163

C

cable television, 118–21
calls, 288
camera left/right, 289
Carlson, Richard, 46–47
Catch-22, 96–97
character arcs, 289
character-driven scripts, 289
Chick Lit, 60–61
children, as primary audience, 99
close-ups, 289
commencement of principal photography, 289
confidence, xviii, 7–8
conglomerates, 3–4
continuity, 290
contracts, 39, 123–38
    flow-through clauses in, 126–27
    negotiating, 125–28, 134–38
    and rights, 133–34
    sample, 128–31
cookbook proposal, 211–18
co-production financing, 106
copyright, 134, 280–81
corporate mergers, 3–4
cover, 290
coverage, novel, 267–76
crew, 290
criticism, dealing with, 62–67
cue, 290
Curtis, Christopher, 181, 188

D

dailies, 290
deal memo (sample), 128–31
deal negotiation, 133–38
DeStefano, Anthony, 26
Detz, Joan, 219
development deals, 97–98
development hell, 290
dialogue directors, 290
director of photography, 291
directors, 104–5, 291
Directors Guild of America (DGA), 291
dissolve, 291
dolly, 291
dramatic series, proposal for, 255–66
dramaturgy, 89–91
dubbing, 291

E

earn out, 281
editorial board meetings, 5–6
editors
    agents and, 32–33

authors and, 34
gaining attention of, 13
elevator pitches, 27–28
e-mail attachments, 18, 49
endorsements, 280
episodic TV, 95, 118
See also television series
Errors and Omissions Policies, 91
establishing shots, 291
executive producers, 292

F

fade in/out/up, 292
faith in self, xviii, 7–8
Fatal Freeway (Salerno), proposal for, 165–79
fiction, 59–67
See also novels
categories of, 59–60
choosing agent and publisher for, 61–62
dealing with criticism and writing, 62–67
rewrites, 63–64
sample proposal for, 235–38
trends in, 60–61
film industry, xxi–xxii
See also Hollywood
advice about, 108–9
contracts, 123–38
development deals, 97–98
financing in, 106–8
novel coverage for, 267–76
players in, 77–81
as relationship business, 29, 121
royalties, 127–28
similarities between publishing industry and, 112

success stories, 89
trends in, 98–100
film options, not exercised, 103
film potential, writing books with, 58
film production, costs of, 102–3
film rights, 84, 89–90, 133–34
film studios, 80, 296
financing, for films, 106–8
first proceeds, 281
first-time novels, 9–11
floor, 281
flow-through clauses, 281
follow shots, 292
foreground, 292
foreign markets, 62
foreign rights, 127
frames, 292
freight pass-through, 282

G

genre fiction, 14, 282
Gilmore, Christopher Cook, 38
green-light, 292
gross profits (GP), 292
Guide To Book Publishers, Editors, & Literary Agents (Herman), 24
Guide to Literary Agents (Writer's Digest), 24
guild scale, 292–93
Guste, Roy, 211–12, 218

H

health book proposal, 223–34
Helter Skelter, 96
high concept, 293
historical fiction, 61

Hollywood, 36
See also film industry;
television industry
advice about, 108–9
choosing representative for,
84–87
contracts, 123–38
deal negotiation in, 133–38
do's and don'ts, 135–38
financing in, 106–8
package deals in, 101–9
players in, 77–81
realities of, 83–100
as relationship business, 29,
121
hooks, 13
housekeeping deal, 293
how-to book proposal, 219–22
*How to Write and Give Great
Speeches* (Detz), proposal for,
219–22

I

indies, 293
Inside Man, The (Schmetterer),
120
proposal for, 255–66
in the can, 293

J

joint accounting, 280
joke books, 56–57

L

letters of commitment, 293
literary auctions, 7, 280
literary fiction, 282

literary managers. *See* agents/
managers
literary marketplace
researching, for nonfiction
books, 44–46
understanding, xix, 14–15
location, 293
looping. *See* dubbing
Los Angeles. *See* Hollywood
low concept, 294

M

Mac Tactics Volume One (Wiser
and Curtis), proposal for,
181–210
managers
See also agents/managers
vs. agents, 29, 287
manuscripts
handwritten, 18
neatness of, 19–20
one-page synopsis of, 10
pagination of, 19–20
preparing for submission,
xix–xx, 17–21
protocol for, 17–20
Marchetti, Albert, 223
marketing
See also promotion
screenplays, 111–16
viral, 286
marketing plans, 282
mass appeal, 13–14
miniseries, 95–96
movie industry. *See* film industry;
Hollywood

N

names attached, 294
net profits (NP), 294

net royalty, 282
network deals, 294
networking, 37
New Orleans Creole Cookery (Guste), proposal for, 211–18
New York, 24, 36
New York Times bestseller list, 283
nom de plums, 284
nonfiction books, 43–58
  biographies, 53–54
  business books, 53
  film and television potential of, 58
  fitting into market, 50–51
  pop culture, 54–55
  proposals for, 11, 46–50
  religious books, 55
  researching market for, 44–46
  specialty books, 56–57
  sports books, 52
  true-crime books, 55–56
  types of, 43, 51–57
no profits, 294
novels
  See also fiction
  adapting for screenplays, 88–91
  coverage of, 267–76
  editing, 63–64
  proposals for, 9–11

O

off-network syndication, 120–21
options, 283
option to purchase, 294
output deals, 294–95

P, Q

package deals, 101–9
  advice about, 108–9

financing and, 106–8
  role of story in, 103–6
packagers, 107–8
packaging, xxi, 295
pay and play, 295
pay or pay, 295
performance bonuses, 280
Perry, Roland, 7–8
persistence, xviii
Pickett, Rex, 105–6
pigeonholing, 14
pitch letters, 283
pitch meetings, 295
pitch season, 295
platforms, 5, 283
points, 295
pop culture, 54–55
Power of Breakthrough (Sayle and Kumar), 50–51
pre-empt, 283
pre-production start date, 296
pre-sales, 296
producers, 81, 103–4, 296
production companies, 80, 103–4, 296
production costs, 106
production designers, 296
production managers, 296
profit participation clauses, 127–28
promotion
  of fiction, 62
  importance of, 6–7
property masters, 297
proposals
  addressing needs in, 46–47
  biography proposal (sample), 141–63
  cookbook proposal (sample), 211–18
  creating a sellable, 9–15

proposals, continued
  developing, 11
  fiction proposal (sample),
    235–38
  health book proposal
    (sample), 223–34
  how-to book proposal
    (sample), 219–22
  neatness of, 19–20
  nonfiction, 11, 46–50
  for novels, 9–11
  presentation of, xix–xx, 17–21
  self-help/relationship book
    proposal (sample), 181–210
  synopsis in, 10
  for television series (sample),
    239–53
  true-crime book proposal
    (sample), 165–79
  for TV movie (sample), 255–66
pseudonyms, 284
publishers, choosing between, 62
publishing industry
  breaking into, 12–15
  changes in, 4–5
  decision-making in, 5–6
  finding a place in, 6–7
  mergers in, 3–4
  realities of, xvii, 3–8
  royalties in, 125–27
  similarities between film
    industry and, 112
  understanding, xix
put deals, 294–95
query letters, 9–10
See also proposals

R

readers, 297
rejection, xviii, 120

religious books, 55
representatives. *See* agents/
  managers
research, on marketplace, 44–46
reserve against returns, 284
retail royalty, 284
rewrites, 63–64
right of first refusal, 284
rights, optioning, 133–34
Robinson, Jennifer, 63
Rosenberg, Nancy Taylor, 69–73
royalties, 125–28
  net, 282
  retail, 284
royalty escalation, 285
royalty ladder, 285
rushes. *See* dailies

S

Salerno, Steven, 165, 179
scene, 297
Schmetterer, Jerry, 120, 255
Screen Actors Guild (SAG), 297
screenplays
  marketing, 111–16
  as part of package, 108
  rewrites of, 112–13
  selling, xxi–xxii, 88–89
  spec scripts, 113
  vs. treatments, 114
  turning into novels, xxi–xxii
  turning novels into, 89–91
  writing, 115–16
screenwriters, 78–79
script supervisors, 297

self-help/relationship book
    proposal, 181–210
series deals, 286
sets, 297
set-up, 297
SFX, 297
shots, 298
slate, 298
sound mixer, 298
special sales clauses, 285
specialty books, 56–57
spec scripts, 113
sports books, 52
star names, for packages, 104–5
story board, 298
studio deals, 298
studios, 80, 296
submissions
    See also manuscripts;
        proposals
    presentation of, 17–21
subsidiary rights, 285
success stories, 6, 69–73
syndicated television, 118–21
synopsis, 10

television movie, proposal for,
    255–66
television series, sample proposal
    for, 239–53
tilt, 299
topping, 285
trades, 299
trailers, 299
treatments, 299
    sample, 255–66
    vs. screenplays, 114
    television, 91–93
trends
    in fiction, 60–61
    in nonfiction, 54–55
    in television and film, 98–100
true-crime books, 55–56
    sample proposal for, 165–79
True Murder Mysteries project, 120
    proposal for, 239–53
umbrella deals, 296
video, 299
viral marketing, 286
voice-on-camera (VOC), 299
voice-over (VO), 299

T, U, V

W

talent, 299
television industry
    advice about, 108–9
    breaking into, 91–95, 117–21
    cable television, 118–21
    development deals, 97–98
    made-for-television projects,
        88
    players in, 77–81
    series writers, 79
    syndicated television, 118–21
    trends in, 98–100
television miniseries, 95–96

Wiser, Rob, 181, 188
wrap, 299
Writer Guild of America (WGA),
    85, 96–97, 113
writers
    See also authors; screenwriters
    five steps to becoming
        successful, xvi–xxii
    Hollywood, 77–79
    television, 91–95, 117–21
writers' conferences, 27–28
writing, reasons for, 12

Photo © Bernard Auroux

About the Author

Known as "The Literary Lion," **Peter Miller** has been an extraordinarily active literary and film manager for more than thirty years. He is President of PMA Literary and Film Management, Inc. and Millennium Lion, Inc.; he and his company have successfully managed more than 1,000 books worldwide as well as dozens of motion picture and television properties. These works include eleven *New York Times* bestsellers, and eleven produced films that Miller has managed or executive produced. Three of those films have been nominated for Emmy Awards: *Goodbye, Miss Fourth of July* (The Disney Channel, with four nominations); *A Gift of Love* (Showtime, two nominations); and *Helter Skelter* (CBS, one nomination). In addition, Miller has a number of film and television projects currently in active development, with some nearing production, in association with Warner Bros. Features, Sony Pictures Television, Warner Bros. Television, DreamWorks, and many other producers and production companies.

Peter Miller spends most of his time in New York or Los Angeles, but he also frequently tours the country to speak at writers' conferences and workshops. He regularly attends publishing gatherings such the BookExpo America convention and the Frankfurt Book Fair, as well as various film festivals including those at Cannes, East Hampton, and Sundance. For more information about Peter Miller's work, visit his Web site at *www.pmalitfilm.com*.